$20^{\circ\circ}$

THE SIGNBOARDS OF
OLD LONDON SHOPS

SHOP SIGNBOARDS IN CORNHILL *CIRCA* 1750.
(*From a contemporary print by Thomas Bowles.*)

THE SIGNBOARDS OF OLD LONDON SHOPS

A Review of the Shop Signs employed by the London
Tradesmen during the XVIIth and XVIIIth Centuries.
Compiled from the author's collection of contemporary
trade-cards and billheads

by

SIR AMBROSE HEAL, F.S.A.

PORTMAN BOOKS
LONDON

First published 1957
This edition published 1988 by
Portman Books an imprint of
B. T. Batsford Ltd
4 Fitzhardinge Street, London W1H 0AH

Printed and bound in Great Britain by
Butler & Tanner Ltd, Frome

ISBN 0-7134-5983-2

CONTENTS

ACKNOWLEDGEMENTS.

The Author desires to thank Mr. Raymond Smith, F.L.A., of the Guildhall Library, for his assistance in selecting appropriate subjects with which to illustrate London streets of the period. To the Publishers, and especially to Mr. W. Hanneford-Smith, F.R.S. (Edin.), he is deeply indebted for their guidance and enthusiastic collaboration.

PLATE II.

SHOP SIGNBOARDS IN FENCHURCH STREET ABOUT THE YEAR 1750
with Ironmongers Hall on the right.

(From a contemporary drawing by I. Donawell. engraved by T. Bowles.)

INTRODUCTION

THE SIGNS OF INNS HAVE AROUSED THE INTEREST of many and much has been written about them, but Shop Signs, being now practically obsolete, are known and recorded only by the few.

In various ways Signboards claim the attention of the curious. The antiquarian is attracted by a coat of arms indicating the local influence of some great family, or by the " Head " of a past celebrity commemorating a passing wave of patriotic or political popularity now subsided. Or, may be, what catches his eye serves as a reminder of some obsolete industry or a pastime of which only the name now survives. The more casual passer-by will perhaps remark upon some out-of-the-way device, or combination of devices, which appears to him to be inexplicable or curiously incongruous. Occasionally it will be the decorative handling of a design which will arrest the attention of the artist.

Nowadays the Signboards of Inns hold the field, they being practically the only ones left to us. As a result our attention has perforce been almost entirely confined to that trade. The subject of Inn Signs has been much favoured for one reason and another and many writers have been drawn to it ; some have dealt with the heraldic or the topographical interests, some with the significance of emblems employed, but the more usual note struck has been the obvious and popular one of the picturesque appeal of the quaint Old English Inn. From these points of view the field of the inn-sign has been well surveyed.

SHOP SIGNS My purpose here is to cover a wider range than that to which the writer on inn-signs has necessarily been limited and to call to notice the signs which were commonly used by other types of trades. The shop signboard has hitherto not received the attention it deserves and the subject has been little explored mainly because the shop sign has almost ceased to exist. Now and again in a country town one will still see hanging out over shops simple objects typifying certain trades, such as the coiled tobacco roll, the barber's pole, a padlock or a kettle at the ironmonger's, a tea canister on the cornice above the grocer's, a large red hat over the hatter's or a fine trout dangling from the fishing tackle shop ; not infrequently there is the hammer and hand poised threateningly at the gold-beater's and, of course, the ubiquitous Three Golden Balls. Other than these homely emblems very few shop-signs are left to us and the craft of the shop sign-painter has practically died out. Even in our museums few curators have deemed the old signs to be of sufficient antiquarian interest to deserve houseroom. And now that the opportunity to preserve good examples has been lost to us it is difficult in these days to realise what a colourful scene the shopping streets of London must have presented when each shop hung out its painted board or displayed its carved and gilded emblem.

The original purpose of the signboard was, of course, for the identification of a business at a time when few people were capable of reading a shopkeeper's name nor he, possibly, of notifying it. The records of the signs which were used upon Trade Tokens issued in the seventeenth century are sufficient in themselves to show how general the practice had become of the shop identifying itself with a particular sign, though it was not until the days of Charles I that the inhabitants of London received a charter making it lawful for them to affix signboards to their houses. It is noticeable, however, that in the earliest London Directory, issued in 1677, *A Collection of the Names of the Merchants Living in and about the City of London*, the only signs mentioned are those of " The Goldsmiths that keep Running Cashes " in whose hands lay the banking business of that time.

In the rebuilding of the City after the Great Fire many of the signs were carved on stone panels built into the fronts of the houses, though the majority still favoured a signboard either hung from an iron bracket or set up on a post before their shops.

These signs became larger and more and more elaborate until they constituted a nuisance by blocking sun and air from the narrow streets and—because of the insecurity of their dilapidated supports—they became a menace to the safety of the public. One enormous sign in Bride Lane fell, bringing down the front of the house and killing four persons. This was in 1718 and resulted in a commission of enquiry being set up but, as with many commissions, nothing immediately came of it. Later on public opinion was aroused and the removal of these dangerous structures was called for. Most people could by that time read sufficiently well to decipher a number or recognise a shopkeeper's name so there was no longer the same necessity for a visual appeal.

HOUSE
NUMBERS
PRESCRIBED

In 1762 a proclamation was issued ordering the removal of the hanging signs within the City of London and a similar decree was made in the City of Westminster.* Paris had recently given London the lead in this reform by an edict of the 17th September, 1761, ordering that within one month all signboards were to be fixed against the walls of the houses with a projection of not more than four inches. The numbering of London houses thus came to be instituted, but the new method was not favourably received by all ;

* cf. Minute Book of the Commissioners for the Paving of Westminster. 17th May, 1763.

many were loath to relinquish the individuality which attached to their sign and were reluctant to depend upon the efficacy of this novel form of address. A scrutiny of the London Directory issued in 1765, entitled *A Complete Guide to all persons who have any Trade or Concern with the City of London and Parts Adjacent*, discloses only 35 instances of numbered addresses and of these the entries under the Inns of Court and Chancery account for 17, probably the staircase numbers. The "Complete Guide" issued in 1768 shows that the numbering system had then taken hold and by 1770 about three-fourths of the houses are so designated.

It is noticeable that in the early days the new method of numbering was more widely adopted in the quieter localities on the outskirts of the town. Occupants of the main business streets in the City, such as Cheapside, Fleet Street, and those beyond the City boundaries such as Holborn and the Strand, were still inclined to rely upon their accustomed signs. Shopkeepers' bill-heads and trade cards, until quite late in the 18th century, often displayed the old shop-sign in addition to the new street number which had been inconspicuously spatchcocked on to the old plate.

A passage from Hatton's *A New View of London*, published in 1708, has often been cited as evidence that the numbering of houses in certain parts of London was in practice at that date, long before the passing of the Acts of 1762 and 1765. The passage referred to reads :—" Prescot Street, a spacious and regular built street on the south side of the Tenter Ground in Goodman's Fields—instead of signs the houses here are distinguished by numbers, as the staircases in the Inns of Court and Chancery." This state-ment is precise and definite, but records of instances at such an early date as 1708 confirming the use of house-numbering, whether in Prescot Street or elsewhere in London, have not survived. It is noticeable, however, in the 1763 Directory, that of the thirty-one numbered addresses given six occur in Prescot Street ; and this lends some colour to Hatton's account. Northouck's *History of London* (1773), pp. 415 and 436, gives references to the various Acts and their incidence in different parishes between 1760 and 1770. Correspondence, which from time to time has run through the volumes of *Notes & Queries*, has brought to light information relating to the numeration of London streets which amends and amplifies that which was available to Larwood & Hotten *History of Signboards* (1867) and other writers in the 19th and in the beginning of the 20th centuries. The earliest instances which I have been able to trace were discovered as the result of examining about two thousand Fire Insurance Policies between the years 1721 and 1727. During that period I found only two cases where the insured property was specified by a house number : one was in Ropemakers' Alley, the other in Burr Street ; the addresses of all the other houses were identified by signs.

The shop sign continued to be very prevalent until the last quarter of the 18th century. The long established custom of displaying emblems indicative of various trades or devices adopted to distinguish individual businesses was slow to die out. These varied symbols, being drawn from all kinds of trades, necessarily give to the shop-signs a wider and more diverse field of interest than the signs of the innkeepers, whose trade is monotonously limited to one sort of business, though the nature of that business is seldom reflected in the emblem selected on the inn sign-board. The " Red Lion," or the " Pig and Whistle," in no way suggests the calling of the innkeeper nor the liquors or victuals he dispenses. It is perhaps the sole distinguishing characteristic of the inn-sign that it is remote from, and in no way associated with, the trade carried on unless it can be said that a note of conviviality is occasionally struck by such devices as the " Three Cups " or the " Barleycorn." Shop-signs, on the other hand, symbolise practically every other calling throughout the range of human requirements. They not only indicate a man's trade and the goods he deals in, but they frequently constitute a record of old-time implements and the development of his craft ; they record for us also the trend of fashion and the passing of social customs.

TRADESMEN'S CARDS   The only contemporary records we have to draw upon to give a representation of the shop-sign, its design and symbolism, are those early trade-cards or bill-heads on which the signboard appears, and these are not very readily come by. They do not always give us an exact reproduction of the actual sign-board itself, but they do give us the engraver's rendering of the sign in black and white. For the very reason that they are not photographic facsimiles of the sign-painter's originals they possess the individual interpretation of the artist-engraver who simplified or embellished as he felt the design of the card required. In the hey-day of the tradesman's card, that is to say about the middle of the 18th century, the work of some of the artists employed ranks highly. Examples are not uncommon which bear the signatures of men like Bickham, Sturt, Benjamin Cole, Fourdrinier and Hogarth.

The term " trade-card " is something of a misnomer, for these productions were not of the small pasteboard type to which we are now accustomed but were well printed on sheets of good paper and of a fair size, ranging from a small octavo up to a large quarto—sometimes even up to folio size. They were, in fact, hand-bills which might be given to a customer as a reminder of the shop or on which he might jot down a note of a price or a purchase. Occasionally the backs of them would be used as a memorandum of an account outstanding, and these are of the greatest interest to us now as they carry their date and also give descriptions and prices of the goods supplied. They would of necessity embody the name and address of the shop and, more frequently than not, illustrate its sign. These trade-cards must not however be confused with the bill-heads of the period, though the latter very frequently carried the shop-sign, and I have drawn upon such bill-heads as well as upon the trade-cards to illustrate my subject. All the reproductions here used are taken from cards or bill-heads in my own collection with the exception of the few very early ones which have been photographed from the small collection made by Samuel Pepys. The originals of these, happily, are preserved for us in the Pepysian Library at Magdalene College, Cambridge, and are contained in Volume II of his Collection of Prints, etc., relating to the Cities of London and Westminster in a section which is labelled "Vulgaria." These rare examples are of the latter half of the 17th century, and all of them necessarily pre-date the death of the diarist in 1703.

Trade-cards then are frankly advertisements. They claim to be nothing more than the plain announcement of the shop-keeper and his wares ; but their importance in this connection is that they constitute for us practically the sole *contemporary* representations that remain extant of the old shop-signs. The drawings in some cases are crude, but they have the virtue of rendering the naïve convention of the sign-painter in a technique which is in sympathy with the original : these more elementary ones are usually woodcuts. The more elaborate engravings on copper sometimes lose a good deal of the simple direct method of the signboard in the endeavour of an accomplished craftsman to give a more distinctive rendering to a prosaic subject.

BILLHEADS   In a somewhat different category from trade-cards come the shopkeepers' billheads which are of a more utilitarian type. Whereas the trade-card was mainly designed to fulfil the purpose of a decorative advertisement, the billhead was a businesslike statement of the customer's account with the tradesman and consequently the engraver restricted himself to a heading which consisted merely of a direct announcement of the man's name, his calling and address, with ample space below for itemising the articles purchased and their price. Severely practical in purpose it yet contrived to achieve a decorative effect solely by means of the spacing of good lettering in combination with the emblem of the shop-sign. The signs engraved on the billheads are usually represented in a more simplified form than that in which they appear on the trade-card, where they are frequently set in a rococo cartouche and linked up with an elaborate frame containing a detailed list of the wares dealt in. The more severe bill-head treatment often takes the form of a direct rendering of the signboard itself, artlessly shown with its hangers and supporting bracket. For these reasons I have, wherever possible, preferred to illustrate the shop-sign in its more direct rendering rather than the stylised version adopted for the trade-card. As previously pointed out the all-important feature of the billhead is that it fixes precisely the date when it was in use.

The bills themselves are of very considerable interest as records of the makers or vendors of the goods, the various materials used, their trade names, or the topical terms they were known by and the prices at which they were supplied. It is fascinating, too, to trace the history of a firm as the business passed from one hand to another or partnerships were entered into ; to follow its fluctuations in fortune or the changes in address as the flow of trade or fashion affected different localities. In some few cases names which are household words to-day can be traced back to their early beginnings or through various vicissitudes. Old established businesses such as Berry's and Lock's in St. James's Street, Twining's in the Strand, Fribourg & Treyer's of the Haymarket, Garrard's the silversmiths, and others, provide early and interesting records which take us back a couple of hundred years—in some cases further still.

On the other side of the counter the tradesman's customer may, himself, providentially lead one into interesting by-paths of research when, as it sometimes happens, a box full of family bills which have lain aside for generations come to light, all systematically docketed by some careful housekeeper. Accounts of such *trouvailles* have recently been made known to us through Miss Scott Thomson's *The Russells in Bloomsbury* and *The Purefoy Letters*, edited by Mr. G. Eland. The former prints a number of itemised bills for goods supplied to the Duke's town house during the reigns of the two earlier Georges, and the latter records in detail the dealings of a contemporary Buckinghamshire household with the various London tradesmen—mostly conducted through the medium of the London carrier.

FAMILY BILLS Accumulations of old family bills have come my way from time to time—of these the smallest, but of the greatest personal interest, is a collection of three or four dozen bills from London tradesmen for a variety of commodities which were supplied to Edward Gibbon, the historian, while he was living at No. 7, Bentinck Street—all dated between the years 1772–1783 covering the period when he was engaged upon writing the *Decline and Fall of the Roman Empire*.

As an indication of Gibbon's tastes and way of living it is instructive to note the range of his requirements. In addition to the run of ordinary household supplies the bills include purchases of " a strong parrot cage," spectacles (from Dolland's), green handled knives and forks, six English Pheasants with coop and trough complete, a turbot kettle, wax candles in large quantities, rush lights, flambeaux and the oilman's contract for lighting the lamps over the street door, gold-laced liveries for his servants, velvet breeches, silk stockings and hats in profusion ; more personal supplies are represented by packets of quill pens, a " large bath box with lock and key," and several bills from the tobacconist, John Hardham, maker of the famous " No. 37 Snuff " * in Fleet

---

* The mixture popularised by David Garrick. (See *D.N.B.*)

The CHURCH *of* S.ᵗ *Mary le Bow in Cheapside London*

Printed for The Bowles in S.ᵗ Pauls Church Yard Johⁿ

SHOP SIGNBOARDS IN CHEAPSIDE, WITH THE CHU[R]

(*From a contemporary pri*

PLATE III.

Bowles delin. et Sculp.

L'ÉGLISE de St. Marie Le Bow dans Cheapside Londres.

n in Cornhill. R Sayer in Fleet St.

OF ST. MARY-LE-BOW, ABOUT THE YEAR 1750.

homas Bowles.)

Street.   Other accounts include those for the Nightman's services in " removing 6 tons of soil."

In such ways billheads provide an intimate picture filled in with domestic and prosaic details which are not easily matched from other sources.   Auto-biographies, Diaries and Letters which get published are all subject to editorial oversight, idiosyncracies are apt to be either underlined or modified, irregularities straightened out and iniquities condoned or accounted for, but the tradesman's bill is an account which cannot be questioned.   They contain, perhaps, a lesson to many of us and even form a justification for those who never keep their bills.   Be that as it may, the significance of these humble documents is of value to the student, and the passage of time, while rendering divulgences fairly innocuous, only increases the indebtedness of the investigator.

It will be seen, therefore, that billheads can be a rewarding field to the student of the shop-sign, particularly for those who concern themselves with the actual goods offered for sale.   They have not the decorative quality of the more elaborately engraved trade-card, but they give a closer description of the wares, the actual prices paid for them and the rates at which services were rendered.   They bring out precise and illuminating details of the kind of peruke or the sort of shoes which were being worn at particular periods, the type of wine glass newly brought into fashion, how much a yard paduasoys and prunellas sold for, how prodigious was the charge for a first-class funeral, what were the correct accompaniments, and how costly the trappings.   You may see to a penny what the chimney-sweep charged for his boys' services or the cost of the daily attendance on your doorstep of the purveyor of asses' milk.   In fact there are few minutiæ of the citizen's private life about which one cannot obtain exact and curious information.

OLD SHOPPING STREETS   To the student of London topography the recording of shop-signs brings with it the names and associations of the old streets, so many of which have long since been swept out of existence to make way for civic improvements, or which have been demolished quite recently and will be replanned, some with new names given to them.   The shopkeepers' addresses reflect the gradual drift of the shopping-centres westward from the former resorts of fashion, Cheapside, Fleet Street and the Strand or those in Holborn, Leicester Fields and Covent Garden, to others in Piccadilly or St. James's.   One can trace the gradual growth of Bond Street as it developed northward to the Oxford Road, and finally the transmutation effected by Nash's Regent Street.

At a time when addresses were indicated merely by the name of the street and the sign of the shop, some closer indication of the trader's position in the street was sometimes felt to be required. It is not unusual, therefore, to meet with more circumstantial addresses phrased in such terms as :—

" Over against the New Church in the Strand " ;
" South side of St. Paul's opposite the Clock " ; or
" Near the Watch House in Holborn."

Where such directions are given and the position is still unmistakably identifiable, it is of interest in walking the London streets to remind oneself that here stood So-and-So's the haberdasher's, or on that corner was So-and-So's famous bookshop.

TRADESMEN'S TOKENS
The token coinage of the 17th century has preserved for us the records of shop-signs in a large number of cases. The late Dr. G. C. Williamson's edition of Boyne's *Trade Tokens* yields some four thousand issues in London and Southwark alone. From these we get the name, or initials, of the issuer, usually his sign and an approximate address ; his trade also is often denoted and, almost invariably, the date of issue. Of this large number a heavy proportion—as would be expected—relate to inns and taverns. Unfortunately only a very few illustrations are given, and if we go to the tokens themselves we get only a rather dim idea of the sign ; partly, because of its tiny size—the whole face of the coin is rather smaller than our sixpenny piece—and also because the impression has become defaced with wear. This useful work is a most valuable record, and reference to it is greatly assisted by an admirable system of indexes arranged under twelve headings. Since the publication of Dr. Williamson's volumes in 1889 a certain number of previously unknown issues have been recorded in various numismatic publications. The scope of this democratic coinage in the 17th century ranged over a period of about thirty years (1648–1679) ; the revival of tokens in the late 18th and early 19th centuries does not help us as by that time the shop-sign had already fallen into disuse.

EMBLEMS & EFFIGIES
Various emblems were commonly adopted by different trades and, although the practice was not rigidly adhered to, certain signs carried with them unmistakable indications of the sorts of wares dealt in. For example, there was no mistaking the Bible of the booksellers or stationers, the Sugar Loaves of the grocers, the Beaver of the hatters, the Buck of the breeches-makers, the Case of Knives of the cutlers, the Civet Cat of the perfumers, the Three Combs of the comb-makers, the Cup of the goldsmiths, the Coffins of the undertakers, the Pine-apple of the confectioners, the Hand of the glovers, the Rainbow of the dyers, the Key of the locksmiths or ironmongers, the Sash of the glaziers, the Woolpack of the drapers, the Canister of the tea-men, the Leg of the hosiers, the Peacock of the gold-lace men, the

Maiden's Head of the mercers, the Indian Queen of the linen-drapers, the Olive tree of the oilmen, the Juniper tree of the distillers, the Spectacles of the opticians, the Lock of Hair of the peruquiers, the Dish of the pewterers, the figure of Justice of the scale-makers, the Highlander of the snuff-men, the Coffee-mill of the wood-turners, and many other significant trade emblems which were peculiar to their respective callings. In addition to these there were certain signs which were used more or less indiscriminately and are found common to most trades, such as the Sun, Moon and Stars, the King's or the Queen's Head, the Angel or the Lamb, and those which were originally derived from the badges of noble families.

The history and origins of the signboard are thus wrapped up in the commercial and political development of the City and afford a rich field for the student of economics. The heraldic achievements of the monarchy and nobility, the arms of the great City Guilds, as well as the emblems or devices common to particular trades, all found expression in the craft of the sign-painter though their true origins were not commonly recognised. Signs were taken from regal blazonry such as the White Swan of Edward III; the Portcullis, often termed the Harrow, of John of Gaunt; the White Hart of Richard II; the Antelope of Henry IV; the Blue Boar of Richard III; the Falcon of Edward IV; the Greyhound of Henry VII; the White Roses of the Tudors; the Lion of the Stuarts; and the White Horse of the House of Hanover. Emblems derived from the arms of the City Companies are not always taken for what they are. The Cradle for instance of the Basket-makers; the Cupid and Torch of the Glaziers; the Compasses of the Car-penters; the Goats' heads of the Cordwainers; the Leopards' heads of the Weavers; the Tents of the Upholders; the Doves of the Tallow-chandlers; Adam & Eve of the Fruiterers; the Elephant & Castle* of the Cutlers; the Maiden-head of the Mercers; the Rasp of the Snuff-makers; the Cup of the Goldsmiths; the Teazle of the Clothworkers; the Green Man supporter of the arms of the Distillers, were those most commonly displayed, but their original significance gradually became obscured and the signs miscalled.

The " King's Arms " is a shop-sign which is met with so frequently that it was evidently no more than a general expression of loyalty and was not confined merely to those tradesmen who enjoyed royal patronage. Effigies of past and reigning monarchs naturally figured largely on the signboards. Those most often represented were Henry VIII, Elizabeth and Charles II, whose " Royal Oak " was a favourite emblem long after the Restoration.

Prominent figures in the profession of Arms, dignitaries of the Church and the Law, men of Letters and the Arts and the learned professions,

---

* " Elephants endorst with Towers " (*Paradise Regained*, iii, 329).

celebrities of one sort and another, were commemorated on signboards by their " Heads," though few of them we imagine would be classed as " ad vivum " portraits. Popular heroes to be thus commemorated were the Marquis of Granby ; the Admirals Vernon and Rodney ; the Duke of Marlborough and Lord Nelson, though such warriors were usually deemed to be more appropriate on the signs of taverns than on those of sober shop-keepers. Booksellers borrowed lustre from the names of the literary giants Virgil, Shakespeare, Pope and Ben Jonson, while the scientific instrument makers were inclined to go back to such pioneers as Tycho Brahé, Archimedes and Sir Isaac Newton. The names of famous chemists—Galen, Glauber and Boerhaave—were adopted by many apothecaries, and the Rembrandt's Head and the Hogarth's Head were the effigies which found some favour with the artists' colourmen and the printsellers, though, more generally, the anonymous Golden Head was the sign put up above their shops.

Saints and Martyrs had their followings in particular trades :—St. Blaize the patron of the woolcombers ; St. Crispin and St. Hugh of the shoemakers ; St. Luke of the painters and colourmen ; St. Martin, St. John and St. Paul adopted by the printers and booksellers ; St. Peter and his Keys figure appropriately on the sign of the locksmiths ; St. Laurence and his gridiron, or St. Dunstan with his pincers, were favoured by the smiths ; and St. George and his dragon by all and sundry.

Birds, Beasts, Fishes and Plant Life all have their places on the shop signboard, either alone or in combination, but few of them indicate any particular trade. The Beaver, of course, is inevitably associated with hatters, the Civet Cat with the perfumers ; the mystic qualities of the Dragon and of the Unicorn commended them to the apothecaries, but the more popular Lion, Horse, Bear and Stag have merely their common heraldic significance. The Dove, Falcon, Hen & Chickens, Parrot & Pheasant, occur indiscriminately. Fishes are not commonly met with, though the Salmon, the Dolphin and the Whale occasionally come to the surface. Of Fruits and Flowers—the Pineapple consistently appears on the signboards of confectioners ; the Artichoke and the Olive are emblems most frequently adopted by nurserymen and oilmen. Flowers, curiously enough, occur seldom. Except for the Rose, the Fleur-de-Lys and, very occasionally, the Marigold, their decorative qualities seem to have failed to appeal to the signpainter and shopkeeper alike. Trees, on the other hand, found considerable favour among trades where their appropriate significances were readily recognizable ; so we find the Buckthorn standing for the apothecaries, the Cork tree for the cork cutters, the Fig tree for the grocers, the Olive and the Lemon trees for the Italian warehousemen, the Mulberry for the silk men, and, almost invariably, the Walnut tree for the cabinet-makers.

STRANGE INCONGRUITIES The incongruous association of emblems so frequently found on signboards has more often been speculated upon than explained. Indiscriminate combinations like the Bull & Bedpost, the Lamb & Dolphin, the Three Nuns & Hare, the Whale & Gate, or the Wheatsheaf & Speaking Trumpet, provoke a demand for some rational explanation. To meet enquiry renderings are glibly given which are occasionally far-fetched and usually more conjectural than accurate. Many of these incongruities are susceptible of simple explication. Such puzzling amalgamations frequently arose from a tradesman taking over a shop where a different trade from his own had been carried on previously. He might very well wish to retain the old sign if it had been well known and become almost a landmark in the neighbourhood. While preserving the original sign for the sake of goodwill attached to it he would often add a device more appropriate to his own calling or one for which he had some personal preference. It would be natural enough if, say, a grocer decided to go into partnership with another established grocer, for an amalgamation of the signs of both to be adopted for the joint business, just as the names of partners are joined. Or, again, it was not at all uncommon for a young man starting up in business on his own account to add to the sign he chose to adopt that of the master whom he had served or to whom he had been bound apprentice. Also the tendency of particular trades to congregate in certain streets would easily lead to a local preponderance of the symbol commonly connected with such a trade. Consequently a man would add to it one for his personal identification, and this sometimes produced curious associations.

Irreconcilable alliances were not infrequently due to mere lack of understanding or from perversion of emblems as in the case where the insignia of the Order of the Garter was rendered by the signpainter in a lifelike display of the Leg & Star, which thus became to be commonly so called. Heraldic terms converted into colloquialisms resulted in strange composites. At the beginning of the 17th century signs were used singly and it was only towards the end of the century that compounds were formed and resulted in such incongruities as occasioned this " squib " in the *British Apollo* in 1710.

> " I'm amazed at the Signs
> As I pass through the Town,
> To see the odd mixture ;
> A Magpie and Crown,
> The Whale and the Crow,
> The Razor and Hen,
> The Leg and Seven Stars,
> The Axe and the Bottle,
> The Tun and the Lute,
> The Eagle and Child,
> The Shovel and Boot."

Larwood & Hotten, in their *History of Signboards*, touch upon the complexity of signboard symbols with the word of caution that " the explanations as to origin and meaning are based rather upon conjecture and speculation than upon fact—as only in very rare instances reliable data could be produced to bear them out. Compound signs but increase the difficulty of explanation ; if the road was uncertain before, almost all traces of a pathway are destroyed here . . . As a rule, and unless the symbols be very obvious, the reader would do well to consider the majority of compound signs as quarterings or combinations of others, without any hidden signification."

PAINTERS OF SIGNBOARDS The headquarters of the sign-painter's craft were in Harp Alley, leading off Shoe Lane, in Fleet Street. Here a shopkeeper would find a selection of ready-made signboards to hand or he could commission one to his own fancy. The trade-card of one Thomas Proctor,* at the Black-a-Moor's Head, in Harp Alley, near Fleet Ditch, announces that he " selleth all sorts of signs, Bushes, Bacchus's, Bunches of Grapes and Show Boards at Reasonable Prices." Another, of " Willi Steward,* at the King's Head in Fleet Lane " that he " selleth signes ready painted and Bushes for Taverns, Border Cloths for shops, Constables' Staffes, Laurells for Clubs, Dyall Boards for Clocks, Sugar Loafes & Tobacco-roles." Such as these would be the regular practitioners but the more skilled coach-painters of Long Acre had the better class trade in their hands and where a more elaborate piece of work was called for, or heraldic devices needed to be expertly rendered, the painter accustomed to working on coach panels, or decorating sedan chairs, was better qualified for the job.

Most writers on Inn Signs have drawn attention to exceptional cases where famous artists have been known to contribute signboards, not infrequently—as one gathers—in discharge of their liabilities to the landlord. The names of Morland, David Cox, Hogarth, Richard Wilson, John Crome, Peter Monamy and Samuel Wall are among those most commonly alluded to ; it is known that the last two were actually apprenticed to the trade. No more recent example of the work of a famous painter appearing on a signboard seems to be recorded than that of the St. George and Dragon executed by Sir John Millais for an inn at Hayes in Kent, though it was pleasantly noticeable, during the decade before the recent war, that some capable artists were beginning to be employed on signs for inns and various other trades, and one may now happen upon very accomplished and well designed boards painted in the modern idiom. One particularly good series of inn signs was carried out in Sussex and Kent by Mr. Ralph Ellis.

---

* See page 155.

For the student of signboard lore Larwood & Hotten's
SIGNBOARD *History of Signboards* is the outstanding book of reference
LITERATURE —in fact no other comprehensive work on the subject
has been produced. It was published by John Camden
Hotten in 1867, and although reprinted many times since, it has never been
revised. Useful contributions to various phases of the subject have appeared
from time to time during the interval of nearly eighty years. Dr. Philip
Norman's *London Signs and Inscriptions* is a scholarly work, but it is limited to
sculptured signs and relates only to those which had survived at the time it was
written (1893). A valuable series of articles by F. G. Hilton Price appeared in
London Topographical Records between the years 1903 and 1908, but they dealt
only with certain of the more famous streets in the City of London. The signs
of Fleet Street, Lombard Street and the Strand were published separately.
Only a very limited number of illustrations were given in any of these publications. An ambitious attempt was embarked upon by J. Holden MacMichael,
which treated with the London Signs in alphabetical order. The articles came
out in *The Antiquary*, but their appearance was very sporadic, and although
spread over a period of ten years (1904–1914) they had not quite reached to the
end of the letter C when the magazine ceased publication in November, 1914.
Had this effort reached conclusion MacMichael's work would have ranked as
the standard authority on the history of London signboards. The study of each
sign he investigated was full and bore evidence of close and original research
in the files of contemporary newspapers and other out-of-the-way sources
which had not been previously examined with such careful attention.

As the authorship of the *History of Signboards* has, more than once,
been questioned and quite recently some discussion of it has taken place in
the press, it may not be out of place here to put on record the fact that " Jacob
Larwood " was the English pseudonym of a Dutch writer, J. van Schevichaven.
He was born in 1827 at Nijmegen, where he received the greater part of his
education, and thence passed on to Leyden, where he devoted himself mainly
to the study of modern languages. At the age of twenty-four he came to
London to visit the Great Exhibition of 1851 and then went on to Paris ;
in 1854 he enlisted in the French army for the campaign in the Crimea. Four
years later he returned to London where he remained until 1869. During
this period he collaborated with his publisher, John Camden Hotten, in the
production of the *History of Signboards* and gave a good deal of his time to
the study of drawing and painting. The illustrations in " Signboards "
and another book of his, *The Story of the London Parks*, are by his hand.
For nearly twenty-three years he travelled almost continuously, but in 1893
he returned to his native city where he dwelt until his death, at the age of
ninety-one, in 1918.

From a note that " Jacob Larwood " made in his own copy of the *History of Signboards* to the effect that " This was the first work I wrote in English. Hotten paid me £10 for it and corrected the proofs. He considered that sufficient reason to place his name along with my nom-de-plume on the title page "—it would appear that Larwood had some grounds for dissatisfaction with the treatment he received from his collaborator. Presumably, however, matters were set to rights later on, for he had at least two other works issued over Hotten's imprint and two more were published by Hotten's successors, Messrs. Chatto & Windus.

It has seemed necessary to make clear Van Schevichaven's authorship of the works which appeared under the name of " Jacob Larwood " as some bibliographers of pseudonymous literature have mistakenly attributed them to a certain " L. R. Sadler " ; this, however, was merely another pen-name that Schevichaven had assumed in some earlier work.*

Larwood & Hotten, as has been pointed out, published their *History of Signboards* nearly eighty years ago, and it has remained the recognised authority on the subject ever since. When one considers the general interest which is taken in the signboards of inns, and the curiosity they arouse by the variety and peculiarity of the emblems displayed, one would expect to find that some more recent attempt had been made to deal comprehensively with the whole subject.†

Books incidentally touching upon the signboards of inns and taverns have not been wanting and they cover their own ground admirably. In particular one would refer to a most interesting and beautifully illustrated volume by Professor Richardson and H. D. Eberlein—*The English Inn*—and we are indebted to the researches of the late Dr. Kenneth Rogers for a series of studies on old Inns situated for the most part within the boundaries of the City of London. But these, and similar works, are necessarily and properly confined within the limitations set by their titles.

The explanation of the striking absence of any later contribution to the wider field of the signboard generally is possibly to be found in the warning conveyed by the opening paragraph of Larwood & Hotten's own Preface :—

" Although from the days of Addison's *Spectator* down to the present time many short articles have been written upon house-signs, nothing like a general inquiry into the subject has, as yet, been published in this country. The extraordinary number of examples, and the numerous

---

* For the biographical details given above I am indebted to an article by Lawrence F. Powell, who contributed it to *Notes & Queries* in 1920 ; see 12th Series, vol. vii, p. 441, and vol. viii, p. 509.

† While these pages are in the printer's hands a paragraph has appeared in the Press announcing that a work is in preparation which will revise and develop that portion of Larwood & Hotten's *History of Signboards* which relates solely to the signs of Inns.

absurd combinations afforded such a mass of entangled material, as doubtless deterred writers from proceeding beyond an occasional article in a magazine, or a chaper in a book—when only the more famous signs would be cited as instances of popular humour or local renown."

Despite the intricacies and pitfalls of signboardland, it is greatly to be hoped that someone will follow up the tortuous path which Larwood & Hotten so far explored and that they will succeed in penetrating still further " the mass of entangled material " to be encountered. A good deal of additional material has grown up during the last 80 years, some of it helpful, some misleading. Much discrimination and research will be necessary in order to achieve a new and improved History of Signboards. If no more than a revised edition of Larwood & Hotten were undertaken its usefulness could be greatly enhanced by the provision of an additional index giving references to the various trades.

The intention of the present book is in no way an attempt to emulate the *History of Signboards*, though, partially, it may usefully supplement it. Its object rather is merely to represent those London shop-signs which figure upon billheads and trade-cards and are identifiable by specimens in my own collection. In order that this survey should be as authentic as one can make it, the illustrations are derived solely from engravings which were actually employed by the shopkeepers themselves. Without going beyond my own MS. records of London Shop Signs—of which I have noted more than fifteen thousand from various contemporary sources—it would have been possible to extend considerably the number of emblems and the lists of the tradesmen who used them. I have preferred, however, to confine myself here to a selection from those of which I can produce documentary evidence from the printed originals in my own possession. Keeping within this limit it has, I think, been possible to give a typical cross-section of the signs which were in use and of the various trades which employed them. This somewhat arbitrary selection has provided records of about two thousand signboards distributed over about a hundred and fifty different trades. The aim has been to be representative rather than encyclopædical, and to illustrate the range sufficiently to give a general idea of London signboard iconography.

Beaconsfield, 1945.

PLATE IV.

SHOP SIGNBOARDS IN THE VICINITY OF THE MONUMENT ABOUT THE YEAR 1750.

(From a contemporary drawing by A. Canaletto engraved by G. Bickham.)

The following are among the more usual signs adopted by various trades :—

ANVIL MAKERS	*Anvil & Cross Hammers.*
APOTHECARIES (*see* CHEMISTS).	
ASSES' MILK (Vendors of)	*Ass & Foal.*
BATHS & SHAMPOOERS	*Turk's Head.*
BELL FOUNDERS	*Three Bells.*
BELL HANGERS	*Prince's Arms, Three Bells and Golden Lock & Key.*
BELLOWS MAKERS	*Brush & Bellows.*
BIT & STIRRUP MAKERS	*Bit & Crown.*
BLUE MAKERS	*Blue Anchor & Gate.*
BOOK BINDERS	*Bible (& Dove).*
BOOKSELLERS	*Authors' Heads* (Erasmus, Homer, Horace, Pope, Johnson, Prior, Tully, Shakespeare, Virgil, etc.). *Bible. Bible & Crown. Brazen Serpent. Looking Glass (Speculum).*
BOOT & SHOEMAKERS	*Golden Boot. Old Crispin. Hand & Slipper. St. Hugh. Last. Shoe & Slap.*
BRAZIERS	*Bell & Anchor. Three Bells. Candlesticks & Key. Cross Keys. Frying Pan. Gridiron. Mortar & Pestle. Tea Kettle.*
BREECHES MAKERS	*Breeches & Glove. Buck & Breeches. Roebuck.*

BRUSH & BASKET MAKERS	*Three (or Four) Brushes.*
BUTTON MAKERS	*Golden Lion.*
CABINET MAKERS	*Cabinet.*
	Chair.
	Looking Glass.
	Walnut Tree.
CAP MAKERS	*Fox & Cap.*
CARPENTERS	*Carpenters' Arms (Three Compasses).*
	Four Coffins.
CARVERS & GILDERS	*Architrave (or Golden) Frame.*
	Golden Head.
CHAIN MAKERS	*Chain & Buckle.*
CHEESE MONGERS	*Dairy Maid & Churn.*
	Dairy Maid & Cheshire Cheese.
	Mortar & Pestle.
CHEMISTS	*Buckthorn Tree.*
	Galen's Head.
	Glauber's Head.
	Unicorn.
CHIMNEY SWEEPS & NIGHTMEN	*Golden Pole.*
CHINA MEN	*China Jar.*
	Tea Canister and/or Tea Pot.
CLOCK & WATCHMAKERS	*Dial or Dial & Crown.*
CLOGG MAKERS	*Patten & Crown.*
CLOTHIERS	*Three Kings (Arms of Merchant Taylors' Co.)*
	(Slopmen) Jolly Sailor.
COACHMAKERS	*Arms of Coachmakers' Co.*
COALMEN	*Collier & Cart.*
COFFIN PLATE MAKERS	*Angel & Crown.*
COLOUR MEN	*Blue Coat Boy.*
	Harlequin.
	St. Luke's Head.
	Olive Tree & Colour Barrel.
	Silent Woman (Oilmen).

COMB MAKERS	*Three Combs.* *Elephant.* *Hand & Comb.*
CONFECTIONERS	*Haunch of Venison.* *Golden Pheasant.* *Pine Apple.*
COOPERS	*Bathing Tub & Pail.*
CORK CUTTERS	*Cork Tree.*
COSTUMIERS	*Harlequin.*
CUPPERS	*Bleeder & Star.*
CURRIERS	*Roebuck.*
CUTLERS & RAZOR MAKERS	*Case of Knives.* (See also Sword Cutlers.) *Unicorn.*
DISTILLERS	*Juniper Tree.* *Still.*
DRAPERS (*see* Linen & Woollen Drapers).	
DYERS	*Green Man.* *Peacock.* *Rainbow & Dove.*
ENGINE MAKERS (*see* Millwrights).	
ENGRAVERS	*Golden Head.*
FAN MAKERS	*Golden Fan.*
FEATHER BED MAKERS (or Feather Men)	*Angel.*
FISHMONGERS	*Oyster Girl or Whistling Oyster.*
FISHING TACKLE MAKERS	*Angler & Trout.* *Compleat Angler.* *Golden Fish.*
FRUITERERS	*Lemon Tree.*
FURRIERS	*Three Rabbits.*
GARDENERS (*see* Nurserymen).	
GLASS MAKERS	*Golden Bottle.*

GLAZIERS	*Sash.*
GLOVERS	*Hand & Glove.*
GOLD BEATERS	*Hand & Hammer.*
GOLD LACEMEN (*see* LACEMEN).	
GOLDSMITHS & SILVERSMITHS	*Crown & Pearl (together & separate).* *Golden Cup (or Urn).* *Ring & Pearl (together & separate).*
GROCERS (*see also* TEAMEN)	*Golden Canister.* *Fig Tree.* *Three Sugar Loaves.*
GUNSMITHS	*Cross Guns.*
HABERDASHERS	*Sun & Falcon.* *Three Pigeons.* *Wheatsheaf.* *Woolpack.*
HAIRSELLERS	*Hand & Lock of Hair.*
HATTERS	*Cap in Hand.* *Gold Laced Hat.* *Hat & Beaver.* *Hat & Daggers.* *Hat & Feather.*
HOSIERS	*Golden Fleece.* *Golden Leg.* *Lamb.*
INSTRUMENT MAKERS (*see under* MUSICAL, OPTICIANS & SCIENTIFIC).	
IRONMONGERS	*Anchor & Key.* *Three Anchors.* *Two Candlesticks & Bell.* *Cross Saws & Gridiron.* *Dog's Head in Pot.* *Dust Pan.* *Frying Pan.* *Three Keys.* *Lock & Hinge.* *Padlock.* *Saw & Bag o' Nails.* *Stove Grate.*

ITALIAN WAREHOUSEMEN	*Two Olive Posts.*
	Orange Tree & Oil Jars.
LACEMEN (GOLD)	*Peacock.*
LEATHER SELLERS	*Roebuck.*
LIBRARIES (CIRCULATING)	*Dryden's Head.*
	Otway's Head.
	Pope's Head.
LINENDRAPERS	*Blackmoor's Head.*
	Hen & Chickens.
	Three Nuns.
	Packhorse & Fustian Roll.
	Unicorn.
	Wheatsheaf.
LOCKSMITHS	*Lock or Key.*
LORIMERS	*Bit & Crown.*
MANGLE MAKERS	*Mangle.*
MEASURES MAKERS	*Standard Bushel.*
MERCERS	*Angel.*
	Coventry Cross.
	Eagle & Child.
	Golden Fleece.
	Indian Queen.
MILLINERS	*Blue Bodice.*
	Feathers.
	Hood & Scarf.
	Lamb.
	Lamb & Flag.
	Mary Queen of Scots' Head.
MILLWRIGHTS	*Dial, Mill & Hand-Screw.*
	Man & Mill.
MUSICAL INSTRUMENT MAKERS	*French Horn & Violin.*
	Harp & Hautboy.
	Viol & Flute.
MUSICIANS	*Tabor & Pipe.*

NIGHTMEN (*see* CHIMNEY SWEEPS).

NURSERYMEN & SEEDSMEN	*Artichoke.*
	Hand & Flower.
	Pine Apple.
	Thistle & Crown.
OILMEN	*Neats' Tongues.*
	Oil Jar.
	Olive Tree.
OPTICIANS	*Archimedes & Globe.*
	Sir Isaac Newton's Head.
	Golden Spectacles.
PAINTERS	*Golden Pallet.*
	St. Luke's Head.
PAPER STAINERS	*Rainbow.*
PATENT MEDICINE VENDORS	*Lillie's Head.*

PASTRY COOKS (*see* CONFECTIONERS).

PENCIL MAKERS	*Hand & Pencil.*
PERFUMERS	*City of Seville.*
	Civet Cat.
	Three Arquebusade Bottles.
PERUKE MAKERS	*Blue & White Peruke.*
	Locks of Hair.
PEWTERERS	*Black Boy & Worm.*
	Golden Dish.
PIN MAKERS	*Sun.*
PINKERS & CUTTERS	*Dove & Point.*
PIPE MAKERS	*Three Tobacco Pipes.*
PLAYING CARD MAKERS	*King of Diamonds.*
	Knave of Clubs.
PRINTERS	*Anchor.*
	Falcon.
	St. Martin.
PRINT SELLERS	*Globe.*
	Hogarth's Head.

ROBE MAKERS	*Bishop's Head.*
	Parliament & Judge's Robe.
SADDLERS	*Saddle Royal.*
	Golden Stirrup.
	White Horse.
SAILORS & BOATMEN	*St. Julian.*
SCALE MAKERS	*Angel & Scales.*
	Hand & Scales.
SCULPTORS & MASONS	*Golden Head.*
SCIENTIFIC INSTRUMENT MAKERS	*Globe & Sun.*
	Orrery.
	Quadrant.
	Sir Isaac Newton's Head.
	Tycho Brahé's Head.
SEEDSMEN (*see* NURSERYMEN)	*Orange Tree.*
SHAMPOOERS (*see under* BATHS & SHAMPOOERS).	
SHOEMAKERS (*see* BOOT & SHOEMAKERS).	
SIGN PAINTERS	*Golden Head.*
	St. Luke.
SILK WEAVERS	*Blue Boar.*
SILVERSMITHS (*see* GOLDSMITHS)	*Mulberry Tree.*
SLOP SELLERS	*Jolly Sailor.*
SMITHS	*Hammer.*
	Harrow.
	Lock & Hinge.
	Smoke Jack.
SNUFFMEN (*see* TOBACCONISTS).	
SPATTERDASH MAKERS	*Three Spatterdashes.*
SPUR MAKERS	*Hand & Spur.*
STATIONERS	*Bible.*
	Bible & Dove.
	Falcon.
	Hand & Bible.
	Hand & Penknife.
	Ink Bottle.
	Spread Eagle.

STAYMAKERS	*Bodice.*
	Child's Coat & Rose.
SURGICAL & DENTAL OPERATORS.	*Bleeder & Star.*
	Turk's Head.
SCIENTIFIC INSTRUMENT MAKERS.	*Atlas.*
	Globe.
	Orrery & Globe.
	Quadrant.
	Sir Isaac Newton.

SURGICAL INSTRUMENT MAKERS (*see* CUTLERS).

SWORD CUTLERS	*Cross Daggers.*
	Flaming Sword.
TAILORS	*Drayman & Jacket.*
	Golden Fleece.
	Hand & Shears.

TALLOW CHANDLERS (*see* WAX & TALLOW CHANDLERS).

TEA MEN	*Golden Canister.*
	Golden Fan.
	Grasshopper.
	Tea Chest.
	Three Sugar Loaves & Canister.
TENT, TWINE & ROPE MAKERS.	*Peter Boat & Doublet.*
THREAD MAKERS	*Three Pigeons & Sceptre.*
TIN MEN	*Hog & Porridge Pot.*
	Tea Kettle & Speaking Trumpet.
	Three Lamps.
TOBACCONISTS & SNUFFMEN	*Abel Drugger.*
	Dagger.
	Green Man & Still.
	Highlander.
	Rasp & Crown.
	Tobacco Roll.
	Two Black Boys.

TOOL MAKERS	*Cross Axes.*
	Three Planes.
TOY MEN	*Elephant & Rising Sun.*
	Green Parrot.
	Seven Stars.
TRUNK MAKERS	*Trunk & Bucket.*
TRUSS MAKERS	*Golden Key.*
TURNERS	*Beehive & Patten.*
	Blue Coat Boy.
	Coffee Mill & Nimble Ninepence.
	Rocking Horse.
	St. Catherine.
UNDERTAKERS	*Four Coffins.*
	Naked Boy & Coffin.
UPHOLSTERERS	*Blue Curtain.*
	Crown & Cushion.
	Royal Bed.
	Three Crickets (i.e., Stools).
	Three Tents.
WALLPAPERS (*see* PAPER STAINERS).	
WATCHMAKERS (*see* CLOCKMAKERS).	
WAX & TALLOW CHANDLERS	*Golden Beehive.*
WEAVERS	*Spinning Wheel.*
WHALEBONE DEALERS	*Crown & Whale.*
WINE & SPIRIT MERCHANTS	*Angel & Still.*
	Hoop & Grapes.
	Still & Juniper Tree.
	Two Spies.
WIRE WORKERS	*Black Boy & Bird Cage.*
WOOLCOMBERS	*St. Blaize.*
WOOLLEN DRAPERS	*Golden Fleece.*
	Hand & Shears.
	Naked Boy & Woolpack.
	Seven Stars.
	Woolpack.
WRITING MASTERS	*Golden Pen.*
	Hand & Pen.

PLATE V

SHOP SIGNBOARDS IN THE VICINITY OF THE MANSION HOUSE ABOUT THE YEAR 1750

showing Lombard Street and Cornhill.

(From a contemporary print by T. Bowles.)

AN

ABRIDGED DIRECTORY

OF THE SHOP-SIGNS

OF

LONDON TRADESMEN

WITH THEIR

ADDRESSES AND DATES

SAMUEL BIRD at ye *ANVIL & CROSS HAMMERS* in St. John Street and in Northampton Street, Wood's Close in Clerkenwell.   *c.* 1760

ANVIL & CROSS HAMMERS

APOTHECARIES
See under CHEMISTS

APPRAISER

CASTON HOMASTER, at the *THREE COMPASSES* in Castle Street, Long Acre.   *c.* 1770

ASSES' MILK VENDORS

FRANCIS CHATBURN, at the *ASS AND FOAL* in South Molton Row, near Great Brook Street, Grosvenor Square.   1758

CORNELIOUS DAVIS, at the *ASS AND FOAL* in Wood's Close near Clarken Well Green.   At the Late House of Mr. Jennings (see below).   1758

WILLIAM DAVIS, at the *ASS AND FOAL* in Northampton Street, Clerkenwell.   1776
(Previously at the *Ass and Foal* in Wood's Close near Clerkenwell Green.)

ABRAHAM EASLEY, at the *ASS AND FOAL* in Mary Le Bone Fields, near Cavendish Square.   1775
(Previously at the *Ass and Foal* in Oxford Road near Grosvenor Square in 1748.)

THOMAS EDWARDS (Grandson to the late Mr. Abraham Easley), at the *ASS AND FOAL*, the bottom of Wigmore Street in Marylebone Lane, near Cavendish Square.   1779
(Removed to Quickset Row in the New Road near the Toll Gate between Tottenham Court and Portland Road. 1795.)

JNO. JENNINGS, at the *ASS AND FOAL* in Woods Close, near Clarken Well Green.   1733–1743

JAMES JONES, at the *ASS AND FOLE*, facing the Bird in Hand in Wood's Close.   1768
(Asses Drove to any Person's House in Town or Country.)

JOHN PARKE, at the *ROSEMARY BRANCH*, near Islington.   1769
(Removed to the Hackney Road.)

ASS & FOAL

ASSES' MILK VENDORS

MARTHA PROCKTER & LYDIA EDWARDS, daughter and grand-daughter to Mr. Abraham Easley (see above), at the *ASS AND FOAL* in Mary le Bone Lane, near Cavendish Square.   1775

ASTROLOGER

MRS. CORBYN, from Germany, at the *GOLDEN BALL*, No. 5, Stanhope Street, Clare Market.
                                                    c. 1780

BASKET MAKERS

This trade was commonly combined with that of the Brushmakers, *q.v.*

GEDALIAH GATFIELD, at the *CROWN AND ANCHOR* near Cheapside in Newgate street. 1768

See also under HATTERS

——SUTHERS, at the *DUKE'S HEAD*, Mint street in the Borough.

BATHS & SHAMPOOERS

ALICE NEALE, at the *TURK'S HEAD*, Bagnio, in James Street, Golden Square.   *c.* 1730

JAMES SMITH, at the *TURK'S HEAD & WOOL-PACK*, in Newgate Street.   *c.* 1740

BELL FOUNDERS

LESTER, PACK & CHAPMAN, at the *THREE BELLS* in White Chapel.   1769
(This famous firm of bell founders was established by Richard Phelps in 1700 and became Lester & Pack in 1752 and since 1782 it has been carried on by the family of Mears at Whitechapel, who have been connected with the firm since 1782.)

RICHARD PHELPS, at the *BELL* in Thames Street. Removed to the *THREE BELLS* in Whitechapel.
                                                    c. 1705
(In 1735 he took his foreman, Thomas Lester, into partnership; in 1752 Lester was joined by Thomas Pack.)

BELL HANGER & LOCKSMITH

JOHN WEVER, at the *PRINCES ARMS, THREE BELLS & GOLDEN LOCK & KEY* in Princes Street near Cavendish Square.   *c.* 1740
(Cavendish Square and the adjoining streets were laid out between 1720 and 1730.)

CROWN & ANCHOR

THREE BELLS

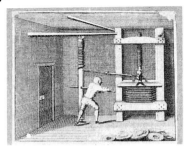

ANGEL & BIBLE

HAT PRESS

RISING SUN

BELLOWS MAKERS

BARTHOLOMEW FLAGGETT, at the *HATT PRESS* in St. John's Lane. *c.* 1770

HANNAH WELLBANK, at ye *BRUSH & BELLOWS*, Red Lyon Street, White Chapel. *c.* 1750
(Both these signs indicate a connection between the trade of the bellows makers and that of the brush and straw hat makers, though it is not evident what the connection was.)

BIT & STIRRUP MAKER (*or* LORIMER)

RICHARD READ, at the *BIT AND CROWN*, near Great Moorgate, London Wall. *c.* 1760

BLACKING MAKER

JOHN KIRBY, at the *WHITE PERUKE*, next the Bear Ale-house by Broad Street, New Buildings, Moorfields. *c.* 1730
(He had been succeeded by John Lee in 1743.)

BLUE MAKERS

RALPH DOUBLEDAY, at the *BLUE ANCHOR & GATE*, against ye Monument, Fish Street Hill. 1762

EDWARD KIRBY, at the *BLUE ANCHOR & GATE*, corner of St. Mary Hill in Little East Cheap. 1767

BOOK BINDERS

J. BIRD, at the *OLD ANGEL & BIBLE*, Ave-Maria Lane, Ludgate Street. 1749

BUDD & CALKIN, at the *CROWN & MITRE*, No. 100, Pall Mall. 1816

WILLIAM COOKE, at the *BIBLE & DOVE*, in Fetter Lane, Fleet Street. 1765

JOHN HURLES, at the *CROWN*, in St. Laurence Lane. *c.* 1700

BOOKSELLERS

JOHN ALLEN, at the *RISING SUNNE*, neare St. Pauls. 1656

BRADLEY THOMAS BATSFORD, at the *BIBLE & CROWN*, 30, High Holborn, and later at 52 and 94 in that street, and now as B. T. Batsford, Ltd., at 15, North Audley Street, Mayfair. 1843.
(Successors to Robert Peake (1611), Piers & Webley (1757), I. & J. Taylor (1770), Priestley & Weale (1825) and John Weale (1860).)

JOHN BRINDLEY, at the *KING'S ARMS* in New Bond Street.   1728
(On Brindley's death in 1759 the business fell into the hands of his shopman James Robson (see below), who carried it on into the nineteenth century. From 1872 until a few years ago it was known to all booklovers as Ellis's of Bond Street and still retained its old double fronted bow windows.)

JOHN BROTHERTON, at *THE BIBLE* next Tom's Coffee House in Cornhill.   1742

JAMES BUCKLAND, at *THE BUCK* in Paternoster Row.   1736–1790

THE BUCK

SAMUEL BUCKLEY, at *THE DOLPHIN*, in St. Paul's Church Yard.   1699

THOMAS COCKERILL, at *YE BIBLE & THREE LEGGS* in The Poultrey, over against Grocers' Hall.   1699

JOHN COLES, at the *SUN & MITRE* against Chancery Lane in Fleet Street.   1745

BENJAMIN CRAYLE, at the *PEACOCK & BIBLE* in St. Paul's Church Yard.   1686

JAMES CROKATT, at the *GOLDEN KEY*, near ye Inner Temple Gate, Fleet Street.   1726

JOHN AND THOMAS CURTIS, at *SHAKESPEAR'S HEAD*, opposite Fetter Lane in Fleet Street. 1760

BIBLE & 3 LEGS

EDWARD DILLY, successor to Mr. John Oswald, at the *ROSE & CROWN* in the Poultry near the Mansion House.   *c.* 1765
(Friend of Dr. Johnson and Boswell.)

ROBERT DODSLEY, at *TULLY'S HEAD*, in Pall Mall.   1740
(Published the works of Pope, Johnson and Swift.)

THOMAS DRING, at the *HARROW* over against the Temple Gate in Fleet Street.   1678

THOMAS EDLIN, at the *PRINCES ARMS* over against Exeter Exchange in the Strand.   1728

JOHN FULLER (1), at the *BIBLE & DOVE* in Ave Mary Lane.   1747
(2) at the *HANGING BIBLE* in Blowbladder Street, between Cheapside and Newgate Street.   1760

PRINCE'S ARMS

PRIOR'S HEAD

ERASMUS' HEAD

LAWTON GILLIVER, at *HOMER'S HEAD* against St. Dunstan's Church in Fleet Street.   1732

JOHN GODWIN, at the *SHAKESPEARE'S MONU-MENT*, No. 171, opposite the New Church in the Strand.   1775

J. GROENEWEGEN & A. VAN DER HOECK, at *HORACE'S HEAD* in the Strand.   1720

SAMUEL HARDING, at the *BIBLE & ANCHOR* on the Pavement in St. Martin's Lane.   1742
(The west side of St. Martin's Lane from Beard's Court to St. Martin's Court was known as " The Pavement " or " The Paved Stones.")

ROBERT HARFORD, at the *ANGEL* on Cornhill, near The Royal Exchange.   1680

GEORGE KEARSLY, at *JOHNSON'S HEAD*, in Fleet Street.   *c.* 1780

JAMES LACKINGTON, at the *TEMPLE OF THE MUSES* in Finsbury Square.   1789
(The pioneer of bookselling on popular lines for cash.)

THOMAS LONGMAN, at the *SHIP & BLACK SWAN* in Paternoster Row.   1725—1775
(The business has been carried on since 1859 under the style of Longman, Green & Co.)

WILLIAM AND JOSEPH MARSHALL, at the *BIBLE* in Newgate Street.   1705

RALPH MINORS, at *PRIOR'S HEAD* in St. Clement's Church Yard, near Temple Bar.   1740

THOMAS MORS, at the *LUTE* on the North side of St. Paul's Church Yard.   *c.* 1740

DAVID MORTIER, at *ERASMUS' HEAD*, near Bedford House in the Strand.   1700

FRANCIS NOBLE, at *OTWAY'S HEAD* in King Street, Covent Garden.   1754
(One of the very earliest Circulating Libraries to be started in London.)

THOMAS NORRIS, at the *LOOKING GLASS* on London Bridge.   1715

JOHN OSBORN, at *THE SHIP* at St. Saviour's, Dock-Head. 1710
(In conjunction with Rivington (*q.v.*), he published Richardson's *Pamela* in 1741.)

ROBERT PEAKE, at the *BIBLE & CROWN* next to the Sunne Tavern, Snow Hill. 1611

H. PIERS, at the *FAN & BIBLE*, near the Bull & Gate, Holborn, and later at the *BIBLE & CROWN* in Holborn, near Chancery Lane. 1742
(Succeeded by Piers & Partner & Henry Webley, at the *Bible & Crown*, Holborn, and later by I. & J. Taylor, Priestley & Weale, John Weale and B. T. Batsford (*q.v.*).)

NATHANIEL PONDER, at ye *PEACOCK* in Chancery Lane. 1669

THE SHIP

EBENEZER POWELL, at the *BIBLE & DOVE* in Crooked Lane. *c.* 1720

JOHN PRIDDEN (successor to Mr. Manby), at the *FEATHERS* in Fleet Street, near Fleet Bridge. 1765

JOHN & JAMES RIVINGTON, at the *BIBLE & CROWN* in Paternoster Row. 1753
(This old established publishing house was founded by Charles Rivington in 1668 and is now carried on at 34, King Street, W.C.2.)

JAMES ROBSON, at the *FEATHERS* in Bond Street. 1764
(Successor to John Brindley, see above.)

RYALL & WITHY, at *HOGARTH'S HEAD & DIAL* opposite Salisbury Court in Fleet Street. 1755

GREYHOUND

WILLIAM SANDBY, at the *SHIP*, Without Temple Bar. 1765
(In 1768 he sold the business to John Murray under which name it is still carried on in Albemarle Street.)

JOHN SAYWELL, at the *GREYHOUND* in Little Britain. 1650

WILLIAM SHEARES, at the *BIBLE* in Bedford Street, Covent Garden. 1661

J. STARKEY, at the *MITRE* at West end of St. Paul's Church. 1660

THREE BIBLES

GOLDEN LEG

SENECA'S HEAD

SAMUEL STILLINGFLEETE, at the signe of the *SAMPSON AND LYON* in the Strand over against the New Exchange.   *c.* 1700

ISAAC TAYLOR, at the *BIBLE & CROWN* in Holborn, near Chancery Lane.   1770
(Succeeded by I. & J. Taylor, Priestley & Weale, John Weale and B. T. Batsford (*q.v.*).)

JOHN TRACEY, at the *THREE BIBLES* on London Bridge.   1722

ROGER TUCKER, at the *GOLDEN LEGG*, at the corner of Salisbury Street in the Strand.   1700

PAUL & ISAAC VAILLANT, at the *SHIP* in the Strand.   *c.* 1740

ABRAHAM VANDENHOECK & GEORGE RICHMOND, at the *VIRGIL'S HEAD*, opposite Exeter Exchange in the Strand.   1727

MATH : VARENNE, at the *SENECA'S HEAD* near Sommerset House in the Strand.   1712

JOHN WALTER, at the *HOMER'S HEAD*, Charing Cross.   1768

ROBERT WALTON, at the *GLOBE AND COMPASSES* on ye North side of St. Paul's Church.
                                                        1670

CÆSAR WARD & RICHARD CHANDLER, at the *SHIP*, between the Temple Gates in Fleet Street.
                                                        1740

A. WEBLEY, at the *BIBLE AND CROWN* in Holborn, near Chancery Lane.   1757
(Succeeded by Piers & Partner and Henry Webley.)

JOHN WILKIE, at the *BIBLE*, near the Chapter House in St. Paul's Church Yard.   1775

EDWARD WITHERS, at the *SEVEN STARS*, over against Chancery Lane in Fleet Street.   1740

HENRY WOODGATE & SAMUEL BROOKS, at the *GOLDEN BALL* in Paternoster Row.   1760

THOMAS WORRALL, at the *JUDGE'S HEAD*, against St. Dunstan's Church, Fleet Street.
(The sign depicts Lord Chief Justice Coke.)   *c.* 1730

RALPH ALDERSEY, at the *CROWN & SLIPPER*, the Lower End of the Minories, near Tower Hill. 1733

ANN ASKEW, at the *BOOT*, next door to the Three Tuns & Rummer in Grace-church Street. 1735

JAMES BAUGHAN (successor to Mr. Willis), at the *ANGEL* in Henrietta Street, Covent Garden. (R. Willis, 1746, see below.) *c.* 1760

JOSEPH CLEMPSON, at the *OLD CRISPIN* in Cranbourn Street, Leicester Fields. 1746 (See also Robt. Jefferson at this address.)

WILLIAM CORP, at the *BOOT* in Aldersgate Street. 1756

JOHN DRAKEFORD, spatterdash maker, at the *THREE SPATTERDASHES*, near Exeter Exchange in the Strand. *c.* 1750 (See also p. 157.)

THOMAS DUNCE & EDWARD HOW, at the *BOOT & CROWN* within Aldgate. *c.* 1760

MICHAEL ELLIS (successor to Mr. Eddis), at the Sign of the *BOOT* in Cannon Street. *c.* 1760

JOHN FLEMING, at the *MOOR & SLIPPER* in Clare Street, Clare Market. *c.* 1765

GOODMAN, at the *ANGEL & SLIPPER*, Shoreditch, facing the Swan tavern. *c.* 1740

THOMAS GRANT (nephew to the late Mr. Richd. Winckley) at the *HAND & SLIPPER* in Chichester Rents, Chancery Lane. *c.* 1770

JOHN GRESHAM, at the *CROWN* in York Street, Covent Garden. 1736 (**In** 1743 he had moved to the *Crown* in Tavistock Street.)

JAMES HARRIOTT, at ye *THREE CROWNS* against St. Paul's Church Yard, Cheapside. 1752 (A pair of Callamanco Clogs, 9s. 6d.)

JUDGE'S HEAD

CROWN & SLIPPER

THE BOOT

HAND & SLIPPER

THE CRISPIN

THE PEACOCK

BENJAMIN HASLOP (1), at the *PEACOCK* at Water Lane End in Fleet Street.   1728
(2) at the *PEACOCK*, near the White Horse Inn, Fleet Street.   1740
(See also John Strange (1727) and Samuel Wolfe (1759).)

ROBERT HOUSE, at the *HAND & SLIPPER* in Tothill Street, Westminster.   1746

E. HUGHES, at the *HAND & SLIPPER* in Norris Street, near St. James's Haymarket.   *c.* 1760

JOHN HUME & DAVID HENDRIE, at the *ROYAL BOOT* in Pall Mall.   1758

ROBERT JEFFERSON, at the *CRISPIN* in Cranborn Alley, Leicester Fields.   *c.* 1770
(See also J. Clempson at this address.)

RICHARD KITCHIN, at the *GOLDEN BOOT* in Great Turnstile, Holbourn.   *c.* 1760

SAMUEL PRICE, at the *GOLDEN BOOT* in Devereux Court, Temple.   1767

—— SHARMAN, at the *SHOE & SLIPPER*, opposite Hicks's Hall, St. John's Street. *c.* 1770

TIMOTHY SMITH, at the *CROWN & SLIPPER* opposite St. Mildred's Church, in the Poultry, near Cheapside.   *c.* 1760

JOHN SNOWDON, at the *ANGEL & THREE SHOES* in Cranbourn Alley, near Leicester Fields.   1764

JOHN STRANGE & BENJAMIN HASLOP, at the *PEACOCK* at Water Lane End in Fleet Street.   1727
(See B. Haslop (1740) and S. Wolfe (1759) at this address.)

PHILIP WELCH, at the *SHIP & ANCHOR* in Cornhill.   1787

RICHARD WILLIS, at ye *ANGEL* in Henrietta Street, Covent Garden.   1746
(See James Baughan, *c.* 1760.)

JOSEPH WILLMER, at the *BLUE LAST*, Cranborn Street, Leicester Fields.   *c.* 1760

SAMUEL WOLFE, at the *PEACOCK* in Fleet Street,
near Shoe Lane.   1759
(See Strange (1727) and Haslop (1740) above. Probably the
same shop as their's, for the White Horse Inn stood on the north
side of Fleet Street between Shoe Lane and Water Lane.)

WOOD, Spatterdash & gaiter maker at the
GOLDEN HORSE, Strand.   *c.* 1730

JONATHAN YEATES, at the Sign of the *BOOT* in
the Poultry over against the Bank.   1700

BRAZIERS

ANTHONY ANDREWS, at the *BELL & ANCHOR*,
No. 68 Fore Street, near Little Moorfields.   1772

CHARLES APPLEBEE & SON, at the *WHEAT-
SHEAF*, on Ludgate Hill.   *c.* 1765

JOHN CAUSWAY, at the *TEA KETTLE* in Princes
Street, Drury Lane.   *c.* 1760

EDWARD DERBY, at the *GOLDEN KEY*, Fleet
Ditch, opposite Bridewell.   *c.* 1770

THOMAS DOXSEY, at ye *TWO CANDLESTICKS
& KEY* near Great St. Helens, without Bishopsgate.   1771

THURSTON FORD, at the *CROSS KEYS* in Wood
Street.   1760

PRIOR GREEN, at the Sign of the *TEA KETTLE*,
near Little Moor-Gate in Moor-Fields.   *c.* 1740

JAMES GREENWOOD, at the *CROWN & KEY*,
without Bishopsgate.   1762

HALLETT & Co., at the *HARROW & ANCHOR*,
next Fishmongers' Hall, Upper Thames Street.
                                          c. 1760

JOHN JENKIN, at ye *TWO CANDLESTICKS &
ANCHOR* in Newgate Street.   1768

WILLIAM MILLER, at the *PETER & KEY*, in
West Smithfield.   *c.* 1760

THOMAS PICKETT, late Servant to Mr. Hancock in
Pall Mall, lives at the Sign of ye *FRYING PAN*
in Compton Street, ye corner of Frith Street,
Soho.   *c.* 1740

THE BOOT

CROSS KEYS

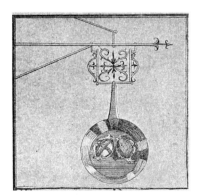

FRYING PAN

CHRISTOPHER ROMLEY, at the Sign of the *THREE BELLS*, in Horseshoe Alley, Middle Moorfields.
c. 1760

WILLIAM SELLERS, at the *MORTAR & PESTLE* in Little Tower Street. 1740

WILLIAM SMITH, at the *CISTERN*, near Russel Court, in Drury Lane. *c.* 1765

THOMAS STEVENSON, living at the *CHAMBER GRATE & GRIDIRON*, in Houndsditch. *c.* 1745

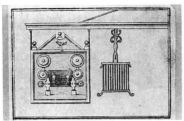

CHAMBER GRATE & GRIDIRON

C. WEAVER, the *GOLDEN EWER*, Badger yard, near St. John's Square. *c.* 1770

WALTER WEST, at the *GOLDEN BELL* in Old Bethlem. 1768

BREECHES MAKERS

JOHN BRISTOW, at the *BUCK & BREECHES*, in Piccadilly, near the Hay Market. *c.* 1750

ROWE BROWN, at the *MITRE & BREECHES*, in Silver Street, Golden Square. 1769

RICHARD COLEMAN, at the *BUCK & BREECHES*, on the Pavement, without Great Moorgate. 1755

THOMAS COLEMAN, at the *BUCK & BREECHES*, 3 doors from Northumberland House, Charing Cross. *c.* 1765

JOHN CURRIE, at the *BUCK & BREECHES*, in Mill Street, behind St. George's church, Hanover Square. *c.* 1750

JOHN EVES, at the *BUCK & BREECHES*, near the end of Hatton Garden, Holbourn. *c.* 1760

BUCK & BREECHES

THOMAS GILBERT, at the *BREECHES & GLOVE*, near the corner of James Street, Long Acre.
c. 1750

THOMAS GILBERT & RICE JONES, at the *BREECHES & GLOVE*, near the corner of James Street, Long Acre. *c.* 1750

RICE JONES, at the *BREECHES & GLOVE*, near the corner of James Street, Long Acre. 1758

PETER HOE, at ye *BREECHES & GLOVE*, removed from White Hart Yard into Brydges Street, near Russell Court, Covent Garden.

c. 1755

MARTHA HOLMES, at the *BELL & BREECHES*, next door but one to ye White Bear Inn, Piccadilly. 1760

THOMAS HURLSTONE, at the *BUCK, BREECHES & GLOVE*, in Pall Mall. 1760

WILLIAM KELLY, at the *BUCK & BREECHES*, in Old Paved Alley, St. James's. 1760

JOHN KING, at the *GLOVE & BREECHES*, at the corner of Conduit Street, near Hanover Square. 1768

JNO. NEWTON, at ye *BLUE ANCHOR & CROWN*, in Shoemaker Row, near Aldgate. 1762

THOMAS POOLE, at the *ROEBUCK*, in New Bond Street, near Grosvenor Square. 1766

JAMES POTTER, at the Sign of the *BOOT & BREECHES*, within 3 doors of Aldgate, in Shoemaker Row. *c.* 1740

WILLIAM ROGERS, at the Sign of the *BREECHES*, No. 17 in Hanway Street, opposite to the end of Great Russell Street, Bloomsbury. 1775

DAVID THOMAS, at the *BUCK & BREECHES*, the corner of James Street, Long Acre. 1780

JOHN THORNILL, at the *BUCK & BREECHES*, in Sheer Lane, Temple Bar. 1758

WALTER WATKINS, at the Sign of the *BREECHES & GLOVE*, on London Bridge, facing Tooley Street. *c.* 1755

JOHN YOUNG, at the *BREECHES*, in Chandois Street, near Covent Garden. 1722

BRICK MOULD MAKER

SAMUEL POWELL, at the *BEAR & RAGGED STAFF*, Whitecross Street, near Old Street.

c. 1760

BELL & BREECHES

BOOT & BREECHES

THREE BRUSHES

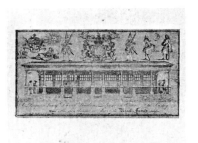

CHELSEA BUN HOUSE

GOLDEN LION

BROKER & APPRAISER

JOHN COX, at the *CROSS KEYS & STAR*, the corner of Spittle Square, Spittlefields. *c.* 1760

BRUSH MAKERS
See also BASKETMAKERS

STEPHEN GIMBER, at the *THREE BRUSHES*, No. 37 Holborn, near Fetter Lane. *c.* 1770

JOHN GRANT (son of the late Mrs. Ann Pitham) at the *FOUR BRUSHES*, the corner of the Square, on London Bridge. 1751

MR. JACKSON, at ye Sign of ye *COFFEE MILL* in Mutton Lane, by Clerkenwell Green. *c.* 1760

BOSWELL JENKINS, at ye *THREE BRUSHES*, in Budge Row, ye corner of Size Lane, near Queen Street. 1753

ABRAHAM SANDERS, at the *THREE BRUSHES & CROWN*, No. 82 Snow Hill, near Holborn Bridge. *c.* 1760

JAMES SMITH, at the *THREE BRUSHES*, No. 28 Fish Street Hill. 1779

NATHAN SMITH, at the *THREE BRUSHES*, on Snow Hill. *c.* 1760

JACOB VALE, at ye *TWO BRUSHES* in Tyler Street, over against Major Fobert's riding house, near Conduit Street. 1768

BUN BAKER

RICHARD HAND, at the *KINGS ARMS* at Chelsea. 1718

(Removed from ye Old Original Chelsey Bunn-house.)

The Chelsea Bun House was kept by four generations of the Hand family. It stood at the corner of Grosvenor Row, on the site now occupied by No. 60, Pimlico Road, and was pulled down in 1839. The Royal Arms are those of George I.

BUTTON MAKERS

GEORGE CATON, at the *GOLDEN LION & CROWN*, the corner of Mays Buildings, St. Martin's Lane, Covent Garden. *c.* 1760

TIMOTHY CATTELL, at the *UNICORN*, Middle Moorfields.   1762

CHARLES FINCH, at ye *QUEEN'S HEAD*, in Great Russell Street, Covent Garden.   *c.* 1760

HUGHES, at the *BLUE ANCHOR*, near the Talbot Inn, in the Strand.   *c.* 1765

THOMAS POWER, at the *DOVE*, in Shoe Lane, Fleet Street.   1750

JOHN STEVENSON, at the *GOLDEN LION*, opposite St. Clement's Church in the Strand.   1766

WILLIAM WRAY, at the *ROSE*, in Knaves' Acre, Soho.   *c.* 1765

THE ROSE

CABINET MAKERS

THOMAS ATKINSON (successor to the late Mr. Belchier *q.v.*), at the *SUN*, South side of St. Paul's, opposite the clock.   1755

JOHN BELCHIER,* at ye *SUN*, on the South side of St. Paul's, near Doctors Commons. 1735–1753

HENRY BELL, at the *WHITE SWAN*, against the South Gate in St. Paul's Church Yard. *c.* 1740
(Succeeded Coxed & Woster, *q.v.*)

ELIZABETH BELL, at the *WHITE SWAN*, against the South Gate in St. Paul's Church Yard.
    c. 1750

ELIZABETH BELL & SON, at the *WHITE SWAN*, against the South Gate in St. Paul's Church Yard.   *c.* 1760

PHILIP BELL, at the *WHITE SWAN*, against the South Gate in St. Paul's Church Yard.   1768

CHARLES BLYDE, at the *CHAIR & TEA CHEST* in Knaves' Acre (Pulteney Street, Golden Square).   *c.* 1760

JOHN BROWN, at the *THREE COVER'D CHAIRS & WALNUT TREE*, the East side of St. Paul's Church Yard, near the School.   1728–1744

WHITE SWAN

3 COVERED CHAIRS & WALNUT TREE

* See *Purefoy Letters*, p. 97 *et seq.*

HAND & CROWN & STAR

THE ANGEL

HENRY BUCK, from the *HAND & CROWN* at the East end of St. Paul's, to the *HAND & CROWN & STAR*, on the South side of St. Paul's Church-Yard.   1741

ANN BUCK (widow of above), at the *QUEEN'S HEAD* near Hatton Garden.   1745

JOHN BURROUGH, at ye *LOOKING GLASS* on Cornhill.   1662
(Cabinet maker to Charles II.)

DAVID CARTO, at the *DRIPPING PAN*, between New [Broad] street and Little Moorgate, in Moorfields.   1745

WILLIAM CAUTY, at ye Sign of the *CHAIR & CURTAINS*, the West end of Somerset House, in the Strand.   1757
(Had removed to King Street, St. James's, in 1774.)

THOMAS CHIPPENDALE & JAMES RANNIE, at the *CHAIR*, in St. Martin's Lane.   1755–1766
(The sign of the Chair was used by Chippendale at his shop in St. Martin's Lane. *Whitehall Evening Post*, 4 Dec., 1756.)

JAMES COMERY, at ye *GOLDEN EAGLE*, in Castle Street, behind Long Acre.   1749–1770

C. COXED & T. WOSTER, at the *WHITE SWAN*, against the South gate in St. Paul's Church Yard.   1724
(Preceded Henry Bell, *q.v.*)

BENJAMIN CROOK, at ye *GEORGE & WHITE LYON*, on ye South side of St. Paul's Church Yard.   *c.* 1740

——DALZIEL, at the *CHAIR* the corner of Wych Street, facing Drury Lane.   *c.* 1760

RICHARD FARMER, at the *HAND & CROWN*, the East end of St. Paul's Church Yard, near the School.   1744
(Formerly in partnership with Henry Buck, *q.v.*)

HUGH GRANGER, at the *CARVED ANGEL*, in Aldermanbury.   1692–1706

WILLIAM GWINNELL, at the *LOOKING GLASS*, ye South side of St. Paul's. 1741

JOHN HATT (successor to Mr. John Arrowsmith), at the *BLUE BALL & ARTICHOKE*, in Aldersgate Street. 1759

WILLIAM HENSHAW, at the *CABINET & CHAIR* on the South side of St. Paul's Church Yard. 1763

THOMAS HOLDEN, at the Sign of the *CHAIR*, in Hanover Street, near Castle Street, Long Acre. *c.* 1760

RICHARD HOLMES, at the *TEA CHEST*, in Barbican. *c.* 1780

PHILLIP HUNT, at ye *LOOKING GLASS & CABINET* at East end of St. Paul's Church Yd. 1720

GEORGE KEMP, at the *GOLDEN BALL*, Cornhill. 1772

WILLIAM KIRK, at the Sign of the *GOLDEN CHAIR*, the corner of Salisbury Street in ye Strand. 1749

LANDALL and GORDON, at ye *GRIFFIN & CHAIR*, in Little Argyle Street, by Swallow Street. *c.* 1740

CHRISTOPHER MARTIN, at the *STAR* by Fleet Market near Fleet Street. 1747

DANIEL MILLS, at the *JAPAN CABINET & CISTERN* in Vine Street, near Hatton Garden, Holborn. 1775

JOHN NEWMAN, at the *FEATHERS & BALL*, the South side of St. Paul's Church Yard. 1755

WILLIAM OLD and JOHN ODY at the *CASTLE* in St. Paul's Church Yard over against the South Gate of ye Church. 1720

JOHN PARDOE, at the *CABINET & CHAIR* next to Temple Barr in ye Strand, remov'd from aga^st St. Clement's Church. 1740

LOOKING GLASS & CABINET

GOLDEN CHAIR

THE CABINET

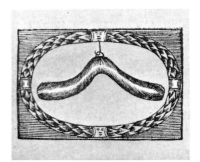

CROOKED BILL

THE CALICO PRINTER

CABINET MAKERS

THOMAS PISTOR, at the *CABINET*, on Ludgate Hill.   1699–1711

FRANCIS PYNER, at the *TENT*, near George Yard, Lombard Street.   1765–1793

BENJAMIN RACKSTRAW, at *SIR ISAAC NEWTON'S HEAD*, the corner of Crane Court in Fleet Street.   1747

THOMAS SILK, at the *BLUE CURTAIN*, No. 4, St. Paul's Church Yard.   1772
(Successor to J. Fall, upholsterer, *q.v.*)

NATHANIEL SKINNER, at the *BLACK LYON* on ye South side of St. Paul's.   *c.* 1720

GEORGE SPEER, at the *SEVEN STARS*, No. 2, Great Tower Street.   1779–1802

JOHN SPEER, at ye *LION & LAMB*, West side of Fleet Market.   *c.* 1760

CHRISTOPHER WALLIS, at the *BLUE FLOWER-DE-LUCE*, next Drury Lane, Long Acre. *c.* 1765

STEPHEN WOOD, at the *CABINET*, near the Bridge Foot, Southwark.   1725

CALENDRER

RICHARD IRONS, at the Sign of the *CROOKED BILL*, over against the Cock, in the Great Old Bailey.   *c.* 1700

CALICO PRINTERS

C. HOOKER, at the *ANCHOR & CROWN*, in Ratcliff High Way, between Old and New Gravel Lane.   *c.* 1750

JACOB STAMP, at ye Sign of the *CALLICO PRINTER*, in Hounsditch.   *c.* 1680

CANE WORKER

BENJAMIN FORFIT, at ye *ANGEL & CROWN*, near ye East India House, in Leaden Hall Street.   1749

SAMUEL TOTEN, at the *GOLDEN KEY*, in Dean
Street, Fetter Lane.   *c.* 1760

CARPENTERS

JOHN KING, at the *FOUR COFFINS & HEART*,
in Little Earl Street, near the Seven Dials.
     c. 1720

WILLIAM OVERLEY, at the sign of the *EAST
INDIA HOUSE*, in Leaden-hall Street.   *c.* 1700

HENRY SIDGIER, at the *CARPENTERS' ARMS*,
in Great Shere Lane, near Temple Barr.   *c.* 1765

CARVERS & GILDERS

DAVID CRASHLAY, at *SIR ISAAC NEWTON'S
HEAD*, in Long Acre.   *c.* 1780

——DUFFOUR, at the *GOLDEN HEAD*, in Berwick
Street, Soho.   *c.* 1780

MARTIN FOXHALL, at the *GOLDEN HEAD*, in
Great St. Andrew's Street, Seven Dials.   *c.* 1790

JOAN JAQUES, at the *KING'S ARMS*, No. 14
Holborn, near Gray's Inn Gate.   1790

ROBERT JOHNSON, at the *GOLDEN HEAD*,
Frith Street, St. Ann's.   *c.* 1780

HENRY JOURET, at the *ARCHITRAVE FRAME*,
in Grafton Street, St. Ann's, Soho.   *c.* 1760

WILLIAM MASSA, at the *GOLDEN HEAD*, near
New Inn, in Wytch Street, Drury Lane. *c.* 1780

THOMAS MERLE, at the *GOLDEN KEY*, Leadenhall Street.   1790

RENÉ STONE, at the *GOLDEN HEAD*, Berwick
Street, Soho.   1772

——WATSON, at the *KING'S ARMS*, No. 21, Long
Acre.   *c.* 1790

CHARLES WHARTON, at the *CROWN & TWO
SCEPTRES*, in Queen Street, in the Park,
Southwark.   *c.* 1750

4 COFFINS & HEART

CARPENTERS' ARMS

EAST INDIA HOUSE

THE DOLPHIN

DAIRY MAID & CHURN

THE LAMB

HENRY PRICE, at the *TWO CHAINS & BUCKLES* in King's Gate Street, near Red Lion Square.
c. 1770

CHEESEMONGERS

EDWARD DE SANTÉ, at the *DOLPHIN*, No. 83 Leadenhall Street.   1756

JOHN DOBSON, at the *CHEESE & STAR*, East Smithfield, Tower Hill.   1769

ROBERT GREEN, at the *DAIRY MAID & CHURN*, near the Half Moon Inn, in the Borough.   *c.* 1760

GEORGE KENDAL, at the Sign of the *DOLPHIN*, near ye White Horse Inn, in Fleet Street.
c. 1760

MATTHEWS & HOLMES, at the *THREE HORSE SHOES*, against St. Martin's Le Grand, in Newgate Street.   *c.* 1770

THOMAS MILLER, at the *DAIRY MAID & CHESHIRE CHEESE* at Wapping Old Stairs.

RICHARD PLIMPTON, at ye *RED COW*, in Clare Market.   1739

JNO. SMITH & WM. PALMER, at ye *BLACK BOY* in Thames Street, near ye Custom-house.   1716

CHEMISTS & DRUGGISTS

PETER ARNAUD, at ye *LAMB*, in ye Poultry.   1737

AMOR AUSTWICK, at the *BLACK LION & GOLDEN ANCHOR* facing Gray's Inn Gate in Holborn.   *c.* 1760

VINCENT BARNETT, at the *GOLDEN KEY*, opposite the East India House, Leadenhall Street.   *c.* 1765

SAMUEL BLACKWELL, at the *QUEEN'S HEAD & STAR*, near St. Andrew's Church, Holborn.
1752

SAMUEL BLACKWELL & SON, at above.   1764

SAMUEL BLACKWELL & SON, at the *GOLDEN LION & UNICORN*, over against the West end of the New Exchange in the Strand.   1767
(Successors to Peter Snee at above.)

WILLIAM BLACKWELL, at ye *BUCKTHORN TREE*, Covent Garden, or at his garden, South Lambeth.   1775

STEPHEN BREARCLIFFE, at the *CIVET CAT & THREE HERRINGS* near Cloth Fair in West Smithfield.   *c.* 1760

FENWICK BULMER, at the *BELL & DRAGON* in the Strand.   *c.* 1780

THOMAS CORBYN, at the *BELL & DRAGON* in Holborn.   1755

HENRY CUNDELL, at the *GOLDEN HEAD*, No. 47, the corner of Swan Street, in the Minories.   *c.* 1780

DALMAHOY, at *GLAUBER'S HEAD*, opposite the Old Baily, on Ludgate Hill.   1748

ALEXANDER DOUGLAS, at the *GOLDEN HEAD* [Glauber's] near St. Clement's Church, in the Strand.   1778

F. FERNYHOUGH, at the *WHITE HORSE*, without Newgate.   *c.* 1770

FRENCH & SADLER, at the *GOLDEN KEY*, No. 18, Norton Folgate, near Shoreditch.   *c.* 1780

AMBROSE GODFREY, at the *PHOENIX*, Southampton Street, Covent Garden (see *D.N.B.*).   1747

AMBROSE GODFREY HANCKWITZ (as above).   1721–1741

JOHN HORNIDGE, at *BOERHAAVE'S HEAD*, opposite St. Bride's Church, Fleet Street.   1747
Hermann Boerhaave, Dutch physician (b. 1668—d. 1738).

JOHN KENT & THOS. CALVERLEY, at the *GRIFFIN*, over against the George Inn in ye Borough of Southwark.   *c.* 1750

CIVET CAT & 3 HERRINGS

BOERHAAVE'S HEAD

THE GRIFFIN

LION & UNICORN

GOLDEN KEY

—— LABROW, at the *GLAUBER'S HEAD*, St. John Street.   *c.* 1770

CORNELIUS LYDE, at the *BLACK LYON* in Fleet Street, near Salisbury Court.   *c.* 1740

COLLET MAWHOOD, at ye *GOLDEN LION & UNICORN*, against the New Exchange in the Strand.   1748

JAMES MAWHOOD, at ye *GOLDEN LION & UNICORN*, against the New Exchange in the Strand.   1756

PETER SMEE, at ye *GOLDEN LION & UNICORN*, against the New Exchange in the Strand.   1758

SAMUEL BLACKWELL & SON, at ye *GOLDEN LION & UNICORN*, against the New Exchange in the Strand.   1764
(See also at *Queen's Head & Star*, Holborn.)

GERVASE & VINCENT NEWTON, at the *BLACK LYON & ANCHOR*, facing Gray's Inn Gate, Holborn.   1750

NORRIS & SMITH, at the *SUN* in Cheapside.
                                    c. 1760

CHAS. NOYES & SAML. HOLLAND, at the *STAR*, in Cornhill.   1739

RICHARD PAYNE, at the *GOLDEN HEAD* in Coventry Street, near Piccadilly.   *c.* 1765

ROGER PINDAR, at ye *GOLDEN KEY*, in ye Borough.   *c.* 1755

SARAH SAMPSON, at the *GOLDEN STAR*, No. 46 on Great Saffron Hill, near Hatton Street, Holborn.   1778

RICHARD SIDDALL, at the *GOLDEN HEAD* in Panton Street, near the Hay-Market.   *c.* 1770

PETER SNEE, at the *GOLDEN LION & UNICORN*, against the New Exchange in the Strand.   1764

HENRY & GEORGE SISSON, at the *RED CROSS* in Ludgate Street.   1739

Thomas Stallard, at the *GLAUBER'S HEAD*, opposite Cree Church, in Leadenhall Street.
1761

Thos. Stephenson, at the *GOLDEN HEAD* in Hart Street, near St. Sepulchre's Church.
c. 1755

Thos. Townsend, at the *KING'S ARMS & GOLDEN HEAD*, near Panton Street in the Hay-Market.
1748

Robt. Turlington, at the *KING'S ARMS*, Birchin Lane.
1756

Edward Walmesley, at the *CONDUIT* on Snowhill.
1743

Martha & Hilton Wray, successors to Robt. Turlington & Wm. Wray, at the *KING'S ARMS*, No. 14, Birchin Lane.
1784

John Young, at the *RED CROSS*, against Bow Church, Cheapside.
1744–1753

GOLDEN HEAD

CHIMNEY SWEEPS & NIGHTMEN

John Bates, successor to Robert Stone & Mary Burnett, at the *GOLDEN POLE*, the Upper end of Whitecross Street, near Old Street, St. Luke's.
1763

John Cole, at the *GOLDEN POLE* in Goswell Street, near Old Street.
1740

Samuel Collins, at the *TWO BREWERS*, in Tothill Street, Westminster.
c. 1780

Francis Hallmarke, at the *SUN*, in Oxford Road, near Rathbone Place.
1767

Martha Harrison, at the Sign of the *SUN & FEATHERS*, the corner of David Street, Oxford Road.
1780
[This bill is made out to Mr. Gibbon (the historian) at his house, No. 7, Bentinck Street.]

W. James, at the *GEORGE & GATE*, Gracechurch Street.
c. 1770

GOLDEN POLE

THE WOMAN CHIMNEY SWEEP

THE FLOWER POT

THE CHINA JAR

ROBINS & HARPER, at the *HAMPSHIRE HOG*, Goswell Street.   1787

ROBERT STONE, at the *GOLDEN POLE*, the Upper End of White Cross Street, near Old Street.   1745–1761

ROBERT STONE, at ye Sign of ye *SHIP* in Hartshorn Court, ye upper end of Golden Lane, Old Street.   (?) 1787

JEANE TEMPELL, at the Signe of the *WOMAN CHIMBLEY SWEPER* in Nutners Street, near the Watch House, in Holborn.   *c.* 1740

CHINA MEN

JAMES AMSON, at the *CHINA JARR*, near the New Exchange Buildings, Strand.   1765

ELIZABETH, ANN & MARTHA BAKER, at the *CHINA JARR*, near the Post Office in Lombard Street.   1762

EDWARD CLARKE, at the *CHINA JAR*, on Ludgate Hill.   1768

JNO. CLARKSON, at the *TEA POT*, in Market Street, St. James's Market.   1764

JOHN COTTERELL, at the *INDIAN QUEEN & TEA CANNISTER*, against Stocks Market.   1735

DOYLE'S WAREHOUSE, at ye *FLOWER POT*, in Crown Court, near St. Ann's Church, Soho.   *c.* 1760

ROBERT FOGG, at the *CHINA JARR*, in New Bond Street.   1760

EDMUND MORRIS, at the *CHINA JARR*, in Gray's Inn Passage, coming into Red Lyon Square, Holbourn.   *c.* 1760

BEN : PAYNE, at the *THREE CANNISTERS*, the corner of Chancery Lane, Temple Bar.   1753

JOHN ROBERTS, at the *QUEEN'S HEAD*, in Holborn, near Hatton Garden.   1761

FREDERICK STANTON & JOHN COTTERELL, at the *INDIAN QUEEN*, the corner of Grocers' Alley in the Poultry. 1722–1748

JANE TAYLOR & SON, at the *FEATHERS* in Pall Mall. 1756

CHARLES VERE, at the *INDIAN KING*, the corner of Salisbury Court, Fleet Street. 1757–1764

CLOCK & WATCH MAKERS

GEORGE CLARKE, at the *DIAL & WHEEL*, over against ye Mount, in Whitechappel. *c.* 1720

[JOHN] COWELL, at the *DIAL*, opposite Pope's Head Alley, on Cornhill. 1763

ALEXANDER CUMMING, at the *DIAL & THREE CROWNS*, in New Bond Street. *c.* 1770

WILLIAM DEVIS, at the *DIAL*, opposite St. Dunstan's Church, Fleet Street. 1760

THOMAS FAZAKERLEY, at the *DIAL & CROWN*, in St. John's Street, near Hick's Hall. 1765
Hick's Hall was the Sessions House of the County of Middlesex in St. John's Street, Clerkenwell, from which the milestones on the Great North Road were measured.

THOMAS FOXALL, at the sign of the *SPRING CLOCK*, near East Lane, Rotherhith. *c.* 1760

MATTHEW GAUCHERON, successor to Mr. Vitu, at the *DIAL*, in Tower Street, near ye Seven Dials. *c.* 1760

M. [MARY] GIBSON, at the *DIAL & CROWNS* in Newgate Street. *c.* 1750

GEORGE GRAHAM (successor to Thomas Tompion], at the *DIAL & ONE CROWN*, Fleet Street. 1748

THOMAS HEMINGS, at the *DIAL*, the corner of Air Street, in Piccadilly. 1747

THOMAS JARVIS, at the *DIAL*, Wapping Old Stairs. *c.* 1760

INDIAN QUEEN

DIAL & CROWN

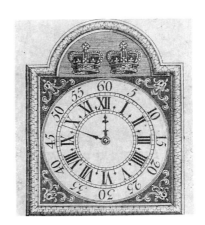

DIAL & CROWNS

THE CLOCK CASE

PATTEN & CROWN

JNO. MONKHOUSE, at the *DIAL* in Gloucester Street, near Red Lyon Square.   *c.* 1760

THOS. MUDGE & WILLM. DUTTON, at the *DIAL & CROWN* in Fleet Street.   1755

CHRISTOPHER PINCHBECK, SENR., at *PINCH-BECK'S HEAD* in Fleet Street.   *c.* 1740
This Christopher Pinchbeck was son of the first Christopher Pinchbeck (died 1732). He added "Senior" to his name to distinguish himself from his brother Edward, the inventor of the well-known alloy, who had succeeded to the business of the original Pinchbeck, senior, at the sign of the "Musical Clock" in Fleet Street.

C. & J. PLUMLEY, at the *CROWN & PEARL*, No. 43 Ludgate Hill.   *c.* 1820

JACOB RIVIERE & WILLIAM SMITH, at the *DIAL* in Princes Street, Cavendish Square, Oxford Road.   *c.* 1780

JAMES ROBINSON, at the *DIAL*, in Graces Alley, Well Close Square.   *c.* 1760

JOSEPH ROSE & SON, at the *DIAL*, in St. Ann's Lane, Foster Lane, near Cheapside.   *c.* 1770

THOMAS & CHARLES RUSSELL [maker of clock cases only], at the *CLOCK CASE*, No. 18, Barbican, near Cripplegate.   1780

JNO. SIMS, at the *GOLDEN CUP*, Lombard Street (successor to Finch & Sims).   1775

JOSEPH STEPHENS, at ye *DIAL & CROWN*, near ye Bars in Whitechappel.   *c.* 1740

RICHARD STREET, at the *DIAL & TWO CROWNS*, over against St. Dunstan's Church, in Fleet Street.   *c.* 1720

[CHARLES ?] THOMPSON, at the *DIAL & CROWN*, in St. Ann's Lane, near Aldersgate.   *c.* 1760

SAMUEL TOULMIN, at the *DIAL*, in Burleigh Street, near Exeter Change, in the Strand. *c.* 1760
(See also under Cockspur makers.)
(Samuel Toulmin was one of the last of the makers of silver cockspurs. He succeeded to the business of the very famous cockspur makers, Smith & Gatesfield, about the year 1750.)

JOHN WAIT, at ye sign of ye *DIAL*, against Gun Dock Yard in Wapping.   *c.* 1765

CLOG MAKER

THOMAS BERRY, at the *PATTEN & CROWNE*, under St. Dunstan's Church in Fleet Street.   *c.* 1700

CLOTHIERS & SLOP-SELLERS

HENRY ATTERBURY, at the sign of the *GOLDEN BALL*, in New Rents, in St. Martin's-le-Grand.   1707

CASALTINE & MATHEWS, at the *LAMB & STAR*, the 2nd shop in Houndsditch, facing Aldgate Church.   *c.* 1750

KENELM DAWSON, at the sign of the *JOLLY SAILOR*, in Monmouth Street.   *c.* 1740

FULLAGAR & TODD, at the *GOLDEN BALL*, near ye India House, in Leadenhall Street.   1767

GEORGE HARTLEY, at ye *ROSE & CROWN* in Monmouth Street.   *c.* 1730

RICHARD HORN, at the *GOLDEN ANCHOR*, in the Borough High Street, next door to the Dog and Bear Inn.   *c.* 1770

HULL & BENNETT, at the Sign of the *HOOP-PETTICOAT*, Houndsditch.   1783

RICHARD LANGRISH, at the Sign of the *THREE KINGS*, in Watling Streete.   1663
(The arms are those of the City of London and the Merchant Taylors' Company.)

COACH BUILDERS

JAMES MARRIOT (successor to Christopher Hall), at the *NAKED BOY*, in Long Acre.   *c.* 1760

THORNTHWAIT & KELWAY, at the *GOLDEN UNICORN*, in Upper Mount Street, Grosvenor Square.   *c.* 1760

SHADRACH VENDEN, at the *ANGEL*, in Holbourn.   *c.* 1750

LAMB & STAR

JOLLY SAILOR

COLLIER & CART

BLACKMOOR'S HEAD

SPOTTED DOG

COAL MEN

JOHN EDWARDS, at the *OLD COLLIER AND CART*, at Fleet Ditch, near Holborn Bridge. 1717

PHILIP FRUCHARD, at the *GOLDEN HEART*, in All-hallows Lane, Thames Street. *c.* 1740

HENRY WILLIAMS, at the *THREE COMPASSES*, at the Ditch Side, near Fleet Bridge. *c.* 1760

COAT SHOP

MARY ANTROBUS & DOROTHY GRAY, at the *BLACKMOOR'S HEAD* in Cornhill. 1735

COCK SPUR MAKER

SAMUEL TOULMIN (successor to Smith & Gatesfield), at the *DIAL & CROWN*, near Hungerford Market, in the Strand.
(He also worked as a clockmaker.)

COFFIN PLATE CHASERS

EDWARD HOPKINS, at the *SPOTTED DOG* on Snow Hill. *c.* 1760

THOMAS NOWELL, at the *ANGEL*, in the Great Old Bayley, without Newgate. *c.* 1740

JOHN OLIVER, at the *ANGEL & CROWN*, near ye Four Lamps, on Snow Hill. *c.* 1760

COLOURMEN

GEORGE BLACKMAN, at the *BLUE-COAT BOY*, No. 362 Oxford Street. 1808

JOHN CALFE, at *ST. LUKE'S HEAD*, Without Temple Barr. *c.* 1690

NATHAN DRAKE, successor to Robert Keating*, at the *WHITE HART* in Long Acre. 1763

At the *WHITE LION* in James Street, Covent Garden, near Long Acre. 1777

ALEXANDER EMERTON, at the *BELL*, near St. Clement's Church in the Strand. 1725

---

* W. T. Whitley, in *Artists and their Friends*, says that Robert Keating is the earliest recorded artists'-colourman (1749–1763).

ELIZABETH EMERTON [widow of above], at the *BELL*, near St. Clement's Church in the Strand.
1741

ALEXANDER EMERTON & COMPANY [son], at the *BELL*, near St. Clement's Church in the Strand.
c. 1750

JOSEPH EMERTON, Brother to the late Mr. Alexander Emerton, at the *BELL & SUN*, over against Norfolk Street, between St. Clement's and the New Church in ye Strand. 1748

THOMAS ETTERIDGE, son in law to the late Mr. Joseph Emerton, at the *BELL & SUN* (as above).
1747

WILLIAM MILLER, at the *DOLPHIN & ROSE*, next door to the George Inn, in the Borough of Southwark. *c.* 1700

JOSEPH PITCHER, at the sign of the *GOOD WOMAN* near St. Giles's Church. 1764
(This sign is alternatively styled *The Silent Woman* and was often adopted by oilmen. The rather far-fetched explanation offered by Larwood and Hotten is that it was in allusion to the *heedless* or foolish virgins in the parable.)

WILLIAM & THOMAS REEVES, at the *BLUE COAT BOY*, No. 80, Holborn Bridge. 1781

REEVES & INWOOD, at the *KINGS ARMS & BLUE COAT BOY*, No. 300 Strand, by the New Church. 1807

SAMUEL RUDD, at the *WHITE LYON & SUN*, without Aldgate. 1740

THOMAS SHARP, at the *THREE KINGS*, opposite the Market in Newgate Street. *c.* 1780

FRANCIS STACY, at the *SAINT LUKE*, the corner of Long Acre next Drury Lane. *c.* 1765

JAMES STONE, at the *OLIVE TREE & COLOUR BARREL*, within Bishopsgate. *c.* 1760

THOMAS WADDELL & SON, at the *ORIGINAL GOOD WOMAN** near St. Giles's Church. 1783

CROOK WILSON, at the *BLUE DOG* in the Minories. 1768

DOLPHIN & ROSE

BLUE COAT BOY

GOOD WOMAN

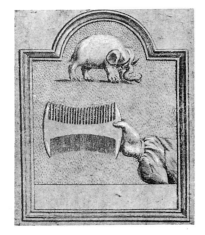

ELEPHANT, HAND & COMB

GOLDEN PHEASANT

WILLIAM BONNER, at the *THREE COMBS &
POWDER FLASK*, over against ye King's Head
Tavern, ye Corner of Chancery Lane, Fleet
Street.   *c.* 1760

WILLIAM BOWERS, at the *CROWN & COMB*,
within Aldgate.   *c.* 1750

THOMAS HEDGES, at the *ELEPHANT, HAND &
COMB*, the Old Shop in St. Martin's-le-Grand.
                                         c. 1730

COMPOSITION ORNAMENT MAKER & PLAISTERER

THOMAS BROWN, at the *GOLDEN HEAD*, in
Ax Yard, King Street, Westminster.   *c.* 1770

CONFECTIONERS & PASTRYCOOKS

THOMAS COLLINS, at the *SUGAR LOAF*, No. 67,
St. Paul's Church Yard.   *c.* 1780

S. CRISPIN, at the *WHEATSHEAF*, between Great
Turn Stile and Chancery Lane, in Holborn.
                                         c. 1740

CHARLES DUBUY, at the *ROYAL BISKET* in
Norris Street, near St. James's Market.   1747

JAMES ERWIN, at the *GOLDEN FAME & PINE
APPLE*, the south corner of Berkley Square. 1760

SAMUEL HANAM, at the *PHEASANT*, No. 186,
Fleet Street.   *c.* 1780

JOHN HOFFMAN, at the *PINE APPLE* in the City
Road, near Dog House Bar, Old Street.   1767

——— JOHNSON, at the *PINE APPLE*, Leicester
Square.   1785

FREDERICK KUHFF, at the *ROYAL ARMS*, in
the Hay Market.   1763

FRANCIS LAWE, at the *EAGLE & CHILD*, in
Fleet Street, near Bride Lane.   *c.* 1750

RICHARD MORLEY (successor to the late Mr.
Weedon, *q.v.*), at the *GOLDEN PHEASANT*,
No. 160, Fleet Street.   *c.* 1765

DOMINICUS NEGRI, at the *POT & PINE APPLE* in Berkeley Square.   1757

At the *PINE APPLE*, Berkeley Square. *c.* 1760

NEGRI & GUNTER, at the *PINE APPLE*, No. 7, Berkeley Square.   1784
(In the London Directories the name of James Gunter does not re-appear at No. 7 Berkeley Square until 1802. From 1817 to 1827 the firm is James & Robert Gunter, from 1827 to 1839 it is Robert & John Gunter. This famous shop remained at No. 7, Berkeley Square until the demolition in 1937.)

NEGRI & WETTEN, at the *PINE APPLE*, No. 7, Berkeley Square.   1789

RICHARD PERRY, at the *PHEASANT*, No. 60, Oxford Street.   *c.* 1800

WILLIAM SMITH, at ye *KING'S ARMS* in Old Bond Street.   1768

THOMAS STREET, at ye *KING'S ARMS* in Old Bond Street.   1756

THOMAS STOKES at the *PINE APPLE*, High Street, Kensington.   *c.* 1760

WILLIAM WEEDON, at the *GOLDEN PHEASANT*, near the Horn Tavern, No. 159 in Fleet Street.   *c.* 1760

ROBERT WILLS, at the *HAUNCH OF VENISON*, over against the North Door of St. Paul's, the corner of Cannon Alley.   1745

PINE APPLE

COOPERS

JOHNS ADAMS (at the late Mr. Pampion's), at the sign of the *BATHING TUB*, near White Chapel Bars.   *c.* 1760

THOMAS HUBBARD, at the *BATHING TUB & PAIL*, in Bishopsgate Street, near Wide Gate Alley.   *c.* 1760

COPPER PLATE MAKER

BENJAMIN WHITTOW, at the *CROWN*, in Shoe Lane, opposite the White Swan, near St. Andrew's Church, Holborn.   *c.* 1760

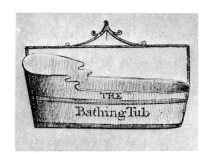

BATH TUB

HARLEQUIN & PIERROT

BEEHIVE & PATTEN

ROE BUCK

CORK CUTTER

JOHN PURSER, at the *CORK TREE* in St. Andrew's Street, Seven Dials. 1760

CORK JACKET MAKER

JOHN WARD, at the sign of the *CORK JACKET*, the foot of London Bridge, Southwark. *c.* 1760

COSTUMIER

JOHN MUMFORD, at ye *HARLEQUIN & PIERROT*, in Tavistock Street, Covent Garden. 1745

CRICKET BAT MAKER & TURNER

CHRISTOPHER THORN, at the *BEEHIVE & PATTEN* in John Street, Oxford Market. 1764

CUPPERS

See under SURGICAL & DENTAL OPERATORS

CURRIERS & LEATHER CUTTERS
See also LEATHER SELLERS

RICHARD DELL (late Wm. Stafford), at the sign of the *RED COW*, in Houndsditch. 1780

JOHN & ANTHONY NEATBY, at the *ROEBUCK*, by the Maze Pond in St. Thomas' Parish, Southwark. 1744–1809

SARAH SIMS (late Larkin), at the *GOLDEN BALL* in Silver Street, near Wood Street. *c.* 1770

CUTLERS, RAZOR MAKERS & SWORD CUTLERS

Sword Cutlers marked †   Surgical Instrument Makers ‡

ALSTON & GRAYHURST, at the *BLUE BOAR*, within Aldgate. 1720

MARK BATES [removed], from the corner of St. Paul's Alley to the *HATT & STAR* in St. Paul's Church Yard. *c.* 1710

ADEY BELLAMY, successor to Jonas Cockerton (*q.v.*), at the *SHIP*, No. 10 in the Poultry, facing Grocers' Alley. 1779

†JOHN BENNETT, at the *CROSS DAGGERS*, in Threadneedle Street, behind ye Royal Exchange. *c.* 1760

Sword Cutlers marked †   Surgical Instrument Makers ‡

NATHANIEL BENTLEY [commonly known as "Dirty
Dick," a well known London character. *See*
D.N.B.] & JOHN FISHER, at the *GOLDEN LYON
& CASE OF KNIVES*, near the Royal African
House in Leadenhall Street.   *c.* 1755

‡JAMES BERNARDEAU at the *PISTOL & L*, in
Russell Court in Drury Lane.   1736
(The sign of the initial L originated with Francis Liege who
was Bernardeau's predecessor at this address in 1712. Cutler's
marks were formed by the initial of the surname.)

‡JOHN BEST, at ye *MACE*, ye corner of Lumbard
Street next ye Stocks Market.   *c.* 1690

†CHARLES BIBB, at ye *FLAMING SWORD*, in
Great Newport Street, near St. Martin's Lane.
                                         1775

‡THOMAS BICKERSTAFF, at the *HALBERT*, in
Princes Street, between Lincoln's Inn Fields &
Drury Lane Market.   *c.* 1700

‡HENRY BODKER, at ye *HEART & STAR*, in
the Poultry, faceing the Old Jewry.   1765

M. BURCHELL, at the *ANODYNE NECKLACE &
CASE OF KNIVES*, in Long Acre, next Drury
Lane.   1744

ALEXANDER BURGES, at the *RED BULL & CASE
OF KNIVES*, the corner of Leadenhall Street,
next to Cornhill.   *c.* 1720

CHARLES CARLETON & SON, at the *CASE OF
KNIVES*, in New Street, Covent Garden. *c.* 1760

‡YEELING CHARLWOOD, at the *G. AND STAR* in
Russell Court, Drury Lane.   1770
(Successor to Jacob Gorden, *q.v.* Charlwood was followed by
H. Underwood at above address and also at No. 56, Haymarket,
where the business is still carried on to-day.)

[JONAS] COCKERTON & BELLAMY, at the *SHIP*,
No. 10 in the Poultry.   1777

HENRY COLE, at the *G.R. AND CROWN*, in
Old Round Court, in the Strand.   *c.* 1760

PISTOL AND L

CASE OF KNIVES

RED BULL & CASE OF KNIVES

DAGGER & CROWN

FLAMING SWORD

UNICORN

‡JOHN COOKE, at the Signe of the *SHEARS*, in Lombard Street.   *c.* 1700

‡JAMES CORNECK, Hosier, hatter and sword cutler, at the *LEG & BEAVER*, near St. Paul's, Cheapside.   1768

‡RICHARD COURTNEY, at the *DAGGER & CROWN* (?), three doors above Bartlet's Buildings, facing Hatton Garden, Holborn.   *c.* 1710

†NICHOLAS CROUCHER, at ye *FLAMING SWORD*, in St. Paul's Churchyard, the corner of Booksellers' Row, fronting Cheapside.   *c.* 1700

MATTHEW ENSOR, at ye *SEVEN STARS*, in Vere Street, Clare Market.   *c.* 1765

‡JOSEPH GIBBS, at the *HALF MOON & STAR*, in New Bond Street.   1759

JOSEPH GILLETT, at the *CASE OF KNIVES*, in St. James's Market.   *c.* 1750

‡JACOB GORDEN, at the *G. AND STAR*, in Russell Court, Drury Lane.   *c.* 1740
(Predecessor of Yeeling Charlwood, *q.v.*)

‡RICHARD GRANT, at the *G. AND CROWN*, in Crown Court, by St. Ann's, Soho.   *c.* 1745

‡MR. GRENIER, at the Signe of the *TARE* (? Tear).   1698
(No further address given but presumably in St. Martin's Lane.)

‡SAMUEL GROVER, at the *SCEPTER & HEART* on London Bridge.   *c.* 1700

†JOHN HILMAN [at the *FLAMING SWORD*], in New Bond Street, near Hannover Square.   1765

THOMAS HOLLIS, Senr. and Junr. [at the *CROSS DAGGERS*?], in the Little Minories.   1670

JOHN HYDE, at the *ANCHOR & CASE OF KNIVES*, ye corner of Queen Street, Cheapside.   1750

JOHN JACKSON, at the *UNICORN*, corner of Wood Street, Cheapside.   1699

Sword Cutlers marked †   Surgical Instrument Makers ‡

ALEXANDER JOLLY, at the sign of the *UNICORN & CASE OF KNIVES*, in Compton Street, Soho, within 3 doors of the Church passage.   *c.* 1760

HENRY LOOKER, at the *CITY ARMS*, within three doors of the Mansion House, in the Poultry.
                                            c. 1750

—— MILLWARD, at the *M. & STAR*, in King Street, near the Abbey, and also in Westminster Hall.   *c.* 1760

JOHN MOGGRIDGE, at the *EAGLE*, in Fenchurch Street.   *c.* 1770

BENJAMIN NICKLIN, at the *FLEECE & CASE OF KNIVES* in the Long Walk between Christ's and St. Bartholomew's Hospitals.   *c.* 1760

HENRY PATTEN, at the *SAW & CROWN*, in Middle Row, Holborn.   1756
(See also under Fishing Tackle Makers.)

MOSES ROBERTS, at the *FORK & CROWN*, in New Street, near Convent Garden.   *c.* 1720

JOSIAH ROGERSON, at the *CASE OF KNIVES* in the Hay-market, near Pickadilly.   *c.* 1760

‡PAUL SAVIGNY, successor to the late Widow How, at the *HALBERT & CROWN*, in St. Martin's Church Yard.   *c.* 1700

ROBERT SPARLING, at the *CASE OF KNIVES*, in St. James's Haymarket, corner of Norris Street.   1759

THOMAS SQUIRE, at the *CASE OF KNIVES*, opposite Mercers' Chapel in Cheapside. 1787

EDWARD TYMPERON, at the *E.T. & CROWN*, in Russell Court, Drury Lane.   1759

RICHARD WEALE, at the *BLUE GATE* in Cannon Street.   1744

DISTILLERS

THOMAS HOLFORD, at the *GOLDEN LYON*, in Bread Street.   1749

RICHARD PANTON, at the *MAN & STILL*, in Barbican.   1754

FLEECE & CASE OF KNIVES

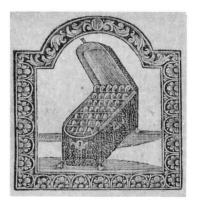

CASE OF KNIVES

PLOUGH & STILL

GROVES WHEELER, at the *PLOW & STILL*, in Leadenhall Street.   (Illustration p. 61.)   1754

EDMUND WOODS, at the *JUNIPER TREE*, in Warwick Lane, near Newgate Street.   1740

DRAWING MASTER

THOMAS JOHNSON, at the *GOLDEN BOY*, in Charlotte Street, Bloomsbury.   *c.* 1780

DYERS, SCOURERS & SILK DYERS

JOHN ALLAN, at the *CHERRY TREE*, No. 99, Leadenhall Street.   1777
(Successor to the late Mr. Osmond.)

ALLAN & OSMOND, at the *CHERRY TREE*, No. 99, Leadenhall Street.   1790

SAMUEL BEARD, at the *BLUE BALL* on Snow Hill.   *c.* 1740

INDIAN QUEEN

ANN & JOHN BOYER, at the *GREEN MAN* in Ivy Lane, Newgate Street.   1760

CHARLES CARPUE, at ye *CROWN* in Duke Street, Lincoln's Inn Fields.   1747–1785

VALENTINE COLE, at the *RAINBOW & DOVE*, near St. George's Church, Ratcliff Highway.   1765

BARNABY DARLEY, (1) at the *TURKS HEAD*, in Portland Street, near Berwick Street, Soho.   *c.* 1765

(2) At the *INDIAN QUEEN*, in Maiden Lane, Covent Garden.   1773

CATH: & EDWD. DARLEY, successors to B. Darley, at the *INDIAN QUEEN*, in Maiden Lane.   1773

GEO: DICKINSON, (1) at the *UNICORN*, in Stanhope Street, Clare Market.   *c.* 1760

(2) At the *DOVE*, in Blackmoor Street, Clare Market.   *c.* 1770

RAINBOW & DOVE

JOHN EDWARDS, at the sign of the *RAINBOW & DOVE*, in Aldersgate Street.   *c.* 1700

EDWARD EDWARDS, at the *RAINBOW & DOVE* in Fetter Lane, near Holbourn. *c.* 1760

WILLIAM FOXWELL, successors to Mr. Dew, deceased, at ye *INDIAN QUEEN* in Little Queen Street, Holborn. 1753

JOHN HILL, at the *PIDGEON*, opposite Crown Court, in Little Pultney Street, near Golden Square. *c.* 1760

RICHARD HORRABIN, at the *RAINBOW & DOVE* in Great Eastcheap, the upper end of Cannon Street. *c.* 1720

JAMES HUMMERSTONE, at the *GREEN MAN* in Lothbury. *c.* 1765
(Late servant to Mr. Jefferys, *q.v.*)

THE GREEN MAN

THOMAS JEFFERYS, at the *GREEN MAN* in Lothbury. *c.* 1760

WILLIAM MARSH, at the *RAINBOW & BUSH* in Brook Street, Holborn. *c.* 1780

JOHN PARKIN, at the *GREEN MAN*, near the May-Pole, in East Smithfield. *c.* 1720

RICHARD PEPYS, at ye *WHITE LION*, in Leadenhall Street, near Lime Street. *c.* 1760

GEORGE POWELL, at the Signe of the *DYERS ARMS* in the Litle Ould Baly neare Snow Hill. *c.* 1720

THOMAS ROBINS, at ye *RAINBOW & DOVE*, near Bridewell Bridge, Fleet Ditch, Blackfriars. *c.* 1760

RICHARD ROMMAN, at ye *RAIN BOW & ANCHOR*, near Barking Church in Tower Street. *c.* 1730

RAINBOW & ANCHOR

JAMES SAVAGE, at the *CROWN*, Sherrard Street, Golden Square. 1778

JOHN STOCKMAN, at the *SUN* in Sherrard Street, near Golden Square. *c.* 1740

JOHN TAYLOR, at the *PEACOCK* in Swallow Street, the corner of Maddox Street, near Hanover Square. 1790

MAN & MILL

EUSTACE TILLER, at the *RAINBOW & DOVE*, the corner of Magg Pye Alley, in Fetter Lane.
c. 1760

JOHN WALKER, at the *CROWN* in Leaden Hall Street, over against Billiter Lane.   c. 1700

JOHN WILDBLOOD, at the *RAINBOW & THREE PIDGONS* in St. Clement's Lane, in Lombard Street, who Married the Widdow Harrinton, Silk Dyer.   c. 1720

EMBROIDERER

LEVI ISAACS, at the *STAR* in Denmark Court, near Exeter Exchange, in the Strand.   c. 1750

ENAMELLER

ROBERT HIENS, at the *LAMB & DIAL*, in New Street, Covent Garden.   c. 1760

ENGINE MAKERS & MILLWRIGHTS

JOHN BRISTOW, at the *KING'S ARMS* in Ratcliff-Highway.

JONATHAN ELY, at ye *MAN & MILL* in Crooked Lane, near ye Monument.   c. 1740

JOHN ELY, at the *MILL & HAND-SCREW* in Crooked Lane, near the Monument.   1763

RICHARD HUGHES, at the *MILL, HAND-SCREW & BLUE BALL* in Crooked Lane, near the Monument.   c. 1760

PETER LYON, at the *DIAL, MILL & HAND-SCREW* in Tooley Street, near the Bridge Foot, Southwark.   c. 1760

(*See also under* MANGLE MAKERS)

ENGRAVERS

It is characteristic of the trade-cards of engravers that they rarely depict the trade-sign but rather tend towards ornamental or fanciful devices.

[WILLIAM] AUSTIN, at the *GOLDEN HEAD* in Great George Street, Hanover Square.   c. 1770

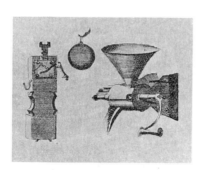

MILL, HAND-SCREW AND
BLUE BALL

HENRY BURGH, at the *CANISTER*, the corner of Magpye Yard, Fetter Lane.   *c.* 1750

ABRAHAM CATLETT, at ye *ROSE, CROWN & GARTER*, at the East Piller of the Royall Exchange.   *c.* 1740

ROBERT CLEE, at the *GOLDEN KEY* in Panton Street, near Leicester Fields.   *c.* 1760

BENJAMIN COLE, at the *SUN & KEY*, near Snow Hill conduit.   *c.* 1740

J. COUSE, at the *INDIAN QUEEN* in White Horse Yard, Stanhope Street, Clare Market.
                    c. 1750

WILLIAM & CLUER DICEY, at the *MAIDEN HEAD* in Bow Church Yard.   *c.* 1730

THOMAS HARPER, at the *BIBLE*, in King Street, Seven Dials.   *c.* 1760

WILLIAM HOGARTH, at ye *GOLDEN BALL*, ye corner of Cranbone Alley, Little Newport Street.
                    1720

(*cf.* R. Broughton, hatter, at this address, c. 1760.)
Hogarth was apprenticed to Ellis Gamble, silversmith, in 1712 and according to the D.N.B. this trade-card was his earliest work.

THOMAS OUGHTIBRIDGE, at ye sign of ye *SUN* in Brooks Market, near Holborn.   *c.* 1730

WILLIAM PENNOCK, at the *TOBACCO ROWLE* in Panier Alley in Newgate Street.   *c.* 1710

JOHN SAVAGE, at ye *GOLDEN HEAD* in St. Paul's Church Yard.   *c.* 1700

CHRISTOPHER SETON, at the *GOLDEN HEAD* in Suffolk Street, near Charing Cross.   *c.* 1760

R. SIMPKINSON, at the *SHIP*, near St. Dunstan's Church, Fleet Street.   1761

JOHN TINNEY, at the *CARVED GOLDEN LION*, near the Globe Tavern in Fleet Street.   1741

J. WARBURTON, at the *KING'S ARMS* in More Street, St. Ann's, Soho.   *c.* 1740

ROSE, CROWN AND GARTER

THE MAIDENHEAD

SUN & FAN

SWAN & GOLDEN FAN

JAMES BROOKER, at the *SUN & FAN*, the corner of St. Paul's Church-Yard, near Cheapside. 1735

BLANCH KEMP, at the *WHITE BEAR & STAR*, opposite the India House, Leaden Hall Street.
c. 1760

MRS. PHILLIPS, at the sign of the *FAN*, No. 5, Orange Court, Leicester Fields. *c.* 1770

ROBERT PICKEARD, at the *SWAN & GOLDEN FAN*, in Cheapside, near ye Conduit. *c.* 1720

MARY SANSOM, at ye *GOLDEN FAN*, next door to ye Nagg's Head Tavern in Cheapside. *c.* 1760

MARTHA SLEEPE, at the *GOLDEN FAN & SEVEN STARS*, next door to the Black Swan, the North Side of St. Paul's Church Yard. *c.* 1760

ESTHER SLEEPE, at the *GOLDEN FAN & SEVEN STARS*, opposite the Old Jewry in the Poultry.
c. 1760

FEATHERMAN

FRANCIS CURREY, at the *INDIAN QUEEN* in Ludgate Street, near St. Paul's. 1768

FEATHER BED MAKER

JOHN ROWE, at the Sign of the *ANGEL*, by Fleet Ditch, near Fleet Street. *c.* 1690

FIREWORKS MAKER

SAMUEL CLANFIELD, engineer to Ranelagh, Cupers and Marylebone Gardens, at the *ROYAL FIREWORKS* in Hosier Lane, West Smithfield. *c.* 1760

FISHMONGERS

CLARK, at the *OYSTER GIRL*, No. 13, Charles Street, Soho Square. *c.* 1790

JAMES PETO [" OYSTERICUS "] at the *POST BOY*, opposite the back gate of the General Post Office, Sherborne Lane. 1760

ANGEL

JOHN BRAILSFORD, at the *FISH & CASE OF KNIVES*, in the broad part of St. Martin's Court, Leicester Fields. 1769

WILLIAM BROWNE, at the Sign of the *FISH*, in the lower end of Black Horse Alley, at the steps near Fleet Bridge. 1693–1710

JOHN CHESHIRE & WILL BUSICK, at the *ANGLER & TROUT* in Crooked Lane. 1754

W. J. GEE & Co., at the *PERCH*, 19, St. Andrew Street, St. Martin's Lane. 1817

GEORGE GIMBER, at the *GOLDEN FISH* (?), No. 38, Crooked Lane. 1777

—— GREGORY, at the *DIAL & FISH*, opposite St. Clement's Church in the Strand. 1771

JOHN HERRO, at the *FISH & CROWN*, in Bell Yard, near Temple Bar. 1734

JOHN HIGGINBOTHAM, at the *GOLDEN FISH*, opposite Southampton Street, No. 91, Strand. *c.* 1785

GEORGE HUTCHISON, at ye *AMBERLEY TROUT* on Snow Hill. 1762

BARTHOLOMEW LOWE, successor to Stephen Penstone, at the sign of the *GOLDEN FISH*, against Wych Street, in Drury Lane. 1762

HENRY PATTEN, at the *SAW & CROWN* in Middle Row, Holborn. 1771
He combined this trade with that of Cutler. See p. 61.

HENRY STONE & CHAS. IVERSON, at the *OLD COMPLEAT ANGLER* (successors to Mr. Knight), a corner shop in Crooked Lane. *c.* 1760

ONESIMUS USTONSON (successor to Mr. John Herro), at the *FISH & CROWN*, the bottom of Bell Yard, near Temple Bar. 1775

FRUITERERS

JAMES COOK, at the *LEMON TREE*, Covent Garden. *c.* 1770

ANGLER & TROUT

FISH & CROWN

COMPLEAT ANGLER

JOHN COOK, at the *LEMON TREE*, Covent Garden.   1820

ANDREW HEARSEY, at the *BELL*, corner of Botolph Lane, Lower Thames Street.   1794

ELEANOR OGLE, at the *LEMON TREE*, Covent Garden.   1761

WHALE & RAVEN

FURRIERS

JAMES ARNOLD, at the *THREE RABBITS*, the corner of Cornhill.   1754

JOHN GOODSCHWED, at the *QUEEN'S HEAD*, opposite ye Cannon Tavern, Spring Gardens, Charing Cross.   *c.* 1750

ROBERT NORRIS, at the *KING'S ARMS & THREE RABBITS*, in Walbrook.   *c.* 1760

GARDENERS

See NURSERYMEN

GIRDLER & BELTMAKER

JOSEPH LAWRENSON, at ye *WHALE & RAVEN*, next door to Bow Church, in Cheapside. *c.* 1700

GLASS MAKERS & CUTTERS & SELLERS

HANNAH ASHBURNER, at the *ROSE*, the corner of Fleet Bridge.   1745
(Here Hannah Glasse published her famous work, " The Art of Cookery," in 1747.)

ASHBURNER & TODD, at the *ROSE & FAN*, the corner of Fleet Bridge.   1754

WILLIAM BALL, at the *GOLDEN BOTTLE*, No. 29, Within Aldgate.   1777

THOMAS BETTS, at the *KINGS ARMS*, opposite Pell Mell, Charing Cross.   1744–1765

JONATHAN COLLET, successor to the late Thos. Betts.   1765–1793

ANN GARRETT, at the *SHIP*, within Bishopsgate.   *c.* 1750

THE ROSE

C. & D. HEADY, the *KINGS ARMS*, No. 287
Strand, near Norfolk Street   1778

HEADY & LAFONT, at above.   1804

JAMES HIGGINBOTHAM, at the *GOLDEN BOTTLE*,
in Bishopsgate Street, near Cornhill.   1760

MAYDWELL & WINDLE, at the *KINGS ARMS*,
against Norfolk Street in the Strand.   1751–1778
(Succeeded by C. Heady, *q.v.*)

BENJAMIN SHERWILL, at the late house of Mr.
Markham Eles deceas'd, ye *CROWN*, the corner
of St. Mary Hill, Little Tower Street.   1739

TODD & LAMBDEN (successors to Ashburner &
Todd), at the *ROSE & FAN*, ye corner of
Fleet Bridge.   1756–1767

GLAZIERS

EDWARD MARSHALL, at the sign of the *SASH*,
in King Street, Seven Dials.   *c.* 1760

EDWARD THORNTON & SON, at the sign of the
SASH, in Old Bedlam, Moorfields   1722

GLOVERS

JOHN ANDREWS, at the sign of the *STAR &
GARTER*, over against Durham Yard, in the
Strand.   1742

CUE & RUTT, at the *HAND & GLOVE* in
Fenchurch Street.   1760

ISAAC DALVY, at ye *ANGEL & GLOVES*, in
Little Newport Street, Soho.   *c.* 1700

JAMES DALVY, at the *CROWN & THREE
GLOVES*, the corner of James Street in St.
James's Haymarket.   *c.* 1750

THOMAS FAIKNEY, at the *HAND & GLOVE*
[remainder of address wanting].   1729

H. JAFFRAY, at the *GLOVE & FAN*, near
Durham Yard, in the New Buildings, Strand.
(*See* illustration, p. 70.)   1745

GOLDEN BOTTLE

HAND & GLOVE

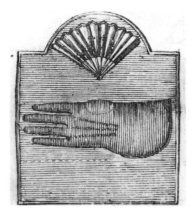

GLOVE & FAN

PRINCE'S ARMS & GLOVE

HAMMER & CROWN

GEORGE JENINGS, at the *ANGEL*, opposite Exeter Exchange, in the Strand.   1764–1792

WILLIAM JONES, at the *CROWN, GLOVE & ANCHOR*, in Cheapside, near St. Paul's.
1761–1772

WILLIAM MASSEY, at ye *GOLDEN BALL & STARR*, near Norfolk Street, in the Strand.   1756

JAMES PARNELL, at ye *LAMB & GLOVE*, near Spittle Square, Without Bishopsgate.   *c.* 1760

MARK SHOLTON, at the *BUCK & GLOVE*, near Old Round Court, in the Strand.   1767

SAMUEL SKINNER, at the *HAND & GLOVE*, the corner of Queen Street, Cheapside.   1781

WILLM. STEPHENSON, at the *ANGEL*, facing Exeter Exchange, in the Strand.   1755
(He was succeeded by G. Jenings, *q.v.*)

JOHN STRICKLAND, at the *BALL & GLOVE*, Great Turnstile, Holborn.   1779

THOS. TREDWAY, at the *HAND & GLOVE*, in Leadenhall Street.   *c.* 1750

GEORGE VEALE, at the *LAMB*, opposite Southampton Street, in the Strand.   *c.* 1760

WILLIAM WILLIAMS (late E. Knowles & W. Williams) at ye *PRINCE'S ARMS & GLOVE*, ye corner of Chancery Lane, Fleet Street.   1740

JAMES WINSTON, at ye *PRINCE'S ARMS*, ye corner of Chancery Lane, Fleet Street.   1735

GOLD BEATERS

ROBERT EVANS, at the *HAMMER & CROWN*, No. 74 Long Acre, near Drury Lane.   *c.* 1770

ROBERT FEARN, at the *HAND & HAMMER*, at No. 44 in Cow Lane, near the Four Lamps, Snow Hill ; from the Great Old Bailey.   *c.* 1760

JOHN SHENTON, at the *HAND & HAMMER* in New Street, Shoe Lane.   *c.* 1760

GERVAS SNAPE, at the *GOLDEN HAMMER* in
Long Acre.   *c.* 1750

JOHN WHITE, at the *HAMMER & HAND* in
the Poultry.   1755

GOLD LACEMEN
See LACEMEN

GOLDSMITHS & SILVERSMITHS

JOHN ALDERHEAD, at the *RING & PEARL* in
Bishopsgate Street, near the South Sea House.
                                                1750–1766

EDWARD ALDRIDGE, at the *GOLDEN EWER*,
in Lilly-pot Lane, in Noble Street, near Goldsmiths' Hall,   1739–1743
    In Foster Lane.   1743–1762

WILLIAM ALLDRIDGE, at the *BLACKMOOR'S
HEAD*, in Red Lion Passage, Holborn.
                                                1751–1773

ALSTON & GRAYHURST, at the *BLUE BOAR*,
within Aldgate.   1720
(Existing successors, Harvey & Gore, Vigo Street.)

STEPHEN ARDESOIF, at the *GOLDEN CUP*, on
the New Pavement, Charing Cross.   1762

HENRY BARLOW, at the *THREE GOLDEN
ANCHORS*, next door but one to the Bull Inn,
White Chappel.   *c.* 1760

EDWARD BENNETT, at ye *BLUE LION &
CROWN*, ye corner of Tooley Street, London
Bridge.   1747

—— BINGANT, at the *STAR OF MYSTERY* in
Salisbury Street, in the Strand.   *c.* 1760

ANTHONY BLACKFORD, at ye *GOLDEN CUP &
CROWN*, in Lombard Street.   1702
(Succeeded by Sheer & Arnold, *q.v.*)

RICHARD BOULT, at the *BLUE ANCHOR &
STAR*, opposite Wood Street, Cheapside.
                                                1744–1753

GOLDEN EWER

BLUE LION & CROWN

GOLDEN CUP & CROWN

THE 3 KINGS & GOLDEN BALL

UNICORN & PEARL

—— BOURNE, successor to Mr. Boursot, at the *CROWN & PEARL* in New Street, St. Martin's Lane.   *c.* 1760
(New Street became continuation of King Street, Covent Garden.)

JOHN BRISCOE, at the *THREE KINGS & GOLDEN BALL*, over against Foster Lane, in Cheapside.   1752

BRISCOE & MORRISON, at above.   1749

STAFFORD BRISCOE*, at the *GOLDEN BALL ONLY*, the corner of Friday Street, Cheapside.
1732–1767

WILLIAM BROWN, at above.   1769

JAMES BUFFAR, at the *KINGS ARMS*, in Cheapside.   1748

JOHN BUHL, at the sign of ye *TWO GOLD CANDLESTICKS AND BLUE COFFEE POT* in St. Martin's Lane.   1768

THOMAS CALDECOTT, at the *CABINET*, the South side of St. Paul's Church Yard.   *c.* 1760

CHARLES CALLAGHAN, at the *SILVER LION*, No. 463 Strand.   1792

JOHN CARMAN, at the *EWER & SWORDS*, near Bartlett's Buildings, Holbourn.   *c.* 1760

BENJAMIN CARTWRIGHT, at the *CROWN & PEARL*, near ye George Inn, West Smithfield.
1754

CHALMERS & ROBINSON, at the *RING & CUP*, in Walker's Court, Berwick Street, Soho. *c.* 1760

CHALMERS & ROBINSON, at the *GOLDEN SPECTACLES*, in Sidney's Alley, Leicester Fields.
1773

THOMAS CHESSON, at the *UNICORN & PEARL*, near Queen Street, Cheapside.   1736

* See *Purefoy Letters*, p. 122.

THOMAS CHESSON, at the *GOLDEN SALMON &
PEARL*, on Ludgate Hill. 1753
(Succeeded by Henry Hurt, *q.v.*)

THOMAS CLARK, at the *GOLDEN HEAD*, near
Arundel Street, in the Strand. *c.* 1750

M. CLARKE, at the *EAGLE & PEARL*, opposite
Brook Street in Holborn. 1790

LETITIA CLARKE, at above. 1802

JONAS CLIFTON, at the *CROWN*, in Henrietta
Street, Covent Garden, removed from a little
beyond Hungerford, in ye Strand. *c.* 1730

JNO COOKE, at the *GOLDEN BALL & CROWN*,
opposite ye Half Moon Tavern in Cheapside. 1773

SAMUEL COURTAULD [succeeded his father, Augus-
tine Courtauld], at the *RISING SUN*, in Shandois
Street, St. Martin's Lane. 1746–1751

SAMUEL COURTAULD, at the *CROWN* in Cornhill,
facing the Royal Exchange. 1751–1765

LOUISA PERINA COURTAULD [widow of Samuel
Courtauld], at the *CROWN* in Cornhill.
1765–1768

LOUISA COURTAULD & GEORGE COWLES, at above.
1769–1778

JAMES COX, at the *GOLDEN URN*, in Racquet
Court, Fleet Street. 1751

JOHN CURGHEY, at the *SHIP*, near St. Dunstan's
Church, Fleet Street. 1741

THOMAS DANIELL & JAMES WALL, at the *SILVER
LION*, No. 20, Foster Lane. 1781

EDWARD DARVILL, at the *GOLDEN BALL* in
Watling Street, near Bow Lane. 1757–1793

WILLIAM & MARY DEARD, at the *STAR*, the end
of Pall-mall, near St. James's Hay-market.
c. 1750
(The Deards had renowned toy shops both in London and Bath
from 1730–1760.)

THE CROWN

GOLDEN URN

JOHN DE CREZ, at the *HARLEQUIN*, in Prince's Street, near Coventry Street, Leicester Fields.
1775

JOHN DELAFONS, at the *CROWN & PEARL*, near the Four Swans, within Bishopsgate.   1749–1768

PETER DE LA FONTAINE, at the *GOLDEN CUP*, in Litchfield Street, Soho.   *c.* 1740

BASIL DENN, JUNR., at ye *GOLD RING*, on London Bridge.   1743

GOLDEN STAR

ANDREW DESALLEE, at the *RING & PEARL*, in Castle Street, facing Cranbourne Alley.
c. 1750

SIGISMUND   GODHELP   DINGLINGER,   at   ye *DIAMOND CROSS* in St. Martin's le Grand.
1749

EDWARD DOBSON, at the *CROWN, RING & PEARL*, near Shoe Lane, Fleet Street.
1755–1773

—— DUBOIS, at the *GOLDEN STAR*, in Eagle Court in the Strand.   *c.* 1750

ANTHONY ELLINES, at the *CROWN, SUN & SEVEN STARS*, under St. Dunstan's Church facing Corbett's State Lottery Office.   *c.* 1750

THOMAS ELSWORTH, at the *CROWN & PEARL*, in the New Rents, St. Martin's-le-Grand.
c. 1750

GOLD RING

WILLIAM PARK FISHER, at the *EAGLE & PEARL* in Tavistock Street, Covent Garden.   *c.* 1760

JOHN FOSSEY, at the *GOLD RING*, corner of Ball Alley, in Lombard Street.   1747

JOHN FOSSEY, at the *BLACKMOOR'S HEAD & SUN*, corner of Ball Alley, Lombard Street.
c. 1760

ANN FOOTE, at the *RING*, near the Maypole, East Smithfield.   1752

Forster & Johnson, at the *PEARL*, Wood Street, Cheapside. *c.* 1760

John Frost, at the *GOLDEN CUP*, opposite St. Peter's Church, Cornhill. 1757

Ellis Gamble, at the *GOLDEN ANGEL* in Cranbourn Street, Leicester Fields. *c.* 1720

GOLDEN CUP

Phillips Garden, at the *GOLDEN LION*, in St. Paul's Church Yard. 1749–1762
(Succeeded by John Townsend, *q.v.*).

Abraham Gardner, at the *EAGLE & CROWN*, opposite Bow Lane, Cheapside. 1762

Thomas Gardner, at the *DIAL* in the Minories, near Aldgate. 1740–1752

—— Garrard, see Wickes & Netherton.

Charles Geddes, at the *CROWN & PEARL*, in the Strand, near Durham Yard. *c.* 1765

Elizabeth Godfrey, at the *HAND, RING & CROWN*, in Norris Street, St. James's Hay-Market. 1741–1760

John Hannam, at the *GOULDEN CUP*, the North side of St. Paul's Church Yard. 1698

Thomas Harding, at the *CROWN & SPUR*, in ye Minories, 1751–1781

FLOWER DE LIS AND STAR

Thomas Harrache, at the *GOLDEN BALL & PEARL*, in Pall Mall, 1751–1773.

George Heming, at ye *HAMMER & HAND*, opposite ye Black Bear Inn in Piccadilly. *c.* 1760–1773

Thomas Heming, at the *KING'S ARMS*, in Bond Street, facing Clifford Street. 1765–1773
(Existing successors Hemming & Co., Conduit Street.)

David Hennell, at the *FLOWER DE LIS & STAR*, in Gutter Lane, ye corner of Cary Lane, near Cheapside. 1736–1756

HAND & BEADS

ANCHOR & RING

CHRISTIAN HILLAN, at the *CROWN & GOLDEN BALL*, in Compton Street, St. Ann's [Soho]. 1741

JOSEPH HODGES, at the *GOLDEN EAGLE*, in Maiden Lane, Covent Garden.   *c.* 1765

EDWARD HOLMES, at the *PEARL*, in Foster Lane, Cheapside.   1768

GEORGE HOUSTON, at ye *GOLDEN CUP* near St. Dunstan's Church, Fleet Street.   1742–1773

JAMES HOWARD, at the *HAND & BEADS*, on London Bridge.   1735–1760

JOHN HOWARD, from London Bridge, at ye *HAND & BEADS*, next the Monument Yard, Fish Street Hill.   1762–1781

WM. HUNT & SON, at the *GOLDEN LION* in King Street, Cheapside.   1755–1763

WILLIAM HUNTER, at the *ANCHOR & RING*, Lombard Street.   1762

HENRY HURT [succeeded T. Chesson, *q.v.*], at the *GOLDEN SALMON* on Ludgate Hill.   1755
(Succeeded by Thread & Pickett, *q.v.*)

HYDE & LEEDS, at the *ANCHOR & CASE OF KNIVES*, near Royal Exchange, Cornhill.   1750

JNO. JACKSON, at ye *CROWN & PEARL*, in George Street, by Goldsmiths' Hall, Foster Lane.   1734

JOHN JACOB, at the *ACORN*, in Panton Street, near Leicester Fields.   1768

HENRY JEFFERYS & CO., at the *GREAT KNIFE CASE*, No. 91, Fleet Street.   1790

CHRISTOPHER JOHNSON, at the *CROWN & PEARL* in Salisbury Court, Fleet Street.   *c.* 1760

JOHNSTON & GEDDES, at the *GOLDEN BALL* in Panton Street, near Leicester Square.   *c.* 1760

JOHN KENTISH, at ye *STAR*, the corner of Pope's Head Alley, opposite the Royal Exchange, Cornhill.   1758–1793

JOHN LEGRIX, at ye Sign *CHANDELLEIR*, next door to the Golden Leg, opposite Langley Street, in Long Acre. *c.* 1760

SIMON LESAGE, at the *GOLDEN CUP*, the corner of Suffolk Street, near the Hay Market. 1761

JOSEPH LOWE, at the *KING'S HEAD*, near Bartlett's Buildings, Holborn. 1748

WILLIAM LUTWYCHE, at the *ANCHOR & DOVE*, No. 51, Fenchurch Street, near Gracechurch Street. 1771–1783

LEWIS MASQUERIER, at the *RING & PEARL*, in Coventry Street, near the Hay Market. 1753–1785

JNO. MONTGOMERY, at the *ANGEL*, the corner of Cambridge Street, near Golden Square. 1726–1749

JOHN MOORE, at the *HAND & SPUR*, near Exeter Exchange in the Strand. *c.* 1755
(A renowned maker of silver cock-spurs.)

—— MORRIS, at the *KING'S ARMS*, the corner of Norris Street, in St. James's Hay-Market. *c.* 1750

HENRY MORRIS, at the *GOLDEN KEY*, the corner of Salisbury Court, Fleet Street. 1753–1777

JONATHN. NEWTON & THOS. COLE, at the *CROWN & ACORN* in Lombard Street. 1745

Cs NORRIS, at the *ANCHOR & CROWN*, in Lombard Street. *c.* 1770

JOHN ORCHARD, at the *ROSE & CROWN*, in Lumbard Street. 1697

MARY OWEN, at ye *WHEAT SHEAF* in Cheapside. 1745

FRANCIS PAGES, at the *GOLDEN CUP* in Orange Street, near Red Lyon Square. 1731

LEWIS PANTIN, at the *CROWN & SCEPTRES*, the corner of Mitre Court, Fleet Street. 1770–1781

GOLDEN CUP

GOLDEN KEY

STAR & PEARL

BOY & CORAL

PETER PARQUOT, at the *EAGLE & PEARL*, in King Street, St. Ann's [Soho], facing Nassau Street.   1744

ROBERT PARR, at the *DIAMOND CROSS*, near Salisbury Court, Fleet Street.   *c.* 1760

SUSANNA PASSAVANT, at the *PLUME OF FEATHERS*, on Ludgate Hill, opposite the Old Baily.   1755

PATERSON & CRICHTON, at the *CROWN & PEARL*, in Green Street, Leicester Square.
                                                        c. 1765

HUMPHREY & JOHN PAYNE, at the Sign of the *HEN & CHICKENS* in Cheapside.   1753

PICKETT & RUNDELL, *THE GOLDEN SALMON*, No. 32, Ludgate Hill.   1785
(Successors to Thead & Pickett, *q.v.*)

PEZÉ PILLEAU, JUNR., at the *GOLDEN CUP*, on the Paved Stones, corner of Shandois Street, St. Martin's Lane.   1719–1755
(He also practised " ye Art of Making and Setting Artificial Teeth—no ways discernable from Natural Ones ".)

PAUL PINARD, at the *CROWN*, in New Street, Covent Garden.   1760–1784

GEORGE PINNOCK, at the *STAR & PERL*, adjoining to the George & Blue Boar Inn, opposite Red Lion Street, High Holborn.
                                                        c. 1760

THOMAS PITTS, at the *GOLDEN CUP*, in Air Street, Piccadilly.   1767–1793

WILLM. PLUMLEY, at the *CROWN & PEARL*, Ludgate Hill.   1768

PORTAL & GEARING, at the *SALMON & PEARL*, No. 34, on Ludgate Hill.   1774

THOMAS POWELL, at the *PEACOCK*, in Gutter Lane, Cheapside.   *c.* 1760

CHARLES PRESBURY, at the *QUEEN'S HEAD*, No. 9, New Street, Covent Garden.   1811

GEORGE RAGSDALE, at the *GOLDEN VAUSE*, in New Bond Street, near Conduit Street.   1781
(Successor to Chadd & Ragsdale.)

JOHN RAYMOND, at the *BOY & CORALL*, in Gutter Lane.   *c.* 1750

JOHN RAYNES, at the Sign of *PALLAS*, in Foster Lane.   1725–1740

GEORGE ROBERTSON, at the *CROWN & PEARL*, near ye corner of the Hay Market, faceing Piccadilly.   1755

JOHN ROBINSON, at the *STAR & RING*, in New Bond Street, St. George's, Hanover Square. 1759

FRANCIS RUFFIN, at the *CROWN & CHAINS*, in Cary Lane, near Goldsmiths' Hall.   *c.* 1760

RUNDELL & BRIDGE, at the *GOLDEN SALMON*, No. 32 Ludgate Hill,   1791
(Successors to Pickett & Rundell, *q.v.*)

JOSEPH SAVORY, at the *GOLDEN FLEECE*, No. 48, Cheapside.   1783

RICHARD SEVERN, at the *CROWN & PEARL*, the corner of Pauls-Grave Head Court, near Temple Barr.   *c.* 1755

SHAW & PRIEST, at the *UNICORN*, in Wood Street, near Maiden Lane.   1749–1758

HENY. SHERE & HENY. ARNOLD, at the *CUP & CROWN*, in Lombard Street.   1751–1768
(Successors to A. Blackford, *q.v.*)

JAMES SHRUDER, at ye *GOLDEN EWER*, in Greek Street, Sohoe.   1739

JAMES SMITH, at ye *ANGEL*, in ye Great Old Bailey, near Newgate.   1746

WILLIAM SMITH, at the *BLACK MOOR'S HEAD*, opposite Gutter Lane, Cheapside.   1760–1769

JOHN SOTRO, at the *ACORN*, in St. Paul's Church Yard.   1750

JOHN STAMPER, at the *STAR*, the corner of Hind Court, opposite Water Lane, in Fleet Street.   1743–1772

PALLAS ATHENE

CUP & CROWN

THE STAR

THE ACORN

JOHN STEERES, at the *BLUE LION*, in Old Round Court, Chandos Street.   1771

JAMES STONES, at the *GOLDEN BALL*, in Maiden Lane, near Goldsmiths' Hall.   *c.* 1760

CHARLES STOREY, at the *SUN*, in Sidneys Alley, Leicester Fields.   1758

JOSEPH SUTTON, at the *ACORN*, in New Street, Covent Garden.   1754–1784

JOHN TAYLOR, at the *GOLDEN CUP*, against Southampton Street, in ye Strand.   1740

THEED & PICKETT, successors to Mr. Henry Hurt (*q.v.*), at the *GOLDEN SALMON*, on Ludgate Hill.   1759

JAMES THOMASSON at ye *GOLDEN CUP & KEY*, in Fen Church Street, near Cullum Street.   1753

JOHN TOWNSEND, at the *GOLDEN LION*, North side of St. Paul's Church Yard.   1762
(Succeeded Phillips Garden, *q.v.*)

JONATHAN TRENHOLME, at the *CASE OF KNIVES & FORKS & GOLDSMITHS' ARMS*, in Wood Street.   *c.* 1760

MARIE ANNE VIET & THOS. MITCHELL, at ye sign of ye *DIAL & KING'S ARMS* on Cornhill, near ye Royal Exchange.   1742

WARRE, at the *GOLDEN LYON*, the fifth door from Devereux Court, near Temple Barr. *c.* 1760

JOHN WHITE, at ye Sign of ye *GOLDEN CUP* in Arundell Street in ye Strand.   1719–1724

THOMAS WHIPHAM, remov'd from Ave-mary Lane to the *GRASSHOPPER*, near White Friars, on the South side in Fleet Street.   1751–1784

GEORGE WICKS & SAML. NETHERTON, at the *KINGS ARMS*, Panton Street.   1751–1759
(Succeeded by Parker & Wakelin, later Wakelin & Garrard; present day, Garrard & Co.)

WILLIAM WIGHT, at the *CROWN*, in King Street, Cheapside.   *c.* 1770

SAMUEL WILDMAN, at the *SUN*, opposite Lawrence Lane in Cheapside.   1792

WILLIAM WILLIAMS, at the *SPREAD EAGLE* in Foster Lane.   1742–*c.* 1760

JAMES WILLMOT, at ye *FLYING HORSE*, between the Savoy and ye Fountain Tavern in the Strand.   1741

THOMAS WINTLE, at the *PEARL & RING*, No. 9, in the Poultry.   1760–1790

JOHN WORSLEY, at the *RING & PEARL & CASE OF KNIVES*, opposite Mincing Lane, Fenchurch Street.   *c.* 1780

JOSEPH WRIGHT, successor to the late Mr. Tisdale, at the *RING & CHAIN*, in Cross Street, Hatton Garden.   *c.* 1750

PAUL WRIGHT, successor to Mr. Edward Smith, at the *PARROT & PEARL*, No. 12 Foster Lane, Cheapside.   1771

H. YOUNG, at the *STAR & GARTER*, near St. Paul's, No. 18, Ludgate Street.   1781

SPREAD EAGLE

GOWN & HABIT MAKERS

POWELL BEMONT, at ye *STAR & GARTER*, in Tavistock Street, Covent Garden.   *c.* 1750

JOSEPH BRACKSTONE, at the *GOLDEN ANCHOR*, in York Street, Covent Garden.   *c.* 1750

HANNAH GLASSE, at the *PRINCE OF WALES' ARMS*, in Tavistock Street, Covent Garden.   1747–1751
(Better known as the anonymous author of "The Art of Cookery," first published in 1747.)

MARY & ANN HOGARTH, from the Old Frock Shop, the corner of the Long Walk facing the Cloysters—Removed to ye *KINGS ARMS*, joyning to ye Little Britain Gate, near Long Walk [Smithfield].   1725
(Mary, born 1699, and Ann, born 1701, were sisters of William Hogarth.)

GOLDEN ANCHOR

M. NORMAN, at the *GOLDEN LION & CROWN* in Tavistock Street, Covent Garden.   *c.* 1760

JNO. SCHERZBERG, at the *GOLDEN LION*, in Tavistock Street, Covent Garden.   1764

GROCERS

See also TEAMEN

EDWARD ALDERSON, at the *THREE SUGAR LOAVES*, No. 102 Oxford Street, corner of John Street.   1802
(Successor to S. Roberts.)

THREE SUGAR LOAVES

ALLEN & BARNARD, at the *GOLDEN KEY & THREE SUGAR LOAVES*, the corner of Dyers Buildings, near the Barrs, Holborn.   *c.* 1760

THOMAS ANSELL, at ye *GOLDEN CANNISTER*, in Leather Lane, near Hatton Garden.   *c.* 1760

JAMES BAKER, at the *GOLDEN CANISTER & UNICORN*, in Catherine Street, in the Strand.   1746

JOHN BARTON, at the *GREEN CANNISTER & 3 SUGAR LOAVES*, on Ludgate Hill.   1750

GEORGE BLAKISTON, at the *BELL*, in King Street, Covent Garden.   *c.* 1760

MATTHEW BLAKISTON, at the *BELL*, next door to York House, in the Strand.   1744

SAMUEL BOWKER, at the *BLACK BOY & SUGAR LOAF*, ye corner of Warders Street, Soho.   *c.* 1755

DOLPHIN & 3 SUGAR LOAVES

ANN BRERETON, at the *GOLDEN CANISTER & SUGAR LOAVES*, the corner of Brook Street in New Bond Street.   1768

JOSEPH BROWNE, at the *COFFEE MILL*, No. 3, St. James's Street.   1793
(Succeeded J. Clarke, *q.v.*)

JNO. & WM. CHARLTON, at the *DOLPHIN & THREE SUGAR LOAVES*, near the White Horse Inn, in Fleet Street.   *c.* 1750

WILLIAM CHARLTON, at the *CANNISTER &*
SUGAR LOAF, the corner of Crane Court, near
Fetter Lane.   *c.* 1760
(Late partner with J. Charlton, see above.)

EDMUND CHAUNTRELL, at the *SUGAR LOAF*,
the corner of Addle Street, in Wood Street.   1744

JOHN CLARKE, at the *COFFEE MILL*, St. James's
Street.   1783
(Succeeded Pickering & Clarke, *q.v.*)

JOHN COLCRAFT, at the *GREEN CANNISTER* in
Cornhill, near ye Mansion House.   1754

JOHN COLCRAFT, at the *CANNISTER & THREE*
SUGAR LOAVES, in Bishopsgate Street, near
St. Helens.   *c.* 1760

DAVIS & TAYLOR, at the *TEA CHEST*, corner of
Orchard Street, Oxford Road, opposite North
Audley Street.   *c.* 1760

DAVISON, NEWMAN & CO., see T. Rawlinson.

JOHN DYSON, at the *TEA CHEST & SUGAR*
LOAF, in New Street, Cloth Fair [Smithfield].
                                                   c. 1750

MORRIS EVANS, at the *THREE SUGAR LOAVES*,
in Cheapside.   1779

GEORGE FARR, at the *BEEHIVE & THREE*
SUGAR LOAVES in Wood Street, near Cheapside.   1753

GEORGE FARR, JUNR., at the *RED LYON &*
THREE SUGAR LOAVES, ye corner of Watling
Street, near St. Paul's.   1763

THOMAS FODEN, at the *KING'S HEAD*, Without
Newgate.   *c.* 1700

FROST & HARDSTAFF, at the *GOLDEN CANISTER*,
No. 37 Leather Lane, Holborn.   *c.* 1820

JOHN HEIGHAM GRESHAM, at the *GREEN*
CANISTER, against St. Martin's Le Grand,
Newgate Street.   1737

JOHN HALE, at ye *KING'S ARMS*, opposite ye
Cannon Tavern, Charing Cross.   1765

SUGAR LOAF

KING'S HEAD

JOHN HARLING, at the *CHINA MAN & TEA TREE*, next Somerset House in the Strand. 1764

FRANCIS HARRAUD, at ye *THREE SUGAR LOAVES*, in Coventry Street, near Leicester Fields. *c.* 1760

HILL & INGALL, at the *FIGG-TREE & TEA CANISTER*, between Norfolk and Arundel Streets in the Strand. 1744

WADE HOLTON, at the *THREE SUGAR LOAVES*, near Fetter Lane in Holborn. 1763

EDWARD HUMFREYS, at the *THREE SUGAR LOAVES*, the corner of Prince's Street, in Red Lyon Street, Holborn. 1775

WILLIAM HUMFREYS, at same address. 1781

THOMAS HUNT, at the *GOLDEN SUGAR LOAF*, No. 93 Newgate Street, the corner of the Hospital Gate. *c.* 1760

ROBERT INGALL, at the *THREE GOLDEN SUGAR LOAVES*, near Southampton Street, in the Strand. 1748

HUGH JAMES, at the *BLACKMOOR'S HEAD*, near Chancery Lane, No. 192 Fleet Street. 1764

JAMES & GARMESON (at above). 1752
(See North, Hoare & Co.)

THOMAS JEMMITT, at ye *BLACKMOOR'S HEAD*, against Fetter Lane in Fleet Street. 1737–1748

RICHARD JONES, at the *TEA TUB & CANISTER*, between Norfolk and Suffolk Streets, Strand. *c.* 1760

RICHARD KING, at the *BELL & THREE SUGAR LOAVES*, in St. Martin's Le Grand, opposite St. Anns Lane. *c.* 1760
(Successor to G. Pickstock, *q.v.*)

JOSEPH LIVERSEDGE, at the *STAR & SUGAR LOAF*, next door to the Sun Tavern, Upper Shadwell. 1768

BLACKMOOR'S HEAD

CANISTER & CROWN

Joseph Lloyd, at the *CROWN & CANISTER* in Chandos Street, Covent Garden.   *c.* 1760

Henry Lock, at the *CANISTER & CROWN*, opposite Great Turn Stile, near Red Lyon Street, Holborn.   1747

Lumley & Ray, at the *TEA TUB, THREE SUGAR LOAVES & CROWN*, near Cruched Fryars in Mark Lane.   1745
(See also Ray & Lumley.)

Mason & Sharman, at the *GREEN CANISTER*, No. 79, New Bond Street, Three doors from Oxford Street.   1789

Thomas Massett, at the *THREE SUGAR LOAVES & CHINESE MANDARIN*, No. 143, Old Gravel Lane, Wapping.   1795

Francis Morley, at the *GREEN CANNISTER*, against St. Paul's Church Yard, Cheapside.   1766

Roger Nethercoat, at ye *CANISTER, ROSE & THREE SUGAR LOAVES*, in Shoreditch.
                              c. 1750

North, Hoare, Nanson & Simpson (late James & North), at the *BLACKMOOR'S HEAD*, No. 192, the corner of Chancery Lane, Fleet Street.   1779

Robert Owen, at ye *THREE GOLDEN SUGAR LOAVES*, ye upper end of Conduit Street, near Hanover Square.   1738

John Philpott, at the *THREE GOLDEN SUGAR LOAVES*, the corner of Durham Yard in ye Strand.   1736

Pickering & Clarke, at the *COFFEE MILL* in St. James's Street.   1760
(Succeeded by J. Clarke, *q.v.*)
This shop, No. 3, St. James's, stands at the corner of Pickering Place—in 1740 it was occupied by William and John Pickering. The present occupiers are Berry Brothers, the famous wine merchants, who went there in 1801. The shop still retains its old sign of the Coffee Mill.

George Pickstock, at ye *BELL & THREE SUGAR LOAVES*, in St. Martin's le Grand.   1743
(Succeeded by R. King, *q.v.*)

*CANISTER, ROSE &
3 SUGAR LOAVES*

COFFEE MILL

BELL & 3 SUGAR LOAVES

CHINESE PORTER

CORNELIUS PYE, at the *GOLDEN SUGAR LOAF*, over against St. James's Church, in Piccadilly.
1750

THOMAS RAWLINSON, at the *THREE SUGAR LOAVES & CROWN*, in Fenchurch Street, near Mincing Lane.   1740
(His nephew, Sir Thomas Rawlinson, became Lord Mayor in 1763.)

RAWLINSON & DAVISON, at above address.   1752

RAWLINSON, DAVISON & NEWMAN, at above address.   1763

DAVISON, NEWMAN & Co., at above address.
1777
(And under this name the firm has traded ever since. Their present address is No. 14, Creechurch Lane.)

RAY & LUMLEY, at the *TEA TUB, THREE SUGAR LOAVES & CROWN*, near Cruched Fryers in Mark Lane.   *c.* 1750
(See also Lumley & Ray.)

JOHN RICHARDSON, at the *CANISTER & THREE SUGAR LOAVES*, against Hatton Garden, Holborn.   1756

WILLIAM ROBINSON, at the *GREYHOUND & KING'S ARMS*, in Fleet Street.   1750

RICHARD ROOKER, at the *GOLDEN SUGAR LOAF*, Holbourn Bridge.   *c.* 1750

WILLIAM SCOTT, at the *THREE SUGAR LOAVES & CROWN*, near White Chapel Bars.   1763

—— SEDGWICK, at ye *ORIGINAL GRASS-HOPPER*, the corner of Spittle Square, in Bishopsgate Street.   *c.* 1760

SARAH SHARPE, at ye *CROWN & TEA CAN-NISTER* in Fleet Street.   *c.* 1760

JOHN SHAW, at the *THREE SUGAR LOAVES*, Greek Street, Soho, and near the Royal Bun House, Chelsea.   1788

WILLIAM SHAW, at the *CROWN* (?) & *THREE SUGAR LOAVES*, facing St. James's Street, No. 65 Piccadilly.   1781

SHAW & ROBINSON, at the *CROWN* (?) & *THREE SUGAR LOAVES*, near the White Horse Cellar, No. 65, Piccadilly.   1799

JOHN SHOWRD, at the *CHINESE PORTER*, in Cockspur Street, near Charing Cross.   *c.* 1760

THOMAS SILK, at ye *THREE SUGAR LOAVES*, Within Aldgate.   1753

ROBERT SMITH, at the *PLOUGH* & *SUGAR LOAF*, No. 38 Aldersgate Street.   1773

WILLIAM SMITH, at the *SUGAR LOAF* in Aldersgate Street.   *c.* 1760

SMITH & CATHERALL (late White & Smith, *q.v.*), at the *GOLDEN CANISTER*, Pall Mall.   1794

SMITH & HUNT, at ye *SUGAR LOAF* & *TEA CANNISTER*, ye West End of St. Paul's. 1745

GEORGE SNOWBALL, at the *FIGG TREE*, over against Salisbury Street, in the Strand. *c.* 1755

JAMES SPALDING, at the *WEST INDIA PLANTER*, near the White Chapel Bars.   *c.* 1755

SPATEMAN, HOTHAM & Co., at the *BLACKMOOR'S HEAD*, No. 39 Cannon Street. *c.* 1780

SPENCER & JEBSON, at the *GOLDEN LYON* & *THREE SUGAR LOAVES*, the lower end of Grace Church Street.   *c.* 1750

SAMUEL STONE, at the *BLACK BOY* & *SUGAR LOAF*, in Leaden Hall Street.   1754

WILLIAM THORNS, at the *GRASSHOPPER*, White Cross Street.   *c.* 1770

DANIEL TWINING, at the *GOLDEN LION*, in Devereux Court.   *c.* 1750

THOMAS TWINING & SON, at the *GOLDEN LION*, near ye Temple.   1747

THOMAS TWINING & SON, at the *GOLDEN LION*, near ye Temple.   1735

SUGAR LOAF & TEA CANISTER

WEST INDIA PLANTER

THOMAS & DANIEL TWINING, at the *GOLDEN LION*, near ye Temple.   *c.* 1740

("Twinings in the Strand" have been "household words" for over 200 years.)

WHITE & SMITH, at the *GOLDEN CANISTER* in Pall Mall.   1788

(Succeeded by Smith & Catherall, *q.v.*)

THOMAS WILSON, at the *TEA CHEST & SUGAR LOAF*, in Glasshouse Street, near Burlington Gardens.   1764

THOS. & NICHOLAS WILSON, at the *FIGG TREE & SUGAR LOAF*, in Glasshouse Street, near Burlington Gardens.   1757

T. (?THOMAS) WILSON, at the *ROYAL ARMS* in Bridge Street, Westminster.   1791

TITUS WILSON, at the *TEA CHEST*, in Bridge Street, Westminster.   1777

WILSON & THORNHILL,* at the *THREE SUGAR LOAVES* in Fleet Street.   1738

(Successors to John Cossin.)

WILSON & THORNHILL, at the *THREE SUGAR LOAVES*, at the West End of St. Paul's.

(Successors to Charles Wilson.)   1751–1771

WILSON, THORNHILL & WILSON, at the *THREE SUGAR LOAVES*, No. 77, St. Paul's Churchyard.
                                                 1784

GUNSMITHS

EDWARD BOND, at the *GOLDEN BLUNDER-BUSS*, No. 59, Lombard Street.   1777

(Successor to Mr. Bumford.)

TOMPSON DAVIS, at the *CROSS GUNS & PHEASANT*, High Holbourn.   *c.* 1750

JEFFERY DUNN, at ye *CROSS BOW* in ye Hay Market.   *c.* 1760

WILLIAM GUY, at the *GUN*, in Bishopsgate Street, near Cornhill.   *c.* 1750

THOMAS JONES, at the *CROSS GUNS* in Cornhill near ye Royal Exchange.   *c.* 1760

---

* See *Purefoy Letters*, pp. 65–67.

GOLDEN LION

CROSS BOW

ALEXANDER ARBUTHNOT, at the *BLUE BOAR &
PEACOCK*, facing St. Paul's Church Yard, No.
153 in Cheapside. 1766

JOSEPH ATKINSON & JAMES ABBISS, at the *LAMB
& STAR*, near St. Peter's Church in Cornhill.
c. 1760

ELIZABETH ATWICK, at the *HALF MOON*, Old
Bond Street, near Piccadilly. 1766

WILLIAM BAYLISS, at the *SUN & CROWN*, No.
47 Fenchurch Street, near Mark Lane. 1769

HANNAH BEALBY, at the *BLACK RAVEN*, No.
144, Drury Lane. *c.* 1780

JOHN BECK, at the *THREE PIGEONS & WOOL
PACK*, opposite Racquet Court, Fleet Street.
c. 1770

EDWARD BLACKSHAW, at the *RAINBOW & FAN*,
opposite Tavistock Court in Tavistock Street,
Covent Garden. 1772
(Preceded by E. Rogers, *q.v.*)

BOURNE & HARPER, at the sign of the *CROWN &
ANCHOR*, the corner of York Street and Catherine Street, Covent Garden. *c.* 1740

BOWER & MELLERSH, at the *STAR & FALCON*,
opposite Furnival's Inn, Holborn. 1772
(Successors to Purnell & Ward, *q.v.*)

—— BRADSHAW, at the *WHEATSHEAF & STAR*,
in Cornhill, near the Royal Exchange. *c.* 1760
(*cf.* J. Brown, gold laceman at this address in 1752.)

ROBERT BRIGHT, at the *GOLDEN FLEECE &
GLOVE*, in Cheapside near the Old Change.
c. 1750
(Afterwards at No. 71, Newgate Street from 1760–1777.)

BROADBELT & CLINTON, at the *SEVEN STARS*,
in Tavistock Street, Covent Garden. 1766

BROADBELT & STANIER, at above address. 1763

ABRAM BURNELL, at the *ANGEL* in New Bond
Street. 1764

CROWN & ANCHOR

STAR & FALCON

ANGEL & CROWN

BLACK BOY

THE SUN

BUTLER & CROOK, at the *GOLDEN BALL*, No. 109 in Pall Mall.   1782
(Successors to James Butler, 1755–1777.)

JOHN CATTS, at ye *SUN*, opposite Canon Row in Bridge Street, Westminster.   *c.* 1760

PERCIFULL CHANDLER, at the *THREE FLOWER DE LUCES*, in Holborne, neere the end of Fetter Lane, formerly dwelling in the Old Bayly.   *c.* 1690

WILLIAM CHEVELY, at the *ANGEL & CROWN*, in Tavistock Street, Covent Garden.   1759

JNO. CLARKE, at the *QUEEN'S HEAD*, in Southampton Row, Covent Garden.   *c.* 1740–1774

CLARKE & TOWNSEND, at the *GOLDEN KEY*, the corner of the Dolphin Inn, Houndsditch, Without Bishopsgate.   *c.* 1730

COGAN & PALMER, at the *FLOWER POT & INDIAN QUEEN*, the corner of White Lion Court, in Cornhill, No. 65.   1768

ELLIS CRISPE, at the *BLACK BOY*, in the Old Bayly, neare the Sessions House.   1669

JAMES CUTTS, at ye *APE ON HORSEBACK* in Henrietta Street, Covent Garden.   1712

WILLIAM DAVIES, at the *HENN & CHICKENS* against the Conduit in the Old Bayley.   1661

DAVISON, BEAMON & ABBOTT, at the *THREE PIGEONS & SCEPTRE*, No. 61 New Bond Street, near Brook Street.   *c.* 1800
(*cf.* Moon & Buckland, linen drapers, 1818.)

CORNELIUS DENNE, at the *SUN*, near Mercers Hall, Cheapside.   1760
(Succeeded by Martha Denne in 1770.)

P. & M. DENSHIRE, at the *CROWN & SCEPTRE*, in Great Russell Street, Covent Garden. *c.* 1790

HENRY DOBSON, at the *SUN*, against the Conduit in Cheapside, next Pater Noster Row.   1705

WILLIAM FABIAN, at the *WHITE HART*, in Fleet Street.   *c.* 1770

FRANCIS FLOWER, at the *ROSE & WOOLPACK*, ye corner of King Street in Holborn.   1753
(Succeeded by B. Godin, *q.v.*)

SUSANNAH FORDHAM, att the *HARTICHOOKE* on ye Royall Exchange.   1700

PHILIP GIBBONS, at the *HOPE*, No. 46 Tottenham Court Road, 4 doors from Windmill Street. 1791

BENJN. GODIN (successor to Flower & Brooks), at the *ROSE & WOOLSACK*, ye corner of King Street, Holborn.   *c.* 1760

GOODYAR & HOULDEN, the *GOLDEN HEART*, corner of Duke Street, Piccadilly.   1766

MARK GREGORY, at the *RAVEN & SUN*, in Drury Lane.   *c.* 1730

HALL & MAGRATH, at the *THREE PIGEONS*, No. 49 Cheapside.   1790
(Successors to Edwd. Sleath, *q.v.*)

J. & J. HARRIS & THOS. KING, at the *WHEAT-SHEAF & SUN* in King Street, facing Bedford Street, Covent Garden.   1763

HARRIS, KING, THOMPSON & PAGET, at above.   1765

HARRIS, KING & THOMPSON, at above.   1766

KING & PADGET, at above.   *c.* 1770

T. W. & R. KING, at above.   1781

J. & R. HARROP, at the *SUN & PEACOCK*, in Coventry Street, near Piccadilly.   1762

BENJAMIN HATWELL, at the *UNICORN*, corner of Butcher-hall Lane, Newgate Street.   1756

INNES, JONES & SLADE (late Middleton & Innes), at the *THREE PIGEONS*, No. 192 Fleet Street.   1820

W. & J. JONES & W. CROSS (late Barrett Walkwood & W. Jones), at the *SUN & FALCON*, against Field Lane, in Holborn, near the Bridge.   1753

ARTICHOKE

RAVEN & SUN

SUN & FALCON

JONES, MEYRICK & CHARLESWORTH, at above.
                                              1772

KING & PADGET.   (*See* Harris, King & Co.)

JOHN LEE, at ye *HEN & CHICKENS*, in ye
Minories, near Aldgate.   *c.* 1760

ANGEL & ROSE

JOHN LEE, at the *THREE PIGEONS & STAR*,
next Temple Gate, Fleet Street.   1784

SIBBELLA LLOYD, MARTHA WILLIAMS & ELIZ.
STOREY, at ye *THREE ANGELS*, against George
Yard in Lombard Street.   *c.* 1745

ROBERT MATTHEWS, at the *SUN & WOOLPACK*,
in Fleet Street, near Bride Lane.   *c.* 1760

RICHARD MEREDITH, at the *ANGEL & ROSE*,
Cheapside, near St. Paul's Church-Yard. *c.* 1750

MIDDLETON & INNES, at the *THREE PIGEONS*,
No. 192 Fleet Street, corner of Chancery Lane.
(Succeeded by Innes, Jones & Co., *q.v.*)   1790

WM. MORFORD, at the *ROYALL POYNT*, in
Cornehill.   1712

—— MORGAN, at the *PARROT*, opposite Somerset
House, in the Strand.   *c.* 1742

DAVID MORRIS, at the *CROWN* in Chandois
Street, Covent Garden.   *c.* 1760

ROYAL POINT

RALPH NEALE, at the *ROYAL POINT*, in Ludgate Street.   *c.* 1730

ALICE PAGE, at the *KING'S ARMS*, in Paternoster
Row, near St. Paul's (successor to Mrs. Forward).
                                     1754

*MATTHEW PEARSON, at the *ROYAL POINT* in
Tavistock Street, Covent Garden.   1774

GILLERY PIGOTT, at the *SUN & PEACOCK*,
between Paternoster Row and Newgate Street,
fronting Cheapside.   1753–1772

* This bill is made out to Mrs. (David) Garrick.

ABRAHAM PINHORN, at the *WOOL-PACK* in Cornhill. 1746

PRICE & PEARSON, at the *WHEAT SHEAF & STAR*, in Tavistock Street, Covent Garden. 1766

PURNELL & WARD, at the *STAR & FALCON*, the corner of Dyer's Buildings, facing Furnivals Inn, Holbourn. *c.* 1755
(Succeeded by W. Ward and later by Bower & Mellersh.)

THOMAS RANDALL, at the *LAMB*, No. 141, in Fleet Street. *c.* 1770

F. RAYNER, at the *GOLDEN PHOENIX*, in Bedford Street, Covent Garden. *c.* 1760

JAMES RAYNOLDS, at the *HAND & PENN* in Rusell Street, Covent Garden. *c.* 1700

ROBINSON, HARRISON & COMPY., late Mr. Cookson's, at the *QUEEN'S HEAD*, in the Cloysters, West Smithfield. *c.* 1760

ELIZABETH ROGERS, at the *RAINBOW & FAN*, opposite Tavistock Court in Tavistock Street, Covent Garden. *c.* 1760
(Succeeded by E. Blackshaw, *q.v.*)

RICHARD ROPER, at the *THREE PIGEONS*, Nos. 146/7 Minories. *c.* 1790

RICHARD ROSE, at the *RISING SUN*, at the corner of the Minories. *c.* 1750

ROSE & BELL, *THE HOPE*, No. 28, Holborn. *c.* 1780

JOHN SAGE & JOHN GOPP, at the *CRANE & ANCHOR*, over against the Half Moon Tavern, in Cheapside. 1748

JOHN SAGE, at above. 1754

EDWARD SAGE & CO., at above [No. 19 Cheapside]. 1780

SAGE & TURNER, at above. *c.* 1770

THOMAS SAGE, at the *SHIP & ANCHOR*, three doors from St. Paul's in Cheapside. *c.* 1760

WOOLPACK

CRANE & ANCHOR

RISING SUN & WOOLPACK

THREE PROTESTANT QUEENS

WHEATSHEAF & BIRD

THOMAS SAUNDERS, at the *RISING SUN & WOOLPACK*, in Cheapside. *c.* 1745

—— SENIOR, at the *THREE PIGEONS*, Bruton Street (from Fleet Street). 1792

EDWARD SLEATH, at the *THREE PIGEONS*, No. 49, Cheapside. 1779
(Succeeded by Hall & Magrath, *q.v.*)

THOMAS SMALL, at the *THREE PROTESTANT QUEENS* in Cheapside, near Friday Street. 1727
(This sign commemorates Queens Elizabeth, Mary and Anne.)

THOMAS SMALLWOOD (late Victor's), at the *GOLDEN BALL*, Little Maddox Street, Hanover Square. 1775

—— SMITH, at the *OLD STAR*, Stockwell Street, Greenwich. *c.* 1790

MARMADUKE SMITH, at the *NEW ROYAL POINT & STAR*, near the Royal Exchange, Cornhill. 1752

JOSEPH SPILSBURY (late Bowen), at the *ROYAL POINT*, in York Street, Covent Garden. 1757

JAMES STANDERWICK, at the *WHEATSHEAF & BIRD*, in Cornhill (No. 74). 1758–1777
(He married the grand-daughter of Daniel Defoe, author of " Robinson Crusoe," etc.)

JOHN STEEL, at the *GOLDEN BALL*, in Crab Tree Row, near Shoreditch Church. *c.* 1780

MARMADUKE TEASDALE, at the *SUN & FALCON*, in Tavistock Street. *c.* 1760

TEASDALE & SQUIBB, at above, No. 16 Tavistock Street. 1770

BARNARD TOWNSEND, at the *SWAN & SUN*, on Ludgate Hill. 1743–1765

RICHARD TOWNSEND, at above (No. 13, Ludgate Hill). 1765–1786

MILDRED TUCKER, at the *ANCHOR & STAR*, by the Cloysters, West Smithfield. *c.* 1760

WILLIAM VALE, at the *SUN* in Tavistock Street, Covent Garden.   1766

JOSEPH VAUX, at the *PACKHORSE & STAR*, in Cornhill, near Leadenhall Street.   1763

JOHN VICTOR, at the *GOLDEN BALL* in Brook Street, turning into Hanover Square. 1760–1772

JOHN VICTORY, at the Signe of the *BLACK RAVEN*, near Bow Church, in Cheapside. *c.* 1700

BARRETT WALKWOOD & WILLIAM JONES, at the *SUN & FALCON*, against Field Lane, in Holborn, near the Bridge.   1750
(Succeeded by Jones & Cross, *q.v.*)

WILLIAM WARD, at the *STAR & FAULCON*, the corner of Dyer's Buildings, facing Furnivals Inn, Holbourn.   *c.* 1750
(Succeeded by Purnell & Ward, *q.v.*)

JNO. WELCH & SAML. SPARKS, at the *ROYAL POINT & ANCHOR*, near the corner of Queen Street, Cheapside.   *c.* 1750

EDWARD WINNOCK, JOSHUA CHANNING & SAMUEL BRENT, at the *SEVEN STARS*, in Bread Street.   1740

HAIR SELLERS

JOHN ALLEN, at the *LOCKS OF HAIR*, on London Bridge.   1755

JOHN HARPER, at the *HAND & LOCK OF HAIR*, in Cock Court, St. Martin's Le Grand. *c.* 1740

JOHN STEAD, at the *LOCKS OF HAIR*, in Newcastle Court, Butcher Row, Temple Bar. *c.* 1750

THOMAS & RICHARD JEFFREYS & JAMES DIXON, at the *HAND & LOCKS OF HAIR* on Snow Hill.   *c.* 1730

HAM & TONGUE SHOP

GODFREY SCHOLEY, at the *HAM & LYON* in St. Nicholas Lane.   1763

SWAN & SUN

BLACK RAVEN

HAND & LOCK OF HAIR

† Straw Hat Makers. ‡ Hatters and Sword Cutlers.

CROSS KEYS

HAT & CROSS DAGGERS

‡J. ADAMS, at the *HAT & BEAVER*, No. 146, Fleet Street, at the corner of Wine Office Court.
1777

W. ALLCOCK, at the *KING'S ARMS*, the North side of St. Paul's Church Yard. *c.* 1755

JOHN BEETSON, at the *HATT & BEAVER*, without Temple Bar. *c.* 1760

SAMUEL BOURNE, at the *CROSS KEYS* in Leaden Hall Street. *c.* 1710

WILLIAM BRACKENBURY, at the *BLACK BOY*, facing Durham Yard, in the Strand. *c.* 1760

ROBERT BROUGHTON, at the *GOLDEN BALL*,* in Little Newport Street, the corner of Cranbourn Alley. *c.* 1760

BENJAMIN CALEY, at the *HAT & BEAVER*, the top of New Bond Street [No. 80]. 1773

WILLIAM CHAMBERLIN, at the *HATT & BEAVER*, in the Poultry. *c.* 1760

THOMAS COLLYER, at ye *KING'S ARMS & BEAVER* in Exchange Alley in Cornhill. *c.* 1700
(The arms are those of King William III.)

JAMES COX, at ye *HAT & STAR*, in Newgate Street, near St. Martin's Le Grand. *c.* 1760

JOHN CRUTCHFIELD, at the *HATT & FEATHER*, in the Back Lane, Lambeth. *c.* 1750

WILLIAM RICHARD DOVE, at the *GOLDEN HEAD*, near St. James's Palace. *c.* 1750

‡EDWARD FAYLE, at the *HAT & CROSS DAGGERS*, near Serjeants Inn, in Fleet Street.
1768

‡DANIEL FRY, successor to Mr. Holden, at ye *TWO EAGLES*, in Ludgate Street. *c.* 1760

†GEDALIAH GATFIELD, at the *CROWN & ANCHOR* in Newgate Street, near Cheapside.
(See also under Basket and Brush makers.) 1768

* *cf.* William Hogarth, engraver and painter, *q.v.*, at this address in 1720.

† Straw Hat Makers.   ‡ Hatters and Sword Cutlers.

STEPHEN GAUDRY, at the *HATT & BEAVER*, in Little Newport Street, near Leister fields.   1757

HENRY GILES, at the *CAP IN HAND*, opposite Lime Street [No. 16], in Fenchurch Street.   1767

GREEN & COMPTON, successors to Mr. Curson, at the *FLEECE & BEAVER*, in New Bond Street, near Conduit Street.   1767

JOHN GRIGSON, at the *HATT & MITRE*, in Butcher Hall Lane, Newgate Street.   *c.* 1750

†ANN GUNNELL, at the *THREE HATTS* (formerly the *ACORN*), in Chandoiss Street, next door to the Coventry Cross [*i.e.*, Atwick's, a famous mercer's shop, *vide* p. 124], Covent Garden.   1768

HALL & LODGE, at the *ACORN*, opposite Gray's Inn Gate, in Holborn.   1759

†JNO. HIGGONS, at ye *HAT & BONHAT*, in Chandois Street, Covent Garden.   *c.* 1755

RICHARD HOAR, at the *HAT & DAGGER*, in Castle Alley, Cornhill.   *c.* 1760

†THOMAS ILIFFE, at ye *HATT & BONNETT*, opposite the Hospital Gate in Newgate Street.   *c.* 1760

‡NICHOLAS LANGFORD, at the *ANGEL & OXFORD ARMES*, near Salsbury Court, in Fleet Street.   *c.* 1740

THOMAS MARTYN, at the *HARE & WOOLPACK*, near Salisbury Court, Fleet Street.   *c.* 1755

—— NOYES, at the *HAT, BONNET & STAY*, in Fore Street, near Moorgate.   *c.* 1750

CHARLES PAGET, at the sign of the *BLACK BOY & HATT*, near Red Lion Street in High Holbourn.   *c.* 1760

EDWARD PAUL, at the *GOLDEN LEG*, in New North Street, near Red Lion Square.   1753

JOHN PERRY, at the *QUEEN'S ARMS*, opposite Southampton Street (No. 88) in ye Strand.   1781 (A maker of " Velvet and other Caps " ; also of " Oil, Silk and Lawn Umbrellas.")

HAT & MITRE

ANGEL & OXFORD ARMS

THE HARE

HAT & BEAVER

FOX & CAP

† Straw Hat Makers.   ‡ Hatters and Sword Cutlers.

†THOMAS PLAYSTED, at the *HATT & BONNET*, against St. Bride's Church near Shoe Lane, in Fleet Street.   1749
(A later bill, *c.* 1760, shows him to be making " Painted floor cloths, Tunbridge wares, Tortoise-shell Combs and all sorts of Sieves and Searces for Apothecaries." " Searce " = fine strainer.)

JOHN PRIEST, at the *RISING SUN*, opposite Grays Inn Gate, Holborn.   1757

NATHANIELL RAIKES, att ye Sign of the *HARE*, neer St. Laurence Lane in Cheapside. *c.* 1700

JOHN ROGERS, at the *HAT & BEAVER*, in Grace Church Street.   1760

ANN & THOMAS ROSSITER, at the *RISING SUN & HAT*, in Newgate Street.   1760

T. F. SALTER, at the *GOLD LACED HAT & FAME* (No. 47), Charing Cross.   1794

DANIEL STUMP, at the *WOOLPACK*, the corner of Harvey Court, opposite the New Exchange Buildings, in the Strand.   *c.* 1750

THOMAS TOWLER, at the *HATT & FEATHER*, in Church Lane, near New Round Court, in the Strand.   *c.* 1755

THOMAS TRONSDALE, at ye *FOX & CAP*, in Long Lane, near West Smithfield.   *c.* 1680

JOHN VENABLES, at the *HAT & BEAVER*, near the Black Bear Inn, Piccadilly.   1782

THOMAS WARNER [at the *HAT & FEATHER*], opposite Campden House Boarding School, Kensington.   *c.* 1760

THOMAS WATSON, at ye *LEG & HAT* in Ludgate Street.   *c.* 1755

JAMES WELDY, at the *HAT & PLUME OF FEATHERS*, under St. Dunstan's Church, Fleet Street, near Temple Barr.   *c.* 1760

JOHN WEST, at the *BEAVER & STAR*, the corner of Monmouth Street, next the Broadway, St. Giles's.   *c.* 1760

† Straw Hat Makers.   ‡ Hatters and Sword Cutlers.

GEORGE WESTRON, at the *GOLDEN ARTI-CHOKE*, near the East end of the New Church, in the Strand.   1746

†JOHN WHITE, at the *STRAW HAT & WHEAT-SHEAF*, against Butcherhall Lane, No. 32, in Newgate Street.   1767

†JOHN & JOSEPH WHITE, at the *STRAW HAT*, against Butcher Hall Lane in Newgate Street.
1763

†JOSEPH WHITE, at the *STRAW HAT*, No. 33 Newgate Street.   1768

PETER WHITE, at the *HAT & BEAVER*, No. 81, Newgate Street.   1768
(John, Joseph and Peter White are all entered in the London Directory, 1768, as separate businesses at their three respective addresses in Newgate Street. Joseph White, at No. 33, claims his to be " the oldest hat warehouse in London.")

JACOB WILD, at the *SPREAD EAGLE* in Brewer Street, opposite Windmill Street, Golden Square.
1754

GEORGE WILSON, at the *HAT & BEAVER*, in Bell Court, St. Martin's Le Grand, near Aldersgate.   *c.* 1760

JAMES WINGFIELD [at the *HAT & FEATHER*], the corner of Brewer Street, near Golden Square.
1768

HOOP MAKER

HORNBY & HARRIS, successors to Mrs. Moody, at the *BLUE SPIRE & GOLDEN BALL* in Compton Street, near Greek Street, Soho.   1775

HOSIERS

JAMES ALLEN, at the *ROE BUCK*, opposite Ivy Lane, in Newgate Street.   1754

ALLEN & HARGRAVE, at the *THREE KINGS*, Fenchurch Street.   1740

GEORGE BANNISTER (successor to Mr. G. Carter), at the *BIRD IN HAND*, the corner of Bedford and Shandois Streets, Covent Garden.   *c.* 1760

HAT & BEAVER

THE STRAW HAT

GOLDEN ARTICHOKE

GOLDEN LEG

LEG & GARTER

ARTICHOKE

—— BARKER, at the *SUN*, corner of Norris Street, St. James's Haymarket.   *c.* 1765

ROGER BASSTONE, at the *THREE KINGS*, over against Great Turn Stile, in Holbourn.   *c.* 1760

E. BENNETT, at ye *GOLDEN FLEECE*, near Tooley Street, on London Bridge.   *c.* 1755

BICKNELL, JAMES & GRIFFITH, at the *KING'S ARMS* (?), the corner of Old Bond Street and Piccadilly.   1758–1769

BICKNELL & JAMES, at above.   1779

BICKNELL & MOORE, at above.   1816
(Succeeded by Moore & Co., hatters, 1827–*c.* 1850, followed by Christy's *c.* 1851–*c.* 1875. In 1875 the name was changed to Scott's whose well known hat shop still occupies this corner site, which has been a hatter's for nearly 200 years.)

WILLIAM BIRCHINALL, at the Sign of the *CATHERINE WHEEL*, opposite the Swan Tavern, in Shoreditch.   *c.* 1770

ROBERT BLUNT, at the *GOLDEN BALL*, facing the Mewse, Charing Cross.   1764

GEORGE BOND, at the *GOLDEN LEG*, at the corner of Pope's Head Alley, over against the Royal Exchange, in Cornhill.   *c.* 1730

M. BOTELER, at the *BEEHIVE*, in Little Newport Street, near Gerrard Street.   *c.* 1780

WILLIAM BRADLEY, at ye *LEG & GARTER*, opposite ye New Church, in ye Strand.   *c.* 1760

ROBERT BRYANT, at the sign of the *LAMB*, (?) No. 77, Chiswell Street.   1776

JAMES BUTLER, at ye *ARTICHOKE*, in Bedford Street, Covent Garden.   1740

RICHARD COOMES, at ye *LAMB*, on Holbourn Hill.   1742

JOHN CORINTON, at *BEN JOHNSON'S* (*sic*) *HEAD*, the corner of St. Clement's Church Yard, in the Strand.   *c.* 1760

JAMES CORNECK, Hosier, Hatter & Sword Cutler, at the *LEG & BEAVER*, near St. Paul's, Cheapside. 1768

SAMUEL CORRALL, at the *LAMB*, in the Cloysters, facing St. Bartholomew's Hospital. *c.* 1760

WILLIAM DODSON, at ye *ANGEL & CROWN*, near ye Bridge Foot, in the Borough of Southwark. *c.* 1740

JOHN ELLWOOD, at the *SHIP & SUN*, in Lombard Street. 1751

BURKITT FENN, at the *RAM*, the corner of Bishopsgate Street, in Cornhill (No. 61), opposite Gracechurch Street and Leadenhall Street. 1768

EDWARD GARDINER, at the *DUKE OF MONTAGUE'S HEAD*, near ye New Exchange, in the Strand. 1725

PETER GAUGAIN, at the *GOLDEN BALL*, near ye Turk's Head Tavern, Compton Street, Soho. *c.* 1765

GEORGE GOSLING, at the *LAMB*, the corner of St. Michael's Alley, Cornhill. 1769

LUKE GRAFFTEY (late Lewis & Grafftey), at the *GOLDEN LEG*, No. 59, the corner of Bow Lane, in Cheapside. 1772

PERCIVAL HASLAM, at ye *BLACK LION*, ye corner of Norfolk Street, Strand. 1732
(Succeeded by W. Wilmot, *q.v.*)

JOHN HOCKER, at the *LAMB & QUEEN'S HEAD*, in the Poultry. *c.* 1760

MARGARET HOOKE & SON, at the *GEORGE*, next door to ye Rose Tavern, Without Temple Barr. *c.* 1760

JOHN HOPWOOD, at ye *GREEN CANISTER*, in Charles Street, Covent Garden. 1742

ANN JAMES, at the *FLEECE*, in Prince's Street, opposite the back of St. Ann's Church (Soho) from the *WOOLPACK*, the corner of Crown Court, Soho. *c.* 1765

ANGEL & CROWN

THE LAMB

DUKE OF MONTAGU'S HEAD

GOLDEN BALL & STAR

RISING SUN

THE STAR

Moses Johnson, at the *CROSS STOCKINGS &
CAP*, in St. John's Street, Clerkenwell.   *c.* 1770

Peter le Quainter, at the *GOLDEN BALL &
STAR*, the end of Duke Street, Piccadilly, St.
James's.   1763

Masters & Nisbet (from the corner of Queen
Street), at the *QUEEN'S HEAD & LEG*, opposite
Laurence Lane, in Cheapside.   1768
(See also Nisbet and Masters.)

George Mason, at the *SUN*, opposite the Pump,
in Leaden-hall Street.   1754

George Maynard, at ye *RISEING SUN*, in
Fenchurch Street.   1747

Ratcliff Medley, at the *GOLDEN FLEECE*,
in James Street, Covent Garden.   *c.* 1760

—— Mitchell, at the *STAR*, in Chandois Street,
Covent Garden.   1757

Robert Moss, at the *ROSE*, Sidney's Alley
(Leicester Fields).   1784

Thomas Moore, at the *BISHOP BLAZE*, Chiswell Street.   1755
(St. Blaize, patron saint of wool-combers.)

Newham & Thresher, successors to Mr. Thos.
Street (*q.v.*), at the *PEACOCK*, next door to
Somerset House in the Strand.   1755
(The firm of Thresher & Glenny still exists near Somerset House.)

Nisbet & Masters, at the *QUEEN'S HEAD*,
Cheapside.   1756
(*cf.* Masters & Nisbet above.)

George Payne, at the *CHARLES II PORTER &
DWARF* (No. 80), Newgate Street.   1783

Palethorp & Co., at the *BISHOP BLAZE*, in
Bread Street, near Cheapside.   1760

Thomas Paris & Edwd. Lewis, at the *GOLDEN
LEG*, ye corner of Bow Lane in Cheapside.   1754

Joseph Potter, at the *GOLDEN LEG*, opposite
Great St. Helen's, No. 99, Bishopsgate Street
Within.   1788

HENRY REDWOOD, at the *THREE PIGEONS*, in Essex Street in the Strand.   *c.* 1765

THOMAS REYNOLDS (successor to the late Mr. Meredith), at ye *GOLDEN FLEECE*, agst. St. Dunstan's Church, No. 24, Fleet Street.   1768
(C. Meredith, "haberdasher of hatts" at this address, is mentioned in the *Purefoy Papers* in 1743. *cf.* James Russell, successor to T. Reynolds.)

WILLIAM ROBERTS, at the *THREE SQUIRRILS* in Jermyn Street.   1775
(Thomas Gray, the poet, on his visits to town used to lodge at Roberts', the hosiers, at the east end of Jermyn Street. See Nicholl's " Reminiscences of Gray," *v.* 49.)

JNO. ROBINSON, at ye *GOLDEN CUP* in King Street, Covent Garden.   1760
(Later the sign was the *Golden Cup & Leg*, c. 1770.)

JAMES RUSSELL, at the *GOLDEN FLEECE*, Fleet Street.   1769
(Successor to Thos. Reynolds, *q.v.*)

WILLIAM SAUNDERS, at the *LAMB & BEEHIVE*, in Houndsditch, near Aldgate.   *c.* 1760

CHARLES SAVIGNAC, successor to Mr. Waller (*q.v.*) at the *GOLDEN LEG*, opposite Catherine Street, No. 147 in the Strand.   1783

JOHN SKYRM, at the *SEVEN STARS*, in Tyler Street, Carnaby Market.   1766
(Tyler Street was the continuation of Foubert's Place eastward.)

HENRY SLACK, at the *LAMB*, South Audley Street, Grosvenor Square.   1789

SLATER & MERRIMAN, at the *WOOLPACK & ANCHOR*, opposite ye Mansion House, in the Poultry.   1763

THOMAS STREET, at the sign of the *PEACOCK*, next Somerset House in the Strand.   1724
(Succeeded by Newham & Thresher, *q.v.*)

RICHARD TAYLER, at the *THREE PIGEONS*, opposite Charing Cross, next door but one to Northumberland House.   *c.* 1750

CHARLES TYRRELL, at the *QUEEN'S HEAD*, Fleet Street (No. 108), near Fleet Bridge.   1760

GOLDEN FLEECE

SEVEN STARS

THREE PIGEONS

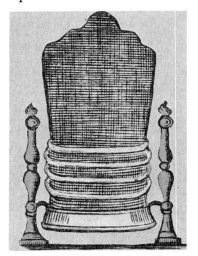

STOVE GRATE

WHITE LION &
THREE FLOWER DE LIS

'*STOW GRATE*'

HOSIERS

VESIE, WYER & SWIFT (successors to Mr. Peter Pope), at the *LAMB*, No. 159, Fenchurch Street.
1785

THOMAS WALLER, at the *GOLDEN LEG*, opposite Catherine Street, in the Strand.   1768
(Succeeded by C. Savignac, *q.v.*)

T. WATSON, at the *LAMB*, in Bedford Street, Covent Garden.   *c.* 1770

WILLIAM WILMOT, at ye *BLACK LION*, ye corner of Norfolk Street, in ye Strand.   1750
(Successor to P. Haslam, *q.v.*)

WILLIAM WOOLLEY, at the *GOLDEN FLEECE* in Cheapside.   1755
(Subsequently No. 48, Cheapside.)

INDIGO MAKER

ADAM MILSOM, at ye *BLUE GATE* in Grace Church Street, near Eastcheap.   1754

INSTRUMENT MAKERS

See under OPTICIANS *and also under*
SCIENTIFIC INSTRUMENT MAKERS

IRONMONGERS

ALEXANDER & SHRIMPTON, at the *ANCHOR & KEY*, Wood Street.   1768
(Successors to Wm. Alexander, 1724–1758.)

FRANCIS BARRON, at the sign of the *STOVE GRATE*, the corner of Surrey Street, near the New Church in the Strand.   1753
(Preceded by Fieldes & Powell at above in 1724.)

NATHANIEL BENTLEY & JOHN FISHER, at the *GOLDEN LYON & CASE OF KNIVES*, near the Royal African House in Leadenhall Street.
c. 1790
(Nathaniel Bentley, an eccentric character, commonly known as " Dirty Dick or The Beau of Leadenhall Street "—See *D.N.B.*)

EDWARD BERRY, at the *TWO CANDLESTICKS & BELL*, ye South Side of St. Paul's Church Yard.   1765

THOMAS BOUCHER, at the *BLACK LION*, corner of Southampton Street in ye Strand.   1712

THOMAS BUTTALL, at the *GRIDIRON*, near Hungerford Market, in the Strand.   1762

JOHN BUTTS & COOKE, at ye *ANCHOR & STAR*, against ye Bolt and Tun Inn, Fleet Street.   1764

JOSEPH CLARKE, at the *GRIDIRON & TROWEL*, in Piccadilly.   *c.* 1740

JOHN ELWELL, at the *LOCK & HINGE*, in the Haymarket.   1766
(Successor to Mr. Thos. Stephens.)
(*cf.* Elwell and Taylor, smiths.)

JOHN GILES & SHADRACH MULLINER, at the *TWO CANDLESTICKS & BELL*, in Addle Street, near Wood Street.   *c.* 1760

RICHARD GORE, at the *GOLDEN BALL*, ye corner of St. Michael's, Crooked Lane, Cannon Street.   *c.* 1740

GORE & PERCHARD, at above.   *c.* 1750

ROBERT HARDING, son (*sic*) & successor to ye late Mr. Wm. Pitches, at the *STOW GRATE*, near to the Brew-house in the Great Minories.
     c. 1750

THOMAS HATTAM, at the *CROSS SAWS & GRIDIRON*, No. 31, Barbican.   1780

JAMES HAWKES, at the *DOUBLET* in Long Acre.
(Successor to Jones & Matthews.)   1765

WILLIAM KINMAN, at the *BELL*, on Snow Hill, near Holbourn Bridge.   *c.* 1760

LEETE & WARBURTON, at the *PADLOCK*, No. 146, Tottenham Court Road.   1838

EDWARD MARTIN, at ye *WHITE LYON & THREE FLOWER DE LIS*, in Foster Lane, Cheapside.   1744

HENRY NETTLESHIP, at the *PARROTT*, the corner of Honey Lane, No. 112, Cheapside.   1770

CROSS SAWS & GRIDIRON

THE BELL

THE PARROT

THREE KEYS

THREE ANCHORS

GABRIEL NICHOLLS, at the *FRYING PAN*, on St. Mary Hill, near Billingsgate.   1768

PHILIP NIND, at the *KING'S ARMS*, the corner of Lancaster Court, near St. Martin's Church in the Strand.   1763

JOHN PEPWELL, at ye *GOLDEN ANCHOR*, at Bell Dock (removed from Gun Dock), Wapping.   1762

JOHN PITTS, at ye *THREE BELLS*, in Great Queen Street, Lincolns Inn Fields.   1768

EDWARD ROGERS, at the *GOLDEN ANCHOR & KEY*, No. 36, in Broad Street, Carnaby Market.   1789

JOHN TAPPENDEN, at the *WHITE LION & GOLDEN KEY*, opposite the Church in Foster Lane, Cheapside.   1753

JOHN THRESHER, at ye *KING'S ARMS & LEATHER DOUBLET*, against Hungerford Market, Strand.   *c.* 1740

TOWNSEND & CROSLEY, at the *THREE KEYS*, No. 3, Gracechurch Street.   1777

A. WALKER, at the *DOG'S HEAD IN THE POT*, No. 25, Great Surry Street, Blackfriars Road.   *c.* 1790

MILES WHITWORTH, at ye *THREE ANCHORS*, in the Poultry.   *c.* 1700

SAMUEL WILSON, at the *CROWN*, ye corner of Crooked Lane, Cannon Street.   1749

WILLIAM WOOD, at the *SAW & BAG OF NAILS*, in Aldersgate Street.   1759
(Successor to Thomas Newnam.)

ITALIAN WAREHOUSEMEN

MRS. HOLT, at ye *TWO OLIVE POSTS*, in ye Broad part of the Strand, almost opposite to Exeter Change.   (?) *c.* 1750

—— LUCERA, at the *ORANGE TREE*, in Air Street, Piccadilly. 1752

BARTO VALLE & BROTHERS, at the *ORANGE TREE & TWO OIL JARS*, in St. James's Hay Market, near Panton Street. 1751

RICHARD WARNER, at the *TWO CIVET CATS & OLIVE TREE*, in New Bond Street, near Grosvenor Street. 1764

LACE MAKERS

M.ˢ LANY, at the *LACE MAKER* in Tavistock Street (No. 11). 1788

WORSLEY, at the *NUN & ANCHOR*, Ludgate Hill. *c.* 1760

TWO CIVET CATS & OLIVE TREE

LACEMEN

(*i.e.*, MAKERS OF GOLD LACE)

JOHN ALISBURY, at the *UNICORN & STAR*, St. James's Street. 1773

AMERY, PITTER & SLIPPER, successors to Mr. K. Brydges (*q.v.*), at the *THREE CROWNS*, corner of Bedford Street, Covent Garden. 1792

EDWARD BARNES, at the *ANCHOR & CROWNE*, over against ye Conduit, in Cheapside, removed from Wood Street. 1707

—— BARRETT, late Basnett's (*q.v.*), at the *GOAT*, corner of Craven Street, in the Strand. 1764–1776

(A bill of Barrett's made out to Edward Gibbon, the historian, when he was living at No. 7, Bentinck Street, is dated 1773.)

WILLIAM BASNETT & COMPANY, at the *GOAT*, corner of Craven Street, in the Strand. 1728–1749

(" Mr. Basnett, laceman to the Prince, is preparing to set out for Paris to observe the French fashions." *Universal Spectator*, 6 June, 1730.)

PERCIVALL BENTLEY & ELIZ. PEARKES, at the *COCK & TURK'S HEAD* in Bedford Street, Covent Garden. 1740–1755

THE LACE MAKER

THREE CROWNS

TURK'S HEAD & COCK

PEACOCK & STAR

BENTLEY & SON, at the *TURK'S HEAD &
COCK*, in Bedford Street.   *c.* 1760–1791

PETER BLUCK, at the *RISING SUN*, near Fetter
Lane, in Fleet Street.   *c.* 1760
(Successor to Wm. Fletcher, *q.v.*)

BLUCK & HOPWOOD, at the *FLEECE & CROWN*,
No. 65, in Long Acre.   1785

BODLEY & ETTY, at the sign of the *BELLOWS
& BALL*, No. 31 in Lombard Street.   1790
(Successors to E. Longdon, *q.v.*)

BRADSHAW & BULLARD, at the *THREE CROWNS*
in the Strand, near Charing Cross.   1755
(Later Thos. Bullard, No. 1, Strand, 1768–1784.)

JOSEPH BROWN, at the *WHEATSHEAF & STAR*
in Cornhill, near the Royal Exchange.   1752
(*cf.* Bradshaw, haberdasher, at this address, *c.* 1760.)

KEMPE BRYDGES (Son-in-law to the late Mr. Saml.
Dawson), at the *THREE CROWNS*, the corner
of Bedford Street, Covent Garden.   1744–1767

BRYDGES & WALKER, at above.   1767
(Succeeded by Amery, Pitter & Slipper, *q.v.*)

WILLIAM COOPER, at the *ACORN*, in Friday
Street, Cheapside.   1777

JOHN DAVISON, at ye *PEACOCK & STAR*, next
door to Pinchbeck's Head, in Fleet Street. 1744
(*cf.* Fletcher & Davison, 1737.)

ISAAC DAY, at the *PEACOCK & TURK'S HEAD*,
the corner of Maiden Lane, Bedford Street,
Covent Garden.   1752

FRANCIS DODSWORTH, at the *SHIPP & ANCHOR*,
in Lombard Street, neere Gracious Street. *c.* 1700

WILLIAM FLETCHER & IOHN DAVISON, at the
RISING SUN, near Fetter Lane, in Fleet Street.
(*cf.* John Davison.)   1737

WILLIAM FLETCHER, at the *RISING SUN*, next
the Horn Tavern, Fleet Street.   1740

GILLES (late A. Jones), at the *LAMB & CROWN*, Long Acre. 1793

ROBERT GLIDE, at the *GOLDEN BOAR'S HEAD*, in Wood Street. 1748

JOHN HASELL, at the *CROSS KEYS*, on Ludgate Hill. 1741

CHRISTOPHER HEDGES, at the *GOLDEN COCK*, on Ludgate Hill. 1755
(Successor to John Ganestock at above in 1722.)

RICHD. & HENRY HEWETSON, at the *SUN*, No. 30, King Street, Covent Garden. 1789
(Successors to Smart & Hewetson at above in 1757.)

TEMPEST HEY, at the *LAMB & CROWN*, in Long Acre. 1752

RICHD. HILL, ROBT. & THOS. PITTER, at the *WHITE HART*, in the Strand, near Charing Cross. 1762
(*c.f.* Pitter & Fox, also Turner, Hill & Pitter.)

ROBERT JAMES, at the *LAMB & CROWN*, in Newgate Street. 1766

WILLIAM JEPHCOTT, at the *SEVEN STARS*, in Wood Street. 1744

THOMAS JONES, at the *BLUE BALL*, in Cross Lane, Long Acre. 1754

THOMAS JONES, at the *LAMB & CROWN*, in Long Acre. *c.* 1770

JOSHUA KNOWLES, at the *PEACOCK*, corner of White Hart Court, No. 40, Lombard Street. 1790

KNOWLES & CHADWICK, at above address. 1777

EDWARD LONGDON, at the *BELLOWS & BALL*, over against George Yard, in Lombard Street.
(*c.f.* Bodley & Etty, above.) 1738

THOMAS NIXON, at the *ARTICHOKE*, near Birchin Lane (No. 60), in Lombard Street. 1763

RICHARD PECK, at the *BLACK BOY*, in Cloth Fair [West Smithfield]. *c.* 1690

SHIP & ANCHOR

SEVEN STARS

CROSS KEYS

BLACK BOY

GOLDEN BALL

JEREMY PEIRCE, at the *GOLDEN BALL*, Ludgate Hill.   1717

EDMUND PELHAM, at the *GEORGE*, against Half Moon Street, in the Strand.   1753
(Half Moon Street was the southern end of Bedford Street previous to 1770.)

PITTER & FOX, at the *THREE CROWNS*, corner of Bedford Street, Covent Garden.   1808
(Successors to Amery, Pitter & Slipper, *q.v.*)

JOHN TOPHAM, at the *ADAM & EVE & STAR*, in Newgate Street, opposite Newgate Market. 1754

WALTER TURNER, RICHD. HILL & ROBT. PITTER, at ye *WHITE HART*, in the Strand, near Charing Cross.   1745
(See also Hill & Pitter at above in 1762.)

GEORGE VAUGHAN, at the *GOLDEN BALL*, near Arundel Street, in the Strand.   1750
(He is several times mentioned in the *Purefoy Letters* between 1743 and 1753.)

MATTHEW WINTER, at the *LAMB & SHUTTLE*, opposite Mercer Street, in Long Acre.   *c.* 1760

WINTER, SON & HAY, at above.   1784

LAMPLIGHTERS
See TINMEN

LEATHER GILDERS

WILLIAM BARBAROUX, nephew and successor to the late Mr. John Hutton, at the *GOLDEN LION*, Fronting the South Door, in St. Paul's Church Yard.   *c.* 1760

THOMAS BROMWICH, at the *GOLDEN LION*, on Ludgate Hill.   1744

BROMWICH & LEIGH, at above.   1759

BROMWICH, ISHERWOOD & BRADLEY, at above. (No. 35, Ludgate Hill.)   1777
(Mr. Bromwich supplied wall papers to Horace Walpole for Strawberry Hill (see Walpole Letters) in 1754–1756.)

JOHN CONWAY, at ye *KING'S ARMS*, the 2nd
Leather Guilders' shop from ye end of Ludgate
Street, ye South side of St. Paul's Church Yard.

1734

JOSEPH FLETCHER & JOHN CONWAY, at above.

1732

ROBERT HALFORD, at the *GOLDEN LION &
BALL*, the South West side of St. Paul's Church
Yard. *c.* 1760

JOHN SCOTT, at the *KING'S ARMS*, in Cheapside,
over against Bow Church Yard. 1746

SAMUEL WILLIAMS, at the *GOLDEN LION &
BALL*, in St. Paul's Church Yard. 1752

THE GEORGE

LEATHER SELLERS
See also CURRIERS

CHURCHER & CHRISTIE, at the *LAMB &
BREECHES*, on London Bridge. *c.* 1750

THOMAS HODGSON, at the *THREE GOLDEN
LYONS*, No. 33, Within Aldgate. 1767

WILLIAM OSBORNE, at the *ROE BUCK*, upon
London Bridge. 1714

LIBRARIES (CIRCULATING)

CHARLES GEARY, at *POPE'S HEAD*, No. 27,
Great Marlborough Street. *c.* 1780
(Successor to Samuel Noble, *q.v.*)

WILLIAM LANE, the *MINERVA*, Leadenhall
Street. *c.* 1780

FRANCIS NOBLE, at *OTWAY'S HEAD*, in King
Street, Covent Garden. *c.* 1750
Removed to *OTWAY'S HEAD*, almost opposite
Gray's Inn Gate, Holborn (see also p. 32) 1768

JOHN NOBLE, at *DRYDEN'S HEAD*, in St.
Martin's Court, near Cranbourne Alley, Leicester
Fields. 1768

ROE BUCK

BLACK MOOR'S HEAD

BLACKAMOOR'S HEAD

Samuel Noble, at *POPE'S HEAD*, in Carnaby Street, near Carnaby Market. *c.* 1770
(Succeeded by C. Geary, *q.v.*)

T. Wright, at the *BIBLE*, in Exeter Exchange, Strand. 1743
(Timperley says Wright established the first circulating library in London, 1740.)

LINEN DRAPERS

Perkins Richard Acton, at ye *BLACK MOOR'S HEAD*, in Henrietta Street, Covent Garden.
 1737

William Alger (late Baker), at the *INDIAN QUEEN*, No. 114, Leadenhall Street. 1800

J. & R. Neale Badcock (late Badcock & Ellis), at the *CROWN & SCEPTRE*, corner of Creed Lane, in Ludgate Street. 1747

Nathaniel Bagshaw, at the *SHIP*, in Bridge Street, Westminster. *c.* 1765

James Bagwell, at the *OLD BELL*, on Little Tower Hill. *c.* 1760

Thomas Balack, at ye sign of ye *NEW EXCHANGE*, in Durham Yard. *c.* 1760

S. Barrow, at the *HEN & CHICKENS*, No. 63, Houndsditch. *c.* 1780
(Removed from the *Two Wax Dolls*, No. 56. *cf.* Bowness Sisters.)

P. Bathurst, at the *BLACKAMOOR'S HEAD* (?), in Little Brook Street, Hanover Square. 1775

Richard Batten, at the *CROWN*, in York Street, Covent Garden. 1752
(Removed from the *Hen & Chickens*, next door.)

Batten & Hughes, at above. 1756
(See also Webb & Batten.)

Thomas Bell, at the *SHIP & ANCHOR*, near York Buildings, in the Strand. *c.* 1755

Thomas Bentley, at the *WHEATSHEAF*, No. 60, in St. Paul's Churchyard. 1796

P. BICKNELL (late Porter & Co., *q.v.*), at the *BLUE ANCHOR*, opposite the Old Change, No. 149, in Cheapside.   1785

JORDAN HEYLAND BIGGER, at ye *ARTICHOKE*, over against ye East India House, in Leaden Hall Street.   1725

RICHARD BINGLEY, at the *KING'S ARMS & ANCHOR*, in Tavistock Street, Covent Garden.   1768

BINGLEY & BRAGG, at above.   *c.* 1755

CHARLOTTE & WILLM. BINGLEY, at the *ANCHOR*, No. 3, Tavistock Street.   1790

JOHN BLAKE, at the *BEEHIVE*, near the Spread Eagle Inn, in Grace Church Street.   1755

WILLIAM BOWKER, at the *GOLDEN ANCHOR*, in Compton Street, St. Ann's [Soho].   1744

BOWNESS SISTERS, at the *TWO WAX DOLLS*, No. 56, Houndsditch.   *c.* 1770
(*cf.* S. Barrow at above.)

WILLIAM BURCHAL, at the *INDIAN QUEEN*, opposite Berwick Street, No. 63, Oxford Street.
(Succeeded by Calthrop & Linton, *q.v.*)   1775

JOSEPH BURNTHWAITE, at the *KING'S HEAD* [Charles II], the corner of Surry Street, in the Strand.   *c.* 1750

CALTHROP & LINTON (successors to Mr. Burchal, *q.v.*), at the *INDIAN QUEEN*, No. 63, Oxford Street.   1781
(This billhead is made out to Edward Gibbon, the historian, when he was living in Bentinck Street.)

ARCHIBALD CAMPBELL, at the *BLACKMOOR'S HEAD*, in the Hay-Market in the Borough of Southwark.   *c.* 1760

JOHN CANCELLOR, at the *SHIP*, in ye Poultry. 1764

WILLIAM CHALONER, at the *HARE*, the corner of Tavistock Street, adjoining to York Street, Covent Garden.   1777

ARTICHOKE

INDIAN QUEEN

THE HARE

HOOP PETTICOAT & CROWN

BLUE BOAR

John Chase, at *D'OYLEY'S HEAD*, in Long Acre. 　　　　　　　　　　1764

Chase & Ashton, at above. 　　*c.* 1770

Benjamin Cole, at the *SUN*, in St. Paul's Church Yard. 　　　　　　　　*c.* 1720

Charles Cole, at the *BLACKMOOR'S HEAD*, ye corner of Fetter Lane in Holborn. 　1726

James Collins, at the *HOOP PETTICOAT & CROWN*, in Bishopsgate Street, near Artillery Lane. 　　　　　　　　　　*c.* 1760

Conington & Radcliffe, at the *HEN & CHICKENS*, two doors from Foster Lane, in Cheapside. 　　　　　　　　　1764

Coward & Pryce, at ye *STAR*, near Great Queen Street, in Drury Lane, opposite Long Acre. 　　　　　　　　　　　1771

Cropley & Craven, at the *SUN*, the corner of York Street, facing Russell Court, Covent Garden. 　　　　　　　　　　　*c.* 1750

B. Davis, at the *STAR*, the corner of Albion and Stamford Streets, Surry side Blackfriars Bridge. 　　　　　　　　　　　1792

Thomas Davis, at the *KING'S ARMS*, New Bond Street. 　　　　　　　　　1782
(This billhead is made out to Edward Gibbon, the historian, when he was living in Bentinck Street.)

Thomas Dawson, at the *BLACK LION & LAMB*, in Blowbladder Street, near Cheapside. 　1754

Dore & Tollerton, at the *FOX*, opposite Bucklersbury, in Cheapside. 　　　　1760

William Dunning, at the *BLUE BOAR*, near Gray's Inn Gate, Holborn. 　　　*c.* 1750

John Edwards, at the *RAVEN & ANCHOR*, in Drury Lane. 　　　　　　　　*c.* 1765

John Evans, at the *GOLDEN ANCHOR*, in Marylebone Street, near Golden Square. 　1769
(Succeeded by Brownbill & Co., 1787.)

Richard Evans, at ye *GOLDEN ANCHOR*, in New Bond Street, next Oxford Road.　1760

Edward Eyre, at the *WHEATSHEAF*, in York Street, Covent Garden.　1739
(Previous to 1738 E. Eyre was in partnership at this address with Peter Webb, *q.v.*)

John Fashion, at the *LION & LAMB*, next the Half Moon Tavern, Cheapside.　1738

Fassett & Addison, at the *HALF MOON*, No. 14, Ludgate Street.　1782

John Fieldsend, at the *NEW BALLOON*, No. 25, Oxford Street, opposite Soho Square.　1786
(Succeeded by T. Foster, *q.v.*)

Finney, Sirdefield & Clarke, at the *UNICORN*, No. 58, Newgate Street, one door from Cheapside.　1777

Fortescue & Hatchett, at the *ANGEL*, in King Street, Covent Garden.　1756

William Fortescue, at above.　1762

Thomas Foster & Co., at the *NEW BALLOON*, No. 25, Oxford Street.　1805
(*cf.* J. Fieldsend above.)

Thomas French, at the *SUN*, opposite Lancaster Court, New Bond Street.　1762

Ralph Fretwell, at the *BLACKMOOR'S HEAD & STAR*, the corner of Castle Yard, Holborn.　1768

R. H. Gedge, at the *THREE PIDGEONS*, No. 1, the corner of Leicester Fields, opposite Sidney's Alley.　1767

—— Gilson, at the *GOLDEN KEY*, No. 95, Minories, near Tower Hill.　1791

Daniel Golden, at the *UNICORN*, near Norfolk Street, in the Strand.　*c.* 1770
(Succeeded T. West at above.)

John Goad, at the *THREE ROSES*, opposite the Green Dragon Inn, Bishopsgate Street.　1762

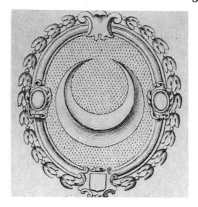

HALF MOON

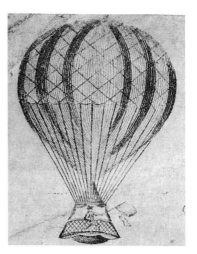

NEW BALLOON

WHEAT SHEAF

TURK'S HEAD

*TWO FUSTIAN ROLLS, ROSE &
CROWN*

WILLIAM GOULD, at the *WHEAT SHEAF*, in Fleet Street. 1734

MICHAEL GREENHOW, at the *GOLDEN WHEAT SHEAF*, near the Barrs, West Smithfield. *c.* 1760

JEREMIAH GREENLAND, at the *HEN & CHICKENS & STAR*, No. 52, in West Smithfield. 1768

GREENWOLLERS, BYAM & DAY, at the *TURK'S HEAD*, in York Street, Covent Garden. *c.* 1760

CHARLES GREENWOOD, at the *BLUE ANCHOR*, No. 149, opposite the Old Change, in Cheapside. (*cf.* P. Bicknell and also B. Porter at above.) 1779

GUBBINS & GUEST, successors to the late Mr. Baxter, at the *NAKED BOY*, in Henrietta Street, Covent Garden. 1768

RICHARD GURWOOD, at the *GOLDEN ANCHOR*, No. 96, Grace Church Street. 1776

NATHANIEL HALL, at the *UNICORN*, in Parliament Street, Westminster. 1772

GEORGE HATCHETT, at the *HEN & CHICKENS*, in Castle Street, facing Cranborn Alley. 1778

HATCHETT & TOMLINSON, at above. 1775
(Preceded by G. A. Hatchett at above in 1770.)

RICHARD HATCHETT, at the *TURK'S HEAD*, in King Street, Covent Garden. 1758

JEREMIAH HEMSWORTH, at the *TWO FUSTIAN ROLLS, ROSE & CROWN*, in White Horse Yard, Drury Lane. *c.* 1750

M. HESELTINE, at the *WHEATSHEAF*, opposite St. Clement's Church, No. 207, Strand. 1810

HODGKINSON & WARRINER, at the *TURK'S HEAD & PLUME OF FEATHERS*, in New Bond Street, near Grosvenor Street. 1786
(Successors to Edd Webster at above, 1765.)

JOHN HOOKER, at the *HARE*, opposite the Half Moon Tavern, No. 23, Cheapside. 1782

STEPHEN HORNE, at ye *BLACKMOOR'S HEAD*, ye corner of Spittle Square, Bishops Gate Street.
c. 1730

WILLIAM HUBBALD, at the *LAMB*, Without Bishopsgate.
c. 1740

WILLIAM HULLS, at the *THREE NUNNS*, in Newgate Street.
1711

ROBT. & MATTH^S HUNTLEY, at the *CROWN*, in Leaden-hall Street.
1750
(Successors to Samuel Huntley at above in 1723.)

HUNTLEY, BROWN & BACON, at above.
1764

—— HUTTON, at the *BLACKMOOR'S HEAD*, No. 94, Minories, near Tower Hill (removed from No. 146).
c. 1770

—— JACKSON, at the *SPINNING WHEEL*, No. 117, Minories, near John Street.
c. 1760

E. JEFFERYS, at the *DOLPHIN*, over against Middle Row, Holborn.
c. 1730

SAMUEL JOHNSON, at the *SUN & ANCHOR*, Without Aldgate.
c. 1755

JOB JONES, at the *THREE KINGS*, opposite Gutter Lane, in Cheapside.
c. 1760

JAMES KETCHER, at the *OLD HEN & CHICKENS*, six doors below the Hospital Gate, West Smithfield.
1777

GABRIEL LA ROCHE, at *QUEEN ELIZABETH'S HEAD*, in (No. 44) New Bond Street.
1772

NATHANAEL LAW, at the *THREE NUNS*, next the Admiralty Office, Whitehall.
1757

RICHARD LAW, at the *THREE CROWNS*, in Coventry Street, faceing the Hay Market. 1769
(Succeeded by M. Scholey at above, *q.v.*)

MICHEL LEJEUNE, at the *HEN & CHICKENS*, the corner of Bedford Street, in King Street, Covent Garden.
1770

BLACKMOOR'S HEAD

DOLPHIN

QUEEN ELIZABETH'S HEAD

OLD BLACK BOY

SPINNING WHEEL

RICHARD LIVELL, at the *GOLDEN KEY*, near Brownlow Street, Holborn.   *c.* 1760

WILLIAM MACDOUALL at the *CROWN*, in New Bond Street, opposite Conduit Street.   1771
(Succeeded A. Scholar, *q.v.*)

JAMES MACKDONALD, at the *RED LYON*, near Durham Yard, in the Strand.   *c.* 1760

MACKINTOSH & HUNTER, at the *GOLDEN ANCHOR*, in Milk Street.   1755

JNO. MAYHEW, at the sign of the *ADAM & EVE*, the corner of Wood Street, Cheapside.   *c.* 1760

JOHN MAYO, at ye *SUN*, next door to ye Half Moon tavern, Cheapside.   1748

MOON & BUCKLAND, at the *THREE PIGEONS & SCEPTRE*, No. 66, New Bond Street, three doors above Brook Street.   1818
(*cf.* Davison, Beamon & Abbott, haberdashers.)

STEPHEN MOORE, at the *BLACKMOOR'S HEAD*, in York Street, Covent Garden.   1757

JOHN MORRIS, at the *OLD BLACK BOY*, in Norton Folgate, near Bishopsgate Barrs, the shop of the late Mr. John Stevens, Deceas'd.   *c.* 1730

THOMAS MOULD, at the *ANGEL & CROWN*, the corner of Gresham College, Bishopsgate Street.
                                    1768
(Gresham College was pulled down in this same year, 1768.)

THOMAS MUNDAY, at ye *TURK'S HEAD*, ye corner of Houndsditch, Without Bishopsgate.
                                    c. 1750

JNO. NEWCOMBE, at the *ARTICHOKE & THREE ANCHORS*, Cheapside.   *c.* 1760

FRANCIS NORRIS, at the *SPINNING WHEEL*, King Street, Covent Garden.   1758

PETER ORTON, at the *BLACKMOOR'S HEAD*, the corner of Bride Lane, in Fleet Street.   1754

RICHARD OVEY, at the *PLUME OF FEATHERS*, No. 22, Tavistock Street, Covent Garden.   1793

JOHN OWEN, at the *PEACOCK*, No. 29, King Street, Covent Garden.   1793

OWEN & FOOTE, at the *HOPE & ANCHOR*, the corner of Southampton Street, High Holborn. (Successors to the late Mr. Thos. Grant.)   1762

JOHN PARKER, at the *TURK'S HEAD*, near the New Church, in the Strand.   *c.* 1750

PAYLER & HEDDON, at the *LAMB & DOVE*, in York Street, Covent Garden.   *c.* 1770

JOHN PERRY, at the *GOLDEN PEAR**, in Portugal Street, facing Lincoln's Inn Back Gate.   1754

GOLDEN PEAR

ABEL PEYTON, at the *CARV'D BLACKMOOR'S HEAD*, West Smithfield.   1749

JOSEPH PHILLIPS, at the *BLACKMOOR'S HEAD*, Aldgate High Street.   1765

JOHN PHIPPS & THOS. FRYER, at the *THREE CROWNS*, Without Bishopsgate, near Devonshire Street.   *c.* 1730

HENRY PLUMPTON, at the *KING'S ARMS*, the corner of Castle Court, in Shandois Street, near Covent Garden.   *c.* 1760
(Successor to J. Rhodes, *q.v.*)

PORTAL & HEBERT, at the *CARVED GOLDEN ANGEL*, facing St. Helen's, No. 98, Within Bishopsgate.   1771

BENJAMIN PORTER, at the *BLUE ANCHOR*, opposite the Old Change, in Cheapside.
                                      1753–1777
(*cf.* C. Greenwood and also P. Bicknell at above.)

JOHN POWELL, at the *PACK HORSE & FUSTIAN ROLL*, New Bond Street. (Illustrated p. 118.)
                                      1764

WILLIAM PRATER, at ye *WHITE LYON*, opposite Northumberland House, Charing Cross.   1769

THREE CROWNS

---

* An apt example of a *rebus* sign.

PACK HORSE & FUSTIAN ROLL

GOLDEN ARTICHOKE

ELLING PRINCE, at the *GOLDEN ARTICHOKE*, in Great Queen Street, Lincoln's Inn Fields.

c. 1730

JNO. RAWLINSON, at the *THREE CROWNS & KEY*, in Newgate Street.   1760

JOHN READE, at the Sign of the *SHIP*, next door but one to ye West end of the New Exchange Buildings, in the Strand.   *c.* 1750

JOHN READSHAW, at the *SUN*, in Blow Bladder Street, near the upper end of Cheapside. *c.* 1740
(Blowbladder Street was the east end of Newgate Street.)

JOSHUA RHODES, at the *KING'S ARMS*, the corner of Castle Court, in Shandois Street, near Covent Garden.   *c.* 1750
(Succeeded by H. Plumpton, *q.v.*)

MRS. ROBERTS, at the *ACORN*, in Salisbury Court, Fleet Street.   1758

JAMES ROBINSON, at ye *BLACKMOOR'S HEAD*, the corner of Norris Street, St. James's Market.
(Successor to J. Lockton at above in 1725.)   *c.* 1760

THOMAS RODGERS, at the *WHEAT SHEAF*, in Great Turnstile, Holborn.   *c.* 1750

ALEXANDER SCHOLAR, at the *WHEAT SHEAF* in New Bond Street, between Conduit and Clifford Streets.   1761

SCHOLAR & MACDOUAL, at above.   1766
(Succeeded by W. Macdoual, *q.v.*)

M. SCHOLEY, at the *THREE CROWNS*, Coventry Street, facing the Hay Market.   1785
(Successor to R. Law, *q.v.*)

ADAM SMITH, at the *GOLDEN LION & CROWN*, in King Street, Golden Square.   1765

CHARLES SMITH, at the *WHEAT SHEAF*, in Conduit Street, Hanover Square, the corner of the Pass leading to Savill Row.   1762

RICHARD SMITH, at the *CROWN*, the North side of St. Paul's Church Yard.   *c.* 1760

RICHARD SPRINGALL, at the *GOLDEN ANCHOR & SUN*, in Bishopsgate Street, near the South Sea House. 1765

WILLIAM STOKES, at ye *BLACKMOOR'S HEAD & STAR*, ye corner of Widegate Street, Without Bishopsgate. *c.* 1750

THOMAS & PUGH, at the *SISTERS*, No. 80, Strand. 1776
(Removed from the corner of Northumberland Street.)

THWAITES, at the *BEEHIVE*, in West Street, Seven Dials. *c.* 1790

GOLDEN ANCHOR & SUN

VINE & HANSARD, at the *THREE PIGEONS*, No. 319, High Holborn, corner of Southampton Buildings. 1787

RICHD. WAINWRIGHT & JOHN WITHERS, at the *SHIP & STAR*, near ye corner of Milk Street in Cheapside. *c.* 1760

WILLIAM WARD, at the *HARE*, in New Bond Street, betwixt Grosvenor Street and Brook Street. 1770

JOSEPH WATERMAN, at the *HEN & CHICKENS*, opposite Oxenden Street in Coventry Street. *c.* 1760

BENJN. WATKINSON, at the *WHEATSHEAF & STAR*, two doors from King Street, in Cheapside. 1759

JAMES WATSON, at the sign of *ST. ANDREW*, the corner of Charles Street, Covent Garden. (Illustration p. 122.) *c.* 1760

PETER WEBB, at the *HEN & CHICKENS*, in York Street, Covent Garden. (Illustration p. 122.)
(Remov'd from the Wheatsheafe, next door.) 1738
(See also Edwd. Eyre.)

THOS. WEBB & RICHD. BATTEN, at above. 1740
(See also R. Batten above.)

EDWARD WEBSTER, at the *TURK'S HEAD & SUN*, in New Bond Street, near Grosvenor Street. 1765

THE SISTERS

ST. ANDREW

HEN & CHICKENS

CROSS KEYS

WEBSTER & HODGKINSON, at the *TURK'S HEAD & PLUME OF FEATHERS*, in New Bond Street, near Grosvenor Street.   1770

SAMUEL WELCHMAN, at the *SHIP*, the corner of Barnard's Inn Gate, Holbourn.   1770

THOMAS WEST, at the *UNICORN*, near Norfolk Street, in the Strand.   *c.* 1755
(Succeeded by Daniel Golden in 1777.)

THOS. WHEAT & JOHN SYMONDS, at the *QUEEN ELIZABETH'S HEAD*, near Laurence Lane, in Cheapside.   1753

GEORGE & HENRY WHEELER, at the *GOLDEN-ARTICHOKE*, St. James's Market.   1773

JNO. WHITING, at the *LION & LAMB & STARR*, near Bow Lane in Cheapside.   1764

FRANCIS WILLIAMS, at the *BLACK LYON*, in Holborn, within the Barrs, opposite Brook Street.   1768

WILLIAM WISEHAM, at the *THREE NUNS*, in ye Poultry.   1744–1760

THOS. WOOLOTON, the *HEN & CHICKENS*, No. 64, Oxford Street.   1781

WOOLOTON & MORTON, at above.   1800

ANN WRIGHT, at the *STAR & BLACKMOOR'S HEAD*, the corner of King's Head Court, near Bartlett's Buildings, in Holbourn.   1738

LOCKSMITHS

EDWD. & WILLM. HILLIARD, at the *CROSS KEYS*, the corner of Bishopsgate Street and Leadenhall Street.   1749

HENRY WALTON, att the Signe of the *BRASS LOCK & KEY*, att the corner of Newportt Streett, att the Upper End of St. Martin's Lane.   1694

JOHN WEVER (*see under* Bellhangers and Locksmiths).

LOCKSMITHS

WOOD & LA ROCHE, at the *GOLDEN KEY*, in Cheapside.   1747

LORIMER

See BIT & STIRRUP MAKER

MALTSTER

IOHN OLDHAM, at the *ADAM & EVE*, without Bishopsgate.   1767

MANGLE MAKER

PETER LYON, at the Sign of the *MANGLE*, No. 20, Great Titchfield Street, Oxford Market. (*See also under* Engine makers.)   1793

MASONS

See SCULPTORS & MASONS

MATHEMATICAL INSTRUMENT MAKERS

See SCIENTIFIC INSTRUMENT MAKERS

MEASURES MAKER

JAMES MARRIOTT & Co., at the *GOLDEN STANDARD BUSHEL*, No. 33, in Eastcheap.
c. 1790

MERCERS

ADAMS, at the *SEVEN STARS*, in Norris Street, near St. James's Hay Market.   *c.* 1760

JOSEPH ALLANSON, at the *GOLDEN LION*, in St. Clement's Church Yard, Strand.   1764

ALLANSON & HARRIS, at above.   1769
(See successors, Harris, Evans & Bourne.)

EDWARD ARGLES, at ye *INDIAN KING*, near Warwick Court, Holborn.   1750
(Successor to Nicklin, see Ryder & Nicklin.)

JOHN ATKINSON & Co., at the *GOLDEN ANCHOR*, the corner of Maiden Lane in Bedford Street, Covent Garden.   1741

STAR & BLACKMOOR'S HEAD

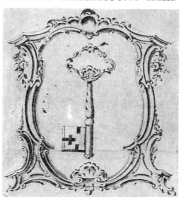

GOLDEN KEY

SEVEN STARS

COVENTRY CROSS

INDIAN QUEEN

THE ANGEL

WILLIAM ATWICK, the *COVENTRY CROSS*, in New Bond Street, near Bruton Street.   1760

ATWICK & HOOPER, at above.   1763
(Succeeded by James Hooper, 1788, *q.v.*)

ELIZABETH ATWICK, at the *HALF MOON* in Old Bond Street, near Piccadilly.   1766

AUSTIN & DEVONPORT, at the *OLD INDIAN QUEEN*, two doors from Bartlett's Buildings facing Hatton Garden, Holborn.   *c.* 1760
(See Garnham Edwards at this address, 1747.)

BAKER, the *THREE CROWNS*, Cranbourne Alley, Leicester Fields.   *c.* 1780

PETER BANISTER, at the *TURK'S HEAD*, near Sadlers' Hall, Cheapside.   1746

BARLOW, ASHBURNER & NELTHORPE, at the *WHEATSHEAF*, King Street, Covent Garden.
(Successors to Swan, Buck & Barlow, *q.v.*)   1776

BELLAMY & SETREE, at the *INDIAN QUEEN*, Shandois Street, the corner of Half Moon Street, Covent Garden.   1763–1764

BELLAMY, SETREE & LANE, at the *INDIAN QUEEN*, No. 1 in Chandos Street, Covent Garden.   1777–1781

BELLAMY & ROBARTS, at above.   1782
(Successors to Setree & Bellamy, *q.v.*)

BELLAMY, ROBARTS & PLOWMAN, at above. 1790

BIRCH & MATHERS, at the *WHEATSHEAF & SUN*, No. 131, Fleet Street, opposite Salisbury Court.   *c.* 1760

MARY BLACKSTONE & WILLIAM HAY, at the *BLUE BOAR*, near the Conduit in Cheapside.
(See also Cotterell & Blackstone.)   1723

THOMAS BOSVILE, at the *ANGEL*, in Bedford Street, Covent Garden.   1747

BOUCHER & ALDERSON, at the *QUEEN'S HEAD*, No. 6, Bridge Street, Westminster.   1791

CARY BOUCHER & HUGH GRONOUS, at the *BLACK LION*, in Shandois Street, Covent Garden. *c.* 1755

JOSEPH BRACKSTONE, at the *ANCHOR*, in York Street, Covent Garden. 1763

ROBERT BRADSHAW, at the *EAGLE & CHILD*, in Maiden Lane, near Wood Street. *c.* 1710

SAMUEL BRIDGES, att the *ANGEL*, in the Strand, neare Summersett House. *c.* 1700

BRYAN & TRINGHAM (successors to Mr. Willm. James), at the *BLUE ANCHOR*, No. 30 in Cheapside, opposite Gutter Lane. *c.* 1760

GEORGE BURTON & C.ᴼᴹᴾ at the *GOLDEN CROSS*, on Ludgate Hill 1741

GEO. CALDECOTT, JNO. BARRODALE, & MATT. VERNON, at ye *NAKED BOY & SEVEN STARS*, in Ludgate Street. 1707

CARR, IBBETSON & BIGGE, at the *QUEEN'S HEAD*, on Ludgate Hill. 1743

CARR, IBBETSON, BIGGE, PICKARD & GIBSON, at above. 1769
(Succeeded by Ibbetson, Barlow & Clarke in 1789, *q.v.*)

ROBT. CARR & JOS. STANFIELD, at the *PARROT*, in Ludgate Street. 1738

G. CARTER, at the *BRITANNIA*, No. 3 in Chandois Street, Covent Garden. *c.* 1770

JAMES CLUTTERBUCK, at the sign of *THREE ANGELS*, against ye New Church, in ye Strand. 1750

CLUTTERBUCK & GASTRELL, at above 1758
(See also J. Hatsell at above, 1772.)

RICHARD COLE, at the sign of the *GREEN MAN*, the Back of St. Clement's, near the New Church in the Strand. *c.* 1760

EAGLE & CHILD

GOLDEN CROSS

QUEEN'S HEAD

LAMB & BLACK SPREAD EAGLE

OLD INDIAN QUEEN

DAVID & PHILIP COOPER, at the *KING'S HEAD*, No. 15, Holliwell Street, St. Clements, Strand.
1785

NATHANIEL COTES, at the *BLACKMOOR'S HEAD*, in Panton Street, the second door from the Hay Market.   1769–1788

BERNARD COTTERELL & CHAS. BLACKSTONE, at the *BLUE ANCHOR & BALL*, near the Conduit, in Cheapside.   1707
(See also Blackstone & Hay, also E. Milward.)

COTTERELL & BLACKSTONE, at the *BLUE BOAR*, near the Conduit in Cheapside.   *c.* 1730
(See E. Milward.)

—— CRANSTON (from Round Court), at the *THREE NUNS & WHEATSHEAF*, in Great Bridge Street, Westminster.   1770

DARE & HITCHCOCK, at the *QUEEN'S HEAD & STAR*, the upper end of Cheapside, next St. Paul's Church Yard.   *c.* 1760

WILLIAM DARE & JAS. PAITFIELD, at the *WHITE LION*, opposite Gutter Lane, in Cheapside. 1748
(See also Paitfield & Dare, *q.v.*)

JOHN THOS. & EDWD. DIVETT, at the *SHIP & BALL*, West Smithfield.   1760–1793

GABRIEL DOUCE, at ye *LAMB & BLACK SPREAD EAGLE*, next door to the Golden Goate, in New Round Court, in ye Strand.   *c.* 1680
(Removed from Shandoies Street.)

GARNHAM EDWARDS, at the *OLD INDIAN QUEEN*, faceing Hatton Garden, Holborn. 1747
(Succeeded by Austin Davenport, *q.v.*)

JOHN EDWARDS, at the *LAMB*, in Oxford Road, near Oxford Market.   1768

FRANCIS ELLERKER, at the *BLACKE SWANNE*, in Paternoster Row.   1664

REBECCA ENGLISH, at the *OLD WHITE SWAN & ROWL*,* over against the Iron Gates on the South-side of St. Paul's Church-yard.   *c.* 1720
(See illustration on p. 128.)

---

* (Rowl = roll of silk.)

Joshua Feary & How Lowfield, at the *WHEAT-SHEAF & STAR*, on Ludgate Hill.   1703

Richard Felton, at the *BLACKMOOR'S HEAD*, Within Aldgate.   *c.* 1750

Samuel Ford, at ye *ANGEL & CROWN*, in Houndsditch, ye second door from Bishopsgate Street.   *c.* 1740
(Succeeded by J. Hunt, *q.v.*)

Jno. Fox & Will^M. Hulbert, at the *WHEAT-SHEAF & SUN*, on Ludgate Hill, faceing the Old Bailey.   1742

Gastrell & Hatsell, at the *THREE ANGELS*, in the Strand.   1763
(See Clutterbuck & Gastrell.)

Richard George, *INDIAN QUEEN & STAR*, Holywell Street, Strand.   *c.* 1800
(See predecessor S. Marriott at above, 1777.)

James Goodchild, at the *BUNCH OF GRAPES*, the Backside of St. Clements Danes.   *c.* 1750

George Haigh, at the *QUEEN CHARLOTTE'S HEAD*, No. 12, Houndsditch, opposite Church Row.   *c.* 1780

Miles Halsey, at the *BLACKMOOR'S HEAD*, in Ludgate Street, near St. Paul's.   1736

Miles Halsey & Phil^P. Palmer, at above.   1745
(See Jenyns & Palmer, also Palmer & Fleetwood.)

Harris, Evans & Bourne (late Allanson & Harris, *q.v.*), at the *GOLDEN LION*, St. Clement's Church Yard, Strand.   1790

John Hartley, at the *INDIAN QUEEN*, the corner of Water Lane, in Fleet Street.   *c.* 1755

John Hartley & Benj. Spencer, at above.   1760–80

John Haskins, at the *GOLDEN FLEECE*, ye corner of Tavistock Court, in Tavistock Street, Covent Garden.   *c.* 1760

BLACK SWAN

ANGEL & CROWN

THREE ANGELS

OLD WHITE SWAN & ROLL

RED LION & STAR

JAMES HATSELL, at the *THREE ANGELS*, opposite the New Church, in the Strand.   1772
(See Gastrell & Hatsell, also Clutterbuck & Gastrell, at above.)

JEREMIAH HAWKES, at the *SEVEN STARS*, in Tavistock Street.   *c.* 1760

JEREMIAH HAWKES, at the *WHEATSHEAF*, in Tavistock Street, Covent Garden.   *1772

WILLIAM HAY, at ye *BLUE BOAR & CROWN*, next door to Sadlers' Hall in Cheapside.   1726
(Formerly Blackstone & Hay, *q.v.*)

JAMES HEBERT, at the *RED LYON & STAR*, in Fenchurch Street.   1740

THOMAS HERBERT, at ye *THREE CROWNS* in Cloath-Faire, near West Smithfield.   *c.* 1700

HERNE & COX, at the *INDIAN QUEEN*, the corner of Kings Gate Street, High Holbourn.
1765

JACOB HEWITT & SON, at the *RED LYON & ANCHOR*, in Gracechurch Street, near Fenchurch Street.   1764

THOMAS HINCHLIFF, removed from the *GREAT WHEATSHEAF*, on Ludgate Hill; to the *WHEATSHEAF*, in Bedford Street. [Later the Hen & Chickens.]   1742

THOS. & WILL.ᴹ HINCHLIFF & JAMES CROFT, at the *HEN & CHICKENS*, Henrietta Street, Covent Garden.   1751

WIDOW HINCHLIFF, removed from above to the *HEN & CHICKENS* in Bedford Street, Covent Garden.   *c.* 1770

HINCHLIFF & RHODES, at the *HEN & CHICKENS & SEVEN STARS*, Bedford Street, Covent Garden.   1778

JAMES HOOPER, at the *COVENTRY CROSS*, No. 149, New Bond Street.   1788
(See Atwick & Hooper at above.)

---

* The 1772 bill is made out to Mrs. David Garrick.

ROBERT HOLDEN, at the *GOLDEN BALL*, next the Crown Tavern, behind the Royal Exchange. 1739

JOHN HUNT [successor to Mr. Saml. Ford, deceased, *q.v.*] at the *ANGEL & CROWN*, No. 77, Houndsditch, 2nd door from Bishopsgate Street. 1776

WILLIAM HYDE, at the *INDIAN QUEEN & STAR*, the corner of Lyons' Inn, behind St. Clement's, Strand. 1760
(Succeeded by S. Marriott, *q.v.*)

IBBETSON, BARLOW & CLARKE, at the *QUEEN'S HEAD*, No. 9, on Ludgate Hill. 1789
(See Carr, Ibbetson & Bigge.)

THOMAS JENYNS & PHILIP PALMER, at the *BLACKMOOR'S HEAD*, on Ludgate Hill. 1737
(Succeeded by Palmer & Fleetwood ; later Palmer & Halsey).

SAMUEL JONES, at the *ROE BUCK* in New Bond Street. 1757

SAMUEL JONES, at the *GOLDEN ROE BUCK*, New Bond Street, near Brook Street. 1760

THO.ˢ & WILL.ᴹ KING, at the *WHEATSHEAF & SUN*, in King Street, Covent Garden. 1787
(Successors to Swann, Buck & Co.)

CHARLES LOWTH & JAMES PITTS, at the *KING'S HEAD*, in Pater Noster Row. 1749

LUCAS, HIGGONS, MASON & GUEST, at the *LAMB*, in Shandois Street. 1772
(Successors to Mason, Lucas & Co., *q.v.*)

THOMAS MALTBY, at ye *LAMB*, in Queen Street, near Cheapside. 1748

SOLOMON MARRIOTT, at the *INDIAN QUEEN & STAR*, corner of Lyons Inn, Hollywell Street, Strand. 1777
(Successor to W. Hyde, *q.v.*)

MILES MASON & BENJN. LUCAS, at the *LAMB*, in Round Court [Strand]. *c.* 1750

MASON, LUCAS & HIGGONS, at the *LAMB*, in Shandois Street. 1756
(See Lucas, Higgons, Mason & Guest.)

ROE BUCK

INDIAN QUEEN & STAR

THE LAMB

BLUE BOAR

TURK'S HEAD

ENOS MILWARD, at the *BLUE BOAR*, near the Conduit in Cheapside.   1741
(Successor to Cotterell & Blackstone, *q.v.*)

PAUL MINIER, at the *EAGLE & CHILD*, in the Strand, over against York Buildings.   *c.* 1750

JOHN MOLYNEUX & THO.ˢ KING, at the *WHEAT-SHEAF & SUN*, in Ludgate Street.   *c.* 1740

FRANCIS & WILLIAM MORIN, at the *LAMB*, in Bedford Street, Covent Garden.   *c.* 1734
(Lately removed from ye *Dove* in Cranburn Street.)

THOMAS NASH, at the *LAMB*, in Bedford Street, in Covent Garden.   1766
(Successor to F. & W. Morin above.)

WILLIAM NEALE & Co., at the *QUEEN'S HEAD & SEVEN STARS*, No. 5, Ludgate Street.   1783

NEALE, WELCH & REDHEAD, at *QUEEN'S HEAD & SEVEN STARS*, in Ludgate Street. 1763
(Successors to T. Welch & Son at above, *q.v.*)

THOMAS NICHOLS, at the *GOLDEN KEY & STAR*, in Carnaby Street, near the Market.   1768

EDWARD NICKLIN & THOMAS RYDER, at the *INDIAN QUEEN* by the Cloysters, West Smithfield.   1748
(Successors to Ryder & Nicklin, *q.v.*)

NICKLIN, WELLS & BALL, at the *INDIAN QUEEN*, where Ludgate stood, No. 23 on Ludgate Hill.   1769

JNO. NOBBES, at the *GOLDEN BELL*, in Bedford Street, Covent Garden.   *c.* 1750

EDWARD NOURSE, at ye *TURK'S HEAD*, near Bow Church, in Cheapside.   *c.* 1750

WILLIAM ORTON, at *QUEEN CHARLOTTE'S HEAD*, behind St. Clement's Church, in the Strand.   1770

LAWRENCE OWEN, at the *GOLDEN BALL*, in Holborn, near Chancery Lane.   1753

JOHN PAGE, at the *BRITTANNIA & KEY*, in Chandois Street, Covent Garden.   1764
(See also **Basil Woodd** & John Page.)

JAMES PAITFIELD & WILLM. DARE, at ye *WHITE LION & BLACKMOOR'S HEAD*, opposite Gutter Lane, in Cheapside. *c.* 1740
(See also W. Dare & J. Paitfield.)

PHILIP PALMER & MILES HALSEY, at the *BLACK-MOOR'S HEAD*, on Ludgate Hill. 1753

PHILIP PALMER & ROBT. FLEETWOOD, at above.
(See also Halsey & Palmer, 1745.) 1754

PAUL & DOWNTON, at the *QUEEN'S HEAD & STAR*, in Chandos Street, Covent Garden. 1762

PAUL & NICCOLLS, at the *QUEEN'S HEAD & STAR*, the corner of Bedford Street in Chandos Street. 1771

HENRY PAULIN, at the *PRINCESS'S ARMS & THE STATUE OF QUEEN ELIZABETH*, in Tavistock Street. 1758

THOMAS PAULIN, at the *STATUE OF QUEEN ELIZABETH*, in Tavistock Street, Covent Garden. 1734

PAULIN & COATES, at the *PRINCESS'S ARMS & STATUE OF QUEEN ELIZABETH*, in Tavistock Street. 1763
(This bill is made out to Mrs. (David) Garrick.)

WILL^M PEERY (& CALEB HOOKER, late of Norwich) at ye sign of ye *GOLDEN WHEAT SHEAF & CROWN* in New Round Court, in the Strand, over against York Buildings. *c.* 1700

J. PHIPPS & J. HENLEY, at ye *INDIAN KING*, in Cheapside, opposite St. Paul's Church-yard. 1741
(Subsequently removed to the *Turk's Head*, opposite Foster Lane in Cheapside.)

JOHN PRESTON, at the *GOLDEN BALL*, the backside of St. Clement's, Strand. 1789

RICHARD PRESTON, successor to Mr. Shaw, at above. 1764

WHITE LION & BLACKMOOR'S HEAD

GOLDEN WHEATSHEAF AND CROWN

THE GEORGE

GOLDEN ANCHOR

JOHN PRITCHARD (removed from Bath), at the *TURK'S HEAD*, on Ludgate Hill.   1763

RANKIN & PARISH, at the *BLACKMOOR'S HEAD*, No. 8, Ludgate Street.   1780

THOMAS RAVENSCROFT & SON, at the *GEORGE*, the corner of Lombard Street.   1741

JOHN RAYNER, at the *BLUE ANCHOR*, the upper end of Steward Street, Spittle Fields.   *c.* 1740

CAREW REYNELL & PARTNERS, at the *BLACK-MOOR'S HEAD*, in Bedford Street, Covent Garden.   1730

ROBARTS & PLOWMAN, at the *INDIAN QUEEN*, No. 1, Chandos Street, Covent Garden.   1796
(Successors to Bellamy & Robarts, q.v.)

WHITEHEAD RUMBALL, at the *GOLDEN ANCHOR*, near the New Church, in the Strand.
c. 1730

RICHARD RYDER, at the *PLOUGH & HARROW*, in Cheapside.   1715

WM. RYDER & THOS. WINGATE, at the *INDIAN QUEEN*, by ye Cloysters, West Smithfield.   1732

WM. RYDER & EDWD. NICKLIN, at above.
c. 1750

CHARLES RYDER (successor to the Widow Henley) at ye *TURK'S HEAD*, opposite Foster Lane, in Cheapside.   1765

RYDER, NICKLIN & WELLS, at the *INDIAN QUEEN*, No. 23 on Ludgate Hill.   1769
(Succeeded by Nicklin, Wells & Ball, q.v.)

CHARLES SALKELD, at the *SEVEN STARS & WOOL PACK*, on Ludgate Hill.   1747

EDWARD SCANDRETT, at the *HEN & CHICKENS*, in Bedford Court, opposite Mays Buildings, near Chandois Street.   *c.* 1770
(See also Wood & Middleton, mercers, at above.)

JOHN SHARE, at the *BLACKMOOR'S HEAD*, near the corner of Chancery Lane in Holborn. (Removed from the *INDIAN KING*, in the Cloysters.) *c.* 1760

SINGER & DAVIS (successors to Edwd. Ingram), at the *TURK'S HEAD*, the corner of Bedford Court, Bedford Street, Covent Garden. *c.* 1760

SMITH & SPENCER, at the *BLACKMOOR'S HEAD*, near ye Blue Coat Hospital, in ye Cloysters, West Smithfield. 1774

FRANCIS SPENLOVE, at ye *QUEEN'S HEAD & STAR*, in Cornhill, near ye Mansion House. 1764

STANSBURY & SMITH, at the *BLACKMOOR'S HEAD*, in the Long Walk, in the Cloysters, West Smithfield. 1761

JAMES STEPHENS (removed from behind St. Clements, Strand), to the *THREE CROWNS* in New Bond Street, near Conduit Street. 1767

ROBERT SWANN & CO., at the *WHEATSHEAF*, in Bedford Street, Covent Garden. 1730

ROBT. SWANN & ROBT. BUCK, at the *WHEAT SHEAF*, in King Street, Covent Garden. 1738

SWANN, BUCK, BARLOW & WHEATLEY, at above. 1757

SWANN, BUCK, BARLOW, ASHBURNER & ELLISSON, at above. 1763
(Succeeded by Barlow, Ashburner & Nelthorpe, *q.v.*, in 1774, and afterwards by T. & W. King in 1777, *q.v.*)

ELLIOTT TAYLOR (from Houndsditch), at the *GOLDEN FLEECE* in Middle Row, Holborn. *c.* 1760

ROBERT TAYLOR, at the *COVENTRY CROSS*, near St. Margaret's Hill, in the Borough, Southwark. *c.* 1760

WILLIAM THOMAS, at the *RISING SUN*, opposite Gravel Lane, Houndsditch. *c.* 1760

INDIAN QUEEN

GOLDEN FLEECE

COVENTRY CROSS

QUEEN ELIZABETH'S HEAD

JOHN THORN, at the *BLACK PRINCE,* in Cloth Fair, near West Smithfield.   *c.* 1760

WILLIAM TRESILIAN, at the *COVENTRY CROSS*, in Shandois Street, Covent Garden.   1750

TRESILIAN & ASHBURNER, at above.   1753

JOSEPH TRIGGE, at the sign of *QUEEN ELIZA-BETH'S HEAD*, within 3 doors of St. Paul's in Ludgate Street.   1742
(This elaborate signboard was the subject of comment in the *Spectator*, 8th January, 1742 :—" The other day going down Ludgate Street several people were gaping at a very splendid sign of Queen Elizabeth, which by far exceeded all other signs in the street, the painter having shewn a masterly judgement, and the carver and gilder much pomp and splendour.   It looked rather like a capital picture in a gallery than a sign in a street.")

HENRY TURNER, at the *MULBERRY TREE*, No. 10 in Cornhill, near the Royal Exchange.
          1777

RICHARD VENN, at the *QUEEN'S ARMS* on Ludgate Hill.   1744

MATTHEW VERNEY & JOSEPH GRIFFIES, att the *QUEEN'S HEAD & HEN AND CHICKENS*, the corner of Old Round Court, Shandoies Street.   1723

ARTHUR WALTER & WILLIAM DARWENT, at the *HALF MOON* in Ludgate Street, near St. Paul's.
          c. 1740

THOMAS WELCH & SON, at the *QUEEN'S HEAD & SEVEN STARS*, in Ludgate Street.   1756
(Succeeded by Neale, Welch & Redhead, *q.v.*)

MILES & JOHN WILLAN, at the *LAMB*, in Panton Street, near the Hay Market.   1779–1784

WILLAN & HAWKSWORTH, at the *GOLDEN LION*, in Chandois Street, Covent Garden. 1768–1790

JOHN WILLETT & JAMES JACKSON, at ye *THREE BLACK LIONS*, near Norfolk Street, in the Strand.   1747
(In 1749 this partnership was dissolved and James Jackson removed to the *Three Black Lions & Wheatsheaf* opposite St. Clement's Church in the Strand.)

GEORGE WILSON, at the *CROWN & ANCHOR*,
No. 252 the Borough, Southwark. *c.* 1750

WOOD & MIDDLETON, at the *HEN & CHICKENS*,
in Chandois Street, Covent Garden. 1763

WOOD & MIDDLETON, at the *HEN & CHICKENS*,
in Bedford Court, opposite May's Buildings, near
Shandois Street, Covent Garden. 1754
(? Succeeded by E. Scandrett, at above, *q.v.*)

BASIL WOODD & JOHN PAGE at the *BRITTANNIA
& KEY*, in Chandois Street, Covent Garden.
(See John Page, mercer, at above, 1764.) *c.* 1760

QUEEN'S HEAD & SEVEN STARS

MILLINERS

ANN BENTLEY, at the *GOLDEN FLEECE*, in
Tavistock Street, Covent Garden. 1753

THOMAS COLE, at the signe of the *KING'S HEAD*,
on Ludgate Hill, neare the Bell Savage. 1663

SUSANNA & MARY CORRIE, at the *PORTER &
DOVE*, in the Cloysters, near the Blue Coat
Hospital. 1793

JANE COX & ELIZABETH HALL, at the *RISING
SUN*, No. 65 in Gracechurch Street, ye corner of
Fenchurch Street. 1769

ELIZABETH DAWES, at the *LAMB*, in Long Walk,
near Christ's Hospital. 1757

SUSAN DOLLAND, at the *ACORN*, between Exeter
Exchange and Catherine Street, in the Strand.
c. 1760

E. & S. HARLEY, at the *HALF MOON & SEVEN
STARS*, No. 26, Castle Street, near Oxford
Street. *c.* 1780

ELIZH. & CATH^N. HEBERT, at the *BLACK
MOOR'S HEAD*, in Fenchurch Street. 1740

JAMES HARTSHORN, at the *THREE NUNS*, in
Wigmore Street. 1787

HARTSHORN & DYDE, at the *THREE NUNS*, in
Wigmore Street. 1779

KING'S HEAD

THE FEATHERS

ROYAL WIDOW AND SUN

THREE GOLDEN LIONS

MARY & ANN HOGARTH (from the Old Frock Shop, the corner of the Long Walk facing the Cloysters). Removed to ye *KING'S ARMS*, joyning to ye Little Britain Gate near Long Walk.

c. 1730

(Mary and Ann were sisters of William Hogarth, who died 1764. Mary was born in 1699 and predeceased her brother. Ann was born in 1701 and died in 1771.)

JOHN MIELL, at the *GOLDEN BALL*, in Northumberland Court, in the Strand.   *c.* 1760

ANN MILNER, at the *FEATHERS* (address wanting).   *c.* 1720

MATTHIAS OTTO, JUNR., at the *ROYAL WIDOW & SUN*,* against Bull Inn Court, in the Strand, from the *ROYAL WIDOW* over the way.

c. 1760

A. PERIN, the *THREE PIGEONS*, No. 66, New Bond Street.   1791

MARY PFAHLER & FRED^K. HAHN, at the *GOLDEN BALL*, in Bedford Court, Bedford Street, Covent Garden.   1763

POWELL & BARROW, at the sign of the *ACORN*, St. James's Street, the corner of St. James's Place.   1766

(Succeeded by Barrow, Powell & Brace, 1772.)

PULLER, at the *MARY QUEEN OF SCOTS HEAD*, in Cranbourn Alley, near Leicester Fields.   1769

—— RICKARD, at the *ACORN & STAR*, in New Bond Street, two doors from Brook Street.   1770

M. ROBERTS, at the *BLACKMOOR'S HEAD*, in Henrietta Street, Covent Garden.   *c.* 1760

(Remov'd from Tavistock Street.)

SAFFORY & WEBB, at the *GOLDEN BALL*, No. 309, near ye New Church, in the Strand.

c. 1770

* The sign of the Royal Widow is probably in allusion to Princess Augusta, daughter of Duke of Saxe-Gotha, who married Frederick Louis, Prince of Wales. He died in 1751 and was survived by his widow for 21 years—until 1772.)

—— SMITH, at the *FEATHERS*, in Panton Street, three doors from Leicester Fields. 1758

WILLIAM STAMPER, at the signe of the *THREE GOLDEN LIONS*, in Fleete-Streete, a little way from the Conduit. 1663
(The Fleet conduit was at the end of Shoe Lane.)

—— TUCKER, at the *STAR* in Holborn, opposite Chancery Lane. c. 1780

SARAH UNDERWOOD, at the *CABINET*, on Ludgate Hill. 1746
(In 1699 this was the address of Thomas Pistor, cabinet maker.)

THE CABINET

MARY VARDEN, at the *CHILD'S COAT & ROSE*, in Houndsditch, near Bishopsgate. c. 1760

MARTHA WHEATLAND & SISTER, at *QUEEN CHARLOTT'S HEAD*, near Wood Street, in Cheapside. 1761

MILLWRIGHTS
See ENGINE MAKERS

MUSICAL INSTRUMENT MAKERS

WILLIAM BULL, at the signe of the *TRUMPETT & HORNE*, in Castal Street, neare the Muyse. 1700
(In 1700 Wm. Bull advertised his removal from the *Horn & Trumpet* in the Hay Market to Castle Street by Leicester Fields.)

CHILD'S COAT AND ROSE

BENJAMIN CARR, at the *VIOLIN & HAUTBOY*, in Old Round Court, Strand. c. 1760

THOMAS COLLETT, at the sign of the *FRENCH HORN & VIOLIN* opposite the Wax Work in Fleet Street. 1787
(Mrs. Salmon's Waxwork Exhibition was at No. 17 Fleet Street from 1785 to 1812.)

WILLIAM COTTON, at the *HAUTBOY & TWO FLUTES*, in Bride Lane Court, near Fleet Street. c. 1780

JNO. COX, at the *VIOL & FLUTE* in Sweeting's Alley opposite the East Door of the Royal Exchange. 1760

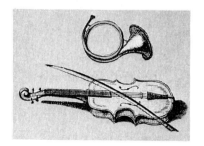

FRENCH HORN AND VIOLIN

ROBERT HORNE, at the *DRUM & COLOURS*,
No. 20, Barbican.   1796

J. HARE, at ye *GOLDEN VIOLL* in St. Paules
Church-yard.   1697

JNO. JOHNSON, at ye *HARP & CROWN*, facing
Bow Church, Cheapside.   1744

RICHARD MEARES, removed from ye *GOLDEN
VIOL* in Leaden-Hall Street to ye *GOLDEN
VIOL & HAUTBOY*, ye North side of St. Paul's
Church-yard.   1706

PETER THOMPSON, at the *VIOLIN, HAUTBOY
& GERMAN FLUTE*, the Westend of St. Paul's
Church yard.   1750

J. WALSH, at the *GOLDEN HARPE & HO-BOY*
in Catherine Street, near Summersett House
in the Strand.   1697

JOHN YOUNG, at the *DOLPHIN & CROWN*,
at the West end of St. Paul's Church.   1699
("There's old young and young young, both men of renown,
Old sells and young plays the best fiddle in town." *Pleasant
Musical Companion,* 1726.)

GOLDEN VIOL

MUSICIANS

HENRY TURNER, at the (?) *VIOL, PIPES &
FLUTE*, in Warwick Street, Charing Cross. 1750

JOHN WARD, at the *VIOLIN & HAUTBOY*, in
ye Old Change, Cheapside.   *c.* 1760

JONATHAN WOOLLS, at the *TABOR & PIPE*,
in the uppermost house in Helmet Court, near
Catherine Street, in the Strand.   1749

NEEDLE MAKERS

EDWARD LANDON, at the *CROWN*, in Bandy Leg
Walk, near Queen Street, in the Park, Southwark.   *c.* 1750

WILLIAM WYLDE, at the *QUEEN'S ARMS*, in
St. Paul's Church Yard, near Cheapside. 1766
(Succeeded by his partner J. Collins in 1796 and later by
Dodson & Sons up till 1832.)

DOLPHIN & CROWN

See Chimney Sweeps & Nightmen.

NURSERYMEN & SEEDSMEN

THOMAS BAILEY, at the *HAND & FLOWER* in Covent Garden.   *c.* 1810

THOMAS BUTLER, at the *THISTLE & CROWN*, Covent Garden Market.   1814

EDDIE, BECK & WRIGHT, at the *WOOL PACK & CROWN*, No. 68, Strand.   1790
(Successors to Wilson & Saunders at above, *q.v.*)

JAMES FISHER, at the *BLACK BOY*, No. 130, Pall Mall.   1785
(Successor to F. Gray.)

JAMES GORDON, at the *THISTLE & CROWN*, No. 25, Fenchurch Street.   1768
(In 1758 Gordon started his nursery at Mile End and his family continued in Fenchurch Street until 1838.)

GRIMWOOD & HUDSON, at the *PINE APPLE*, Arlington Street, Piccadilly.   1783

GRIMWOOD, HUDSON & BARRIT, at above address and also at their Nursery at Kensington.   1790
(Late Williamson & Co.)

WALTER HAY, at the *ACORN*, Parliament Street, Westminster, and at their Nursery Gardens in Lambeth.   1787
(See also Shiells & Hay.)

WARREN LUKER, at the *SUN*, near the late Dog House Bar, in the City New Road.   1777

ARABELLA MORRIS, at the *NAKED BOY & THREE CROWNS* against the New Church, in the Strand.   1748
(Successors to Edward Fuller, at the *Three Crowns & Naked Boy*, near the Maypole, in the Strand, 1683.)

NATHANIEL POWELL, at ye *KING'S HEAD*, near Fetter Lane, in Holborn.   1731

POWELL & LINNELL, at above.   1752
(Later Powell & Eddie, 1761.)

SHIELS & HAY, at the *ACORN*, Parliament Street.   1780
(See W. Hay above.)

PINE APPLE

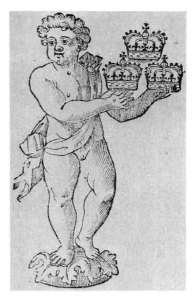

NAKED BOY & THREE CROWNS

WOOLPACK & CROWN

JAR AND 3 PIGEONS

THOS. & JOHN THATCHER, sons & successors to the late Saml. Thatcher, at the *RAVEN*, No. 147 Fleet Street.   1783–1831

WILSON & SANDERS, at the *WOOL-PACK & CROWN*, near Durham Yard, in the Strand. (Succeeded by Eddie, Beck & Wright, *q.v.*)   1760

OILMEN

JOSEPH AUSTIN, at the *FLYING HORSE*, in Catherine Street, in the Strand.   1760

JOHN BEARDMORE & ALEXR. MAINSTONE, at the *OLIVE TREE*, in Thames Street, near Billingsgate.   1757

CHARLES BENNET, at ye *FLOWER-DE-LUCE*, near ye East India House, in Leadenhall Street.   1741

GEORGE BOWLEY, at the *OIL JAR*, No. 61 Within Bishopsgate, three doors from Camomile Street.   1777

JOSEPH CAM, at the *OYL JAR*, ye corner of Tothill Street, near ye Gate House, Westminster.   *c.* 1760

JOHN CRISP, at the *OLIVE TREE*, No. 24 Henrietta Street, Covent Garden.   *c.* 1780

THOMAS ESTCOURT, at the *SHIP*, against Hungerford Market, in the Strand.   *c.* 1740

JOHN FOX, at the *GREEN DRAGON*, Fleet Street.   1763

JOHN GRUNDY, at the sign of the *BELL*, the corner of Fleet Ditch on Ludgate Hill.   *c.* 1760

HAWKINS, at the *OIL JAR*, No. 10 Edward's Street, near Portman Square.   *c.* 1780

RICHARD HOCKETT, at the *GRAND DUKE OF TUSCANY'S ARMS*, agst. Cecill Street, in the Strand.   1720

FRANCIS HUMPHRYS, at the *JAR & THREE PIDGEONS*, near the corner of Warwick Lane, in Newgate Street.   1739

——JONES, at the *OIL JAR*, Charing Cross. *c.* 1740

JOHN LYDE & CO., at the *THREE NEATS'
TONGUES*, opposite Charles Street, in the
Strand. 1768–1823

WILLIAM MACKAY, at the *OLIVE TREE*, opposite
Burlington House, Piccadilly. 1774

NOBBES & HOLLAND, at the *HAM*, in the New
Exchange Buildings, in the Strand. 1766

CHRISTOPHER PACK, at the *HAM & OIL JAR*,
the bottom of Bartholomew Lane, near the Royal
Exchange. *c.* 1760

BARTHO.^W & WILL.^M PRICE, at the *JARR*, on
Holborn Bridge. *c.* 1750

SEARCH & SPENCER, at the *DIAMOND CUT
LAMP*, in Swallow Street, St. James's, West-
minster, faceing Bull Yard, near Glasshouse
Street. 1763

ANTHONY STERRY, at the *OLIVE TREE*, opposite
St. George's Church, No. 156, Borough High
Street. 1793

SAM.^L STRODE, at the *SHIP*, the corner of
Southampton Street, in Holborn, near Bloomsbury Square. 1756

JOHN TISOE, at the *TWO JARRS*, Bloomsbury.
1727

THOMAS WOODHOUSE, at the *BLACK BOY*,
Church Street, Greenwich. *c.* 1760

THE SHIP

OPTICIANS

(*See also* SCIENTIFIC INSTRUMENT MAKERS)

THOMAS ASHLEY, at ye *GOLDEN SPECTACLES*
in Sidney's Alley, near Leicester Fields. *c.* 1760

JAMES AYSCOUGH, at the *GREAT GOLDEN
SPECTACLES*, in Ludgate Street, near St.
Paul's. 1752
Removed from Sir Isaac Newton's Head in the same street.
Succeeded at above by J. Linnell, *q.v.*

THE OIL JAR

*REFLECTING MICROSCOPE &
SPECTACLES*

*GOLDEN SPECTACLES & SEA
QUADRANT*

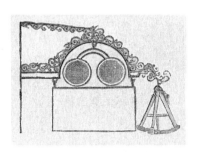

*GREAT GOLDEN SPECTACLES &
QUADRANT*

OLIVER COMBS, at the *SPECTACLES*, in St. Martin's Court, near Leicester Fields.   *c.* 1740

OLIVER COMBS, at the *SPECTACLES*, in the Strand, ye second house from Essex Street, near Temple Bar.   1747

JOHN CUFF, at the sign of the *REFLECTING MICROSCOPE & SPECTACLES*, against Serjeant's Inn Gate in Fleet Street.   1748

PETER DOLLAND, at the *GOLDEN SPECTACLES & SEA QUADRANT*, near Exeter Exchange, in the Strand.   1752
(Removed to No. 59, the North side of St. Paul's Churchyard, *c.* 1755.)

JOSEPH HURT,* successor to Mr. Ralph Sterrop (*q.v.*) at the sign of the *ARCHIMEDES & THREE GOLDEN SPECTACLES*, in Ludgate Street.   *c.* 1730

JOSEPH LINNELL, successor to the late Mr. James Ayscough (*q.v.*) at the *GREAT GOLDEN SPECTACLES & QUADRANT*, No. 33, in Ludgate Street, near St. Paul's.   *c.* 1763

JOHN MARSHALL, at the *ARCHIMEDES & TWO GOLDEN SPECTACLES*, in Ludgate Street.   1675

FRANCIS MORGAN, at the *ARCHIMEDES & THREE SPECTACLES*, No. 27, Ludgate Street.
                                        c. 1740

THOMAS RIBRIGHT, at the *GOLDEN SPECTACLES*, in the Poultry.   1758

MATTHEW RICHARDSON, at *SIR ISAAC NEWTON'S HEAD & GOLDEN SPECTACLES*, against York Buildings, in the Strand.   *c.* 1740

EDWARD SCARLETT, at the *ARCHIMEDES & GLOBE*, near St. Ann's Church, Soho.   *c.* 1710
(In 1724 he was at the same sign in "Maxfield Street" (=Macclesfield Street, Soho).)

SAMUEL SCATLIFF, at *FRIER BACON'S HEAD*, the corner of St. Michael's Alley, Cornhill. *c.* 1750

---

* See *Purefoy Letters*, p. 350.

HENRY SHUTTLEWORTH, at *SIR ISAAC NEW-TON'S HEAD & TWO PAIR OF GOLDEN SPECTACLES*, near the West end of St. Paul's, No. 23, in Ludgate Street.   1780

RALPH STERROP* & JOHN YARWELL, at the *ARCHIMEDES & THREE PAIR OF GOLDEN SPECTACLES*, in Ludgate Street.   1697

SAMUEL WHITFORD, at the *ARCHIMEDES & THREE SPECTACLES*, No. 27, Ludgate Street. (He seems to have succeeded F. Morgan, *q.v.*)   *c.* 1770

WILLDEY & BRANDRETH, at the *ARCHIMEDES & GLOBE*, in Ludgate Street.   1707

FRIAR BACON'S HEAD

PAINTERS & DECORATORS

THOMAS BOWEN, at the *GOLDEN PALLET*, in Shagg Lane, St. James's Hay Market. *c.* 1770

S. MORLEY, at ye *GOLDEN HEAD*, in Salisbury Court, Fleet Street.   *c.* 1780

THOMAS PENSON at the signe of the *KINGS ARMES* on Ludgate Hill.   *c.* 1700

JNO. AUGUSTUS SIMS, at the *KING'S ARMS*, Upper Thames Street.   *c.* 1770

WILLIAM SOUTH, at the sign of *ST. LUKE'S HEAD*, No. 2, Paternoster Row.   *c.* 1780 (Successor to the late Mr. N. Proctor.)

THOS. TILLINGHAST, at the *ST. LUKE'S HEAD*, Swithin's Lane, near Cannon Street.   *c.* 1760

ARCHIMEDES & 3 SPECTACLES

PAPER STAINERS

ARMITAGE & ROPER, at the *BIBLE & CROWN*, No. 65, Within Bishopsgate and in Petticoat Lane.   1777

THOMAS BROMWICH, at the *GOLDEN LION*, on Ludgate Hill.   1744

THOS. BROMWICH & LEONARD LEIGH, at above.   1759

SIR ISAAC NEWTON'S HEAD & TWO PAIR OF GOLDEN SPECTACLES

* See *Purefoy Letters*, p. 351.

KNAVE OF CLUBS

ROSE & CROWN

BROMWICH, ISHERWOOD & BRADLEY, at the *GOLDEN LION*, on Ludgate Hill.   1774
(Mr. Bromwich supplied wall papers to Horace Walpole for Strawberry Hill—see Walpole's correspondence, 1754–1756.)

EDWARD BUTLING, at the *OLD KNAVE OF CLUBS*, at the Bridge Foot in Southwark.   1704

CROMPTON & HODGSON, at the *ANCHOR & SUN* in Castle Street, the corner of Bear Street, Leicester Square.   *c.* 1770
(From Crompton & Spinnage at Charing Cross.)

MATTHIAS DARLEY, at the *ACORN*, facing Hungerford, in the Strand.   1760

SAMUEL HARFORD, at the *EAGLE*, in Milk Street, Cheapside.   1754
(See also under Stationers.)

GEORGE MINNIKIN, at ye *KING'S HEAD*, in St. Martin's-le-Grand, near Aldersgate.   1676
(See also under Stationers.)

JOHN SEAGOOD, at the *GOLDEN BIBLE*, the North Gate of the Royal Exchange.   1760

JOHN SIGRIST, at the *KING'S ARMS*, facing the Castle Inn, No. 218 Piccadilly.   *c.* 1778
(Succeeded by Robson & Hale in 1790.)

JOSEPH SMITH, at the *ROSE & CROWN*, the corner of Angel Street, St. Martin's Le Grand.
                                              1768

WILLIAM SQUIRE, at the *THREE TENTS & LAMB*, in the Poultry.   1777

JOHN TRYMMER, at the *RAINBOW*, in Newgate Street, faceing St. Martin's-Le-Grand.   *c.* 1740

PASTRY COOKS

See CONFECTIONERS

PATENT MEDICINE VENDORS

DOCTOR JOHN CASE, at the *LILLIE'S HEAD*, over against Ludgate Church, in Black Fryers Gateway.   *c.* 1690
(John Case, astrologer, etc., succeeded to the practice of William Lilly, d. 1681. See *D.N.B.*)

LILLIE'S HEAD

ELIZABETH ANDREWS, at the *HAND & PENCIL*, in Houndsditch, near Bishopsgate. *c.* 1770

WILLIAM BAYLIS, at ye *HAND & PENCIL*, against Bridewell Gate, Bride Lane, Fleet Street. 1748

JOSEPH SMITH, at the *THISTLE & CROWN* in Hatfield Street, near Aldersgate Barrs. *c.* 1760

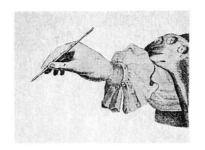

HAND & PENCIL

PERFUMERS

BARNARD, at the sign of the *GOLDEN BALL*, facing the lower end of St. James's, Hay Market, near Pall Mall (kept by his daughter S. Storer). 1696

LEWIS AND DAVID BOURGEOIS, at the *THREE ARQUEBUSADE BOTTLES*, the upper end of the Haymarket. 1777
(Arquebusade was one of the fashionable perfumes—it was imported from Switzerland.)

DIGHTON, at the *CITY OF SEVILLE*, next door to the King's Head tavern, at Chancery Lane end in Fleet Street. 1705
(Later, he became Sworn Perfumer to George I.)

CITY OF SEVILLE

PHILIP DIXON, at the *CIVET CAT*, No. 1, Norris Street, Hay Market. 1790

JOHN GROSVENOR, at the *ANGEL & CROWN*, near Chancery Lane, in Holborn. 1748

J. LEGG, at the *RISING SUN*, in Pall Mall, near St. Alban's Street. *c.* 1770

JAMES SMYTH & NEPHEWS, at the *CIVET CAT*, in Bond Street, near Brook Street. 1766

WM. TRUNKETT'S SISTER, at the *YOUNG CIVET CAT*, without Temple Bar. 1750

WALTER TURNBULL, at the *CIVET CAT*, No. 41, Cornhill, near St. Michael's Church. 1780

VICKERY, at the *ROSE*, No. 119, Bishopsgate Street, near Cornhill, removed from Broad Street, Royal Exchange. 1783

CIVET CAT

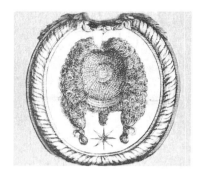

BLACK PERUKE AND STAR

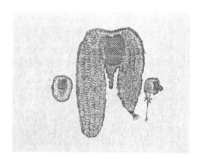

BLUE PERUKE

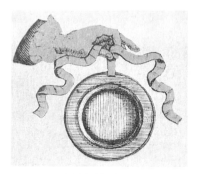

GOLDEN DISH

RICHARD WARREN, at the *GOLDEN FLEECE*, in Mary-le-Bonne Street, Golden Square.   1769

PERUKE MAKERS

WILLIAM BRIGGS, at the *BLACK PERUKE*, near Essex Street, in the Strand.   *c.* 1740

THOMAS BROMFIELD, at the *BLACK PERUKE & STAR*, in Milk Street, near Cheapside. *c.* 1740

JOHN BROWN, at the *BLUE PERUKE & HALF MOON*, the corner of St. Ann's Lane, in Noble Street, near Goldsmiths' Hall.   *c.* 1750

JOHN DELAPORTE, at the sign of the *PHOENIX & LOCKS OF HAIR* in New Round Court, in the Strand.   *c.* 1750

JOHN DOIG JUNR., at the *RISING SUN & LOCKS OF HAIR*, in Panton Street, Leicester Fields.
    c. 1760

THOMAS GIBBON, at the *BLEW & WHITE PERUKE*, in Rosemary Lane [Minories]. *c.* 1740

THOMAS LEWIS, at the *WHITE PERUKE & STAR*, in Ship Yard, Temple Barr.   *c.* 1760

LALLY WOODWARD, at the *BLUE PERUKE*, opposite ye Globe Tavern, in Fleet Street. *c.* 1770

PEWTERERS

HENRY APPLETON, at the *GOLDEN DISH*, in Cheapside.   *c.* 1750
(Later he removed to Fenchurch Street, *c.* 1790.)

RICHARD BOWLER, at the *BLACK BOY & WORM*, in Houndsditch.   1762
(The " worm " was a long winding pewter pipe used in distillation of spirits.)

WILLIAM DE JERSEY, at the *SPREAD EAGLE*, the corner of Lawrence Poulteney Lane.   1744

JOHN JUPE, at the *PEWTER DISH*, in Queen Street, Cheapside.   1761
(Master of the Pewterers' Company in that year.)

RICHARD KING, at the *OSTRICH*, against White Hart Court, in Grace Church Street.   *c.* 1750

JOHN LANGFORD, at the *RISEING SUN*, within Bishopsgate. 1787

FRANCIS PIGGOTT, at the *GOLDEN DISH*, in Pater Noster Row, next Cheapside. 1755
(Master of the Pewterers' Company in 1770.)

THOS. SCATTERGOOD, at the *BLACKMOOR'S HEAD*, near the South Sea House, in Bishopsgate Street. *c.* 1740
(Descendents of this firm are in business to this day.)

EDWARD YORKE, at the *GOLDEN COVER*, by the Four Lamps, on Snow Hill. 1763

THE SUN

PIN MAKERS

WILLIAM GARLAND, at the *SUN*, in Crooked Lane, near the Monument. *c.* 1750

WILLIAM GARLAND, at the *SUN*, No. 21, on Fish Street Hill, between the Monument & London Bridge. 1777
(Succeeded by T. Bennett at above, 1817.)

JOHN JONES, at the *SUN*, in Crooked Lane. *c.* 1720

ANN JONES, at the *SUN*, in Crooked Lane. 1726

HENRY WHITTELL, at the *QUEEN'S ARMS*, 4 doors below Furnivals Inn, in Holborn. *c.* 17—

BLACKAMOOR'S HEAD

PINKERS & CUTTERS & DRAWERS

GEORGE PARAVICINI, at the *BLACKAMORE'S HEAD*, in Bedford Street, sometimes called Half Moon Street. *c.* 1700
(Bedford Street, Strand.)

THOMAS WHEELER, at the *DOVE & POINT*, in Half Moon Street, over against the New Exchange in the Strand. *c.* 1740

(TOBACCO) PIPE MAKERS

THOMAS DORMER, at the *THREE TOBACCO PIPES*, in Brewhouse Yard, near Hermitage Stairs. 1768

JOHN SAVELL, at the *THREE TOBACCO PIPES*, in Featherstone Street, near Moorfields.

DOVE AND POINT

INDIAN QUEEN

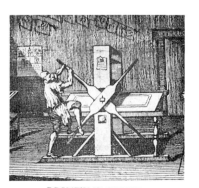

KNAVE OF CLUBS

CHRISTOPHER BLANCHARD, at the *KING'S ARMS*, in Gerrard Street, Soho.   1757
(Succeeded by C. Gibson at above, 1771.)

ABRAHAM FAULCON, at the *ROYAL FAULCONER* [No further address].   *c.* 1700

SAMUEL FULLWOOD, at the *INDIAN QUEEN* [No further address].   *c.* 1700

EDWARD HALL, at the *QUEEN'S ARMS*, Piccadilly.   *c.* 1770

HENRY HART, at the *KNAVE OF CLUBS*, No. 16, Red Lion Street, Holborn.   *c.* 1780

DANIEL WHITTON, at the *QUEEN'S ARMS*, in Charles Street, near St. James's Square. *c.* 1700
(Master of Playing Card Makers' Company in 1691, 1697 and in 1703.)

CHRISTOPHER WRIGGLESWORTH, at ye *KING OF DIAMONDS*, in Fort Street, the Old Artillery Ground, near Spittle Square.   *c.* 1760

PLAISTERER

See COMPOSITION ORNAMENT MAKERS

POTTERS

WEDGWOOD & BENTLEY, at the *QUEEN'S ARMS*, corner of Great Newport Street, next Long Acre.   1772

PRINTERS

JOHN PLUMMER, at the *RISING SUN*, No. 100, Fenchurch Street, opposite the India Warehouse.   1775

RICHARD SHORLEYKER, at the signe of the *FAULCON*, in Shoe Lane.   1632

FRANCIS FOKES, at the *GOLDEN HEAD*, Haughton Street, Clare Market.   *c.* 1770

THOMAS WILLSON, at the *PRINTING PRESS* in White's Alley, Chancery Lane.

PRINTING PRESS

THOMAS BAKEWELL, next to the *HORN* Tavern, in Fleet Street. *c.* 1750

JOHN BOWLES, at the *BLACK HORSE*, in Cornhill. (Succeeded by Carington Bowles—*c.* 1760.) *c.* 1745

FENWICK BULL, at the *WHITE HORSE*, on Ludgate Hill. *c.* 1760

S. W. FORES, at the *CITY ARMS*, No. 3, Piccadilly, near the Hay Market. 1793 (Fores & Co., the well known sporting print shop, were in Piccadilly until 1938 when they removed to No. 123, New Bond Street.)

WILLIAM HANNELL, at the *WHITE HORSE*, under the Piazzas of the Royal Exchange, Cornhill. *c.* 1765

WILLIAM HERBERT, at the *GOLDEN GLOBE*, under the Piazzas, on London Bridge. 1749 (When the houses on the Bridge were demolished Herbert removed to Leadenhall Street—see *D.N.B.*)

MICHAEL JACKSON, at *REMBRANDT'S HEAD*, the corner of Chancery Lane, in Fleet Street. (?) 1747

J. JARVIS, at the *CROWN*, Bedford Court, Covent Garden. *c.* 1760

THOMAS KAYGILL, at the Sign of ye *LAUGHING PAINTER*, in Cross Court, Russell Court, Drury Lane. *c.* 1760

JOHN KING, att the sign of the *GLOBE*, in the Poultry. 1709

DOROTHY MERCIER, at the *GOLDEN BALL*, in Windmill Street, facing Silver Street, Golden Square. *c.* 1740

THOMAS MILLWARD, at the *DIAL & THREE CROWNS*, opposite Salisbury Court, Fleet Street. *c.* 1760

PHILIP OVERTON, at the *GOLDEN BUCK* in Fleet Street. 1744 (Succeeded by M. Sayer, *q.v.*)

JAMES REGNIER, at the *GOLDEN BALL*, in Newport Street, next Long Acre. 1730

THE HORN

REMBRANDT'S HEAD

THE GLOBE

BISHOP'S HEAD*

HAND & PURSE

M. SAYER, at the *GOLDEN BUCK*, in Fleet Street.   1747

R. SAYER & J. BENNETT, at above.   1783

JOHN SMITH, at *HOGARTH'S HEAD*, Cheapside, facing Wood Street.   1752

JOSEPHUS SYMPSON, at the *DOVE*, in Russell Court, in Drury Lane.   1730

THOMAS TAYLOR, at ye *GOLDEN LION*, in Fleet Street, near the Horne Tavern.   1714
(Previously he was on London Bridge.)

ANTHONY TORRE, at the *GOLDEN HEAD*, Market Lane, Pall Mall.   1781

JOHN WALLIS, at *YORICK'S HEAD*, No. 16, Ludgate Street.   1789

PUMP MAKER

JOHN DUMBLETON, at the *THREE CROWNS*, in Castle Street, White Chappel.   *c.* 1720

ROBE MAKERS

ROBERT DUNBAR, at the *BISHOP'S HEAD** in Shoemaker Row, Blackfryers.   *c.* 1700

THOMAS PURSELL, at the sign of the *HAND & PURSE*, in the Olde Change, neere Cheap-side.   *c.* 1700

CHARLES SHUDALL, at the *BISHOP'S HEAD*, in ye back side of St. Clement's, near ye 5 Bells by ye New Church, in ye Strand.   *c.* 1730

SHUDALL & STONE, at the *PARLIAMENT & JUDGE'S ROBE*, in Hollywell Street, near the New Church in the Strand.   1769
(Succeeded by " Wm. Webb, son-in-law to Mr. Francis Stone " at above address.)

SADDLERS

EDWARD ASHWORTH, at the *SADDLE ROYAL* in Fleet Street.   *c.* 1760

---

* This resembles the portraits of Dr. Francis Turner, Bishop of Ely (1684), one of " the Seven Bishops ".

SADDLE ROYAL

JAMES HERGEST, at the *WHITE HORSE*, opposite ye Victualling Office (on Tower Hill).   *c.* 1770

LONDON SADDLE WAREHOUSE, at the *GOLDEN BALL*, in the Middle of the East side of Southampton Street, Bloomsbury.   *c.* 1770

JOHN OLDIS, at the *GOLDEN COCK*, in St. Michael's Alley, in Cornhill.   1745

EDWARD PENNYMAN, at the *GOLDEN LYON* in West Smithfield.   *c.* 1740

JAMES ROBINSON, at the *WHITE HORSE*, in West Smithfield.   *c.* 1760

ROBERT VAUX, at the *GOLDEN STIRRUP* in New Bond Street.   1732

—— WARD, at the *GOLDEN HORSE*, in Bridge Street, Westminster.   *c.* 1770

JOHN WARNER, at the *WHITE HORSE*, No. 76, in Aldersgate Street, near Barbican.   *c.* 1780

SCALE MAKERS

WILLIAM BRIND, at the *HAND & SCALES* in Carey Lane, in Foster Lane, Cheapside.   *c.* 1750

FRANCIS GRAY, at the *ANGEL & SCALES*, Porters Block, Smithfield Bars.   *c.* 1760

WILLIAM HAWKINS, at the *ANGEL & SCALES*, next door to Haberdashers' Hall, in Maiden Lane, near Wood Street.   *c.* 1740

GEORGE KEY, at the *ANGEL & SCALES*, next door to Haberdashers' Hall, in Maiden Lane, near Wood Street.   *c.* 1760

ELIZABETH LAMB, at ye *THREE COCKS*, at Holbourn Conduit.   *c.* 1750

JAS. THOS. MOFFETT, at the *JUSTICE & SCALES*, opposite Haydon Yard, in the Minories.   1793

HENRY OVEN, att the *HEART & SCALES*, in Maiden Lane, over against Goldsmiths' Hall. 1724 (Succeeded by J. Snart, *q.v.*)

WHITE HORSE

GOLDEN LION

ANGEL & SCALES

ANGEL & SCALES

HAND & SCALES

HAND & SCALES

THOMAS OVERING, at the *ANGEL & SCALES*, in Bartholomew Lane, near the Royal Exchange.
c. 1750

JOHN PICARD, at ye *HAND & SCALES*, the corner of Maiden Lane, in Wood Street.   1726

JOSEPH READ, at the *HAND & SCALES*, within Bishopsgate.   *c.* 1760

TIMOTHY ROBERTS, at the *HAND & SCALES*, next ye corner of Queen Street, in Watling Street.   *c.* 1740

E. & J. SANGSTER, at the *KING'S ARMS*, Butcher Row, Temple Barr.   1769

GEORGE SEWELL, at the *HAND & SCALES*, in Bear Street, Leicester Fields.   1777

JOHN SNART, att the *HEART & SCALES*, in Maiden Lane, over against Goldsmiths' Hall.
(Successor to H. Oven, *q.v.*)   *c.* 1740

JAMES TALLMAN, at the sine of the *PORRIGE POT*, on London Bridge.   *c.* 1700

WILLIAM TAYLOR, at ye *HAND & SCALES*, in St. Ann's Lane, by Alders-gate.   *c.* 1710

DANIEL THOMPSON, at the *ANGEL & SCALES*, behind ye Conduit, Snow Hill.   1784

ROBERT VINCENT, at the *HAND & SCALES*, on London Bridge, the second door from the Bear Tavern, Southwark Side.   *c.* 1750
(The Bear tavern was pulled down in 1761.)

THOMAS WILLIAMS, at the *HAND & SCALES*, No. 71, Cannon Street.   1784
(Successor to the late Mr. Harrison.)

JOHN WOOD, at the *ANGEL & SCALES*, in Queen Street, Cheapside.   *c.* 1760

SCIENTIFIC INSTRUMENT MAKERS
(*See also* OPTICIANS)

DUDLEY ADAMS (successor to his father George Adams) at *TYCHO BRAHE'S HEAD*, No. 60 Fleet Street.   *c.* 1790

RICHARD BATES, at the *QUADRANT*, without Newgate, facing the Old Bailey.   1744

JOHN BENNETT, at the *GLOBE*, in Crown Court, between St. Ann's Soho and Golden Square. 1760

JOHN BIRD, at the *SEA QUADRANT*, near Exchange Buildings, in the Strand. 1748

JOHN COGGS, at the *GLOBE & SUN*, over against St. Dunstan's Church, in Fleet Street. *c.* 1730

BENJAMIN COLE, at the *ORRERY* next the Globe Tavern in Fleet Street. 1748
(Successor to T. Wright at same address. Cole was followed by T. Troughton, now Cooke, Troughton & Simms Ld.)

EDMOND CULPEPER, at the Sign of the *CROSS DAGGERS*, in Middle Moorfields. *c.* 1720
(Edmond Culpeper, who was working from 1710 until his death in 1737, has often been confused with his father, Edward Culpeper, who was working as early as 1666.)

EDWARD CULPEPER, at the Sign of the *CROSS DAGGERS*, in Middle Moorfields. *c.* 1666

RICHARD CUSHEE, at the *GLOBE & SUN*, between St. Dunstan's and Chancery Lane. 1732

JOHN GILBERT, at the *MARINER*, Postern Row, Tower Hill. 1763

HENRY GREGORY, at ye *AZIMUTH COMPASS*, near ye India House in Leadenhall Street. 1761

THOMAS HEATH, at the *HERCULES*, next the Fountain in ye Strand. 1735

HEATH & WING, at above (where Heath took Tycho Wing into partnership. They were succeeded by T. Newman). *c.* 1745

NATHANIEL HILL, at the *GLOBE & SUN* in Chancery Lane, Fleet Street. 1756
(He was succeeded by John Newton.)

WILLIAM JOHNSON, at the *GLOBE & QUADRANT*, No. 146 Fenchurch Street. *c.* 1770

JOHN LANE, at the *BLUE COAT BOY & QUADRANT*, in the Great Minories. *c.* 1760

BENJAMIN MARTIN, at the Sign of *HADLEY'S QUADRANT & VISUAL GLASSES*, near Crane Court, in Fleet Street. *c.* 1740

SEA QUADRANT

GLOBE & SUN

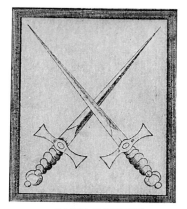

CROSS DAGGERS

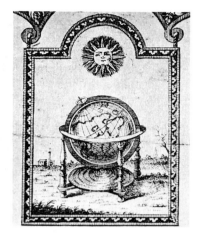

GLOBE & SUN

BLUE COAT BOY & QUADRANT

ORRERY & GLOBE

JOSEPH MOXON, at the *ATLAS* in Warwick Lane.
1692
(Pepys bought a pair of globes for £3 10s. 0d. from Moxon—
see *Diary*, 8 Sept., 1663.)

W. PALMER & J. NEWTON (successors to M^R T.
Bateman) at the *GLOBE & SUN* No. 128 in
Chancery Lane.   *c.* 1780
(*cf.* Nathaniel Hill above.)

THOMAS RIPLEY, at the *GLOBE, QUADRANT &
SPECTACLES*, near Hermitage Bridge, below
the Tower.   *c.* 1760

JOHN ROWLEY, at the *GLOBE*, under St. Dunstan's Church, Fleet Street.   1708

JOHN SENEX, at the *GLOBE*, under St. Dunstan's
1725

JAMES SIMONS, at *SIR ISAAC NEWTON'S
HEAD*, the corner of Marylebone Street, opposite
Glasshouse Street.   1774

JONATHAN SISSONS, at the *SPHERE*, the corner of
Beaufort Buildings in the Strand.   1734
(Succeeded by Jeremiah Sissons in 1747.)

CHRISTOPHER STEDMAN, at the *GLOBE*, on
London Bridge.   *c.* 1750
(When the houses on the Bridge were pulled down he removed
to the *Globe*, near the India House, Leadenhall Street. 1761)

THOMAS TUTTELL, at the *KING'S ARMS &
GLOBE*, at Charing Cross.   1695
(In " Samuel Pepys' Correspondence," I. 167, is note of a debt
to Tuttle the instrument maker. He was drowned whilst
engaged in surveying the coast. *cf. Post-Boy*, 3 Feb., 1702.)

THOMAS WRIGHT, at the *ORRERY & GLOBE*,
near Salisbury Court, in Fleet Street.   1718
(Succeeded by Benjn. Cole, *q.v.* The present day successors are
Messrs. Cooke, Troughton & Simms.)

SCULPTORS & MASONS

JOHN FLAXMAN [senior], Figure Maker, at the
GOLDEN HEAD, New Street, Covent Garden.
1755
(Father of John Flaxman (b. 1755—d. 1826) who worked with
Wedgwood—see *D.N.B.*)

CHARLES HARRIS, at the *ALFRED'S HEAD*,
opposite the New Church in the Strand. *c.* 1780
(See Mrs. Esdaile's *English Monuments since the Renaissance*.)

VINO & PERONNE, at the *GOLDEN VASE*, No.
155, High Holborn.   *c.* 1780

SEEDSMEN
See NURSERYMEN

SERJEANTS AT MACE
See LAW OFFICERS

SHAMPOOERS
See BATHS & SHAMPOOERS

SHOEMAKERS
See BOOTMAKERS

SIGN & ARMS PAINTERS

SYLVANUS MORGAN at the Sign of the *CAMDEN'S
HEAD & CITY ARMS*, at the North-east
corner of the Royal Exchange.   *c.* 1660
  The famous arms-painter and writer on heraldry, b. 162c–
d. 1693—see *D.N.B.*)

EDMOND PICKERING, at ye signe of ye *CITTIE &
SENATORS' ARMES*, in King Street, neere
Guildhall (now removed from his Father-in-
lawes house by ye Royall Exchange).   *c.* 1700

THOMAS PROCTOR, at the *BLACK-A-MOOR'S
HEAD* in Harp Alley, near Fleet Ditch. *c.* 1730
(See page 12.)

WILLIAM STEWARD, at the *KING'S HEAD* in
Fleete Lane, neare the Old Baily.   *c.* 1700
(See page 12.)

JOHN WHITE, at the *GOLDEN HEAD*, Shoe
Lane, Flect Street.   *c.* 1770

SILK THROWERS OR WEAVERS

JAMES BRANT, (late Richd. Finlow's), at the
BLUE BOAR, in Cheapside.   1765
(See also Cotterell and Blackstone, silkmen (under Mercers) at
above address.)

JOHN CALLOWE, at the *ANCHOR & CROWN*,
in Newgate Street.   *c.* 1710

CAMDEN'S HEAD & CITY ARMS

BLACKAMOOR'S HEAD

BLUE BOAR

LOCK & HINGE

HARROW & ANCHOR

SMOKE JACK

FRANCIS RYBOT, at the *CAT*, in Raven Row, ye further end of Smock Alley, Spittle Fields.
c. 1760

SAM^L SPRAGG, THOS. HOPKINS & CO., at the *SHIP*, opposite the Bull Inn, Within Bishopsgate. Also in Masons Court, Spital-Fields.   *c.* 1760

SILVERSMITHS
See GOLDSMITHS

SLOP SELLERS

KENELM DAWSON, at the sign of the *JOLLY SAILOR*, in Monmouth Street.   *c.* 1760
(See R. Kilby under Tailors.)

FULLAGAR & TODD, at the *GOLDEN BALL*, near ye India House, in Leadenhall Street. 1749

SMITHS

GABRIEL DIXON, at the *SMOAK JACK*, in Cherry Tree Alley, Bunhill Row.   *c.* 1760

JOHN ELWELL, at the *LOCK & HINGE* in the Hay Market.   1766

HALLETT & CO., at the *HARROW & ANCHOR*, next Fishmongers' Hall, Upper Thames Street.
c. 1760

JOHN HILL, at the *SMOKE JACK*, in Warwick Lane, Newgate Street.   *c.* 1760

JOHN JOHNSON, at the *SMOAK JACK*, No. 25, Gutter Lane, opposite Goldsmiths' Hall.   1797

HENRY HARTLEY, at the *KING'S ARMS*, in Bruton Mews, near New Bond Street. *c.* 1770

SOUP MAKERS

EDWARD BENNET & SPOUSE (late Dubois), at the *GOLDEN HEAD*, in Fleet Street, opposite Water Lane.   *c.* 1770

BENJAMIN PIPER, (successor to Bennet & Dubois) at the *GOLDEN HEAD*, in Three Kings Court, adjoining to No. 149 in Fleet Street, opposite Water Lane.   1782

JOHN DRAKEFORD, at the *THREE SPATTER-DASHES*, near Exeter Change, in the Strand.

c. 1740

SPUR MAKERS

JOHN MOORE, at the *HAND & SPUR*, near Exeter Exchange, in the Strand. *c.* 1750

SAMUEL TOULMIN, (successor to Smith & Gatesfield) at the *DIAL & CROWN*, near Hungerford Market, in the Strand. *c.* 1750
(Famous maker of silver cock-spurs as well as being a clock-maker. See p. 52.)

SNUFFMEN

See TOBACCONISTS

STATIONERS

JAMES ADAMS, at ye *ADAM & EVE*, near ye Vine Inn, Within Bishopsgate. 1725
(He had removed to the *Adam & Eve* near Three Kings' Court in Lombard Street by 1738. The site is now occupied by the Hongkong Bank.)

THOMAS ATKINS, at the *QUEEN'S HEAD & HALF MOON*, against Bread Street, in Cheapside. 1744
(Succeeded by Charles Powell, *q.v.*)

BAKER & FOURDRINIER, at the *GLOBE*, next door to the General Post Office in Lombard Street 1757
(See Fourdrinier & Co.) (Henry Fourdrinier, who was the son of Paul Fourdrinier, the engraver—see *D.N.B.*)

PHILIP BARRETT, at the *BLACK LYON*, between ye two Temple Gates, neer Temple Barr, in Fleet Street. 1702

JAMES BATE, at the *MITRE*, in Birchin Lane, Cornhill. *c.* 1770

GALPINE BAXTER, at the *DOVE*, No. 58, in Cornhill, the 3rd door from Grace Church Street.

c. 1770

GEORGE BEACHER, at the *BIBLE & CROWN*, in Drury Lane, facing Long Acre. *c.* 1740

THREE SPATTERDASHES

ADAM AND EVE

BLACK LION

ANCHOR AND CROWN

THREE FLEUR-DE-LIS

GOLDEN TURK'S HEAD

EDWARD BEVINS, at the *BIBLE & DOVE*, ye corner of Brownlow Street, near Great Turn-Stile in Holbourn.   1740

ROBY BISHOP, at the *BIBLE*, the upper end of Castle Street, opposite Great Newport Street, near Newport Market.   1768

GEORGE BRETT, at ye *THREE CROWNS*, on Ludgate Hill.   1744

JOHN BROMLEY, at the *BLACK SPREAD EAGLE*, in King Street, Covent Garden.   *c.* 1760
(Successor to Daniel Job, *q.v.*)

JAMES BROOKE, at ye *ANCHOR & CROWN*, near the Square on London Bridge.   1740
(He traded at this address from 1702–1750.)

BENJAMIN BROWNE, at the *THREE FLOWER-DE-LUCES*, in Ludgate Street.   *c.* 1700

SILVANUS CHIRM, at the *GOLDEN HEART*, No. 98, Aldersgate Bars, near Charterhouse Square.
(Succeeded by G. Herdsfield, *q.v.*)   1776

HENRY CLARKE, at the *BIBLE & STAR*, No. 72, in Grace Church Street.   1777

JOHN COMYN, at the *LAMB*, in Grace Church Street.   *c.* 1750

CHRISTOPHER CONINGSBY at the *GOLDEN TURK'S HEAD*, over against St. Dunstan's Church in Fleet Street.   1692

ELIZABETH DARTNALL, at the *BIBLE*, in St. Martin's Court, near St. Martin's Lane.   *c.* 1780

HUGH EDMONDS, at the *PAPER MILL*, near Barnard's Inn, Holborn.   *c.* 1760

WILLIAM EDMONDS, at the *UNICORN*, in the Poultry.   *c.* 1760

WILLIAM FENNER, at the *ANGEL & BIBLE*, in Paternoster Row.   *c.* 1760
(Master of the Stationers' Company in 1786.)

WILLIAM FIELDER, at the *BELL & STAR*, opposite the Royal Exchange, Cornhill.   *c.* 1750
(See W. Mason at above.)

ELIZABETH FIELDER, at the *BELL & STAR*, No. 82, Broad Street, behind the Royal Exchange, removed from No. 26, Cornhill.   *c.* 1770

FOURDRINIER, BLOXAM & WALKER, at the *GLOBE*, No. 11, Lombard Street, the corner of the Post Office.   1793
(See Baker & Fourdrinier at above.)

PHILIP GLASS, at the *BELL*, in Castle Alley, near the Royal Exchange.   1751

RICHARD GREEN, at the sign of the *HAND & PEN-KNIFE*, opposite White Fryars Gateway, No. 154, Fleet Street.   1773
(This bill for quill pens is made out to Edward Gibbon, the historian.)

HAND AND PEN-KNIFE

SAMUEL HARFORD, at the *EAGLE*, in Milk Street, Cheapside.   1754
(See also under Paper-stainers.)

WILLIAM HAYDON, at the *BIBLE*, No. 7, Falcon Court, near St. George's Church, Borough. *c.* 1750

JAMES HENSBOOM, at the *BLACKMOOR'S HEAD* in Catherine Street, three doors from the Strand.   *c.* 1760

GEORGE HERDSFIELD, at the *GOLDEN HEART*, No. 112, Aldersgate Bars.   1782
(Nephew and successor to S. Chirm, *q.v.*)

NAG'S HEAD

WILLIAM HORNER, at ye *NAG'S HEAD*, in Leadenhall Street, near Aldgate.   *c.* 1700

DANIEL JOB, at ye *SPREAD EAGLE*, in King Street, opposite Bedford Street, Covent Garden.   *c.* 1720

(Succeeded by J. Bromley, *q.v.*)

WILLIAM KIRBY, at ye *THREE CROWNS*, over against Jonathan's Coffee House, in Exchange Alley.   *c.* 1740

MONTAGU LAWRENCE, at the *GLOBE*, near Durham Yard, in the Strand.   *c.* 1760

CHARLES LENS, at the *GOLDEN LION*, Fetter Lane.   *c.* 1770

SPREAD EAGLE

INK BOTTLE

KING'S HEAD

BIBLE & CROWN

WILLIAM LEPARD, at the *HAND & BIBLE*, facing Battle Bridge, in Tooley Street, Southwark.

1757

(In 1799 the firm became Lepard & Smith, under which style the business is still being carried on.)

ARTHUR LYON, at the sign of the *INK BOTTLE*, facing Sweeting's Alley, Threadneedle Street.

c. 1750

(His sign shows the ink bottle carried by the early stationers.)

WILLIAM MASON, at the *BELL & STAR*, opposite the Royal Exchange, Cornhill.   *c.* 1760

(See Willm. & Eliz. Fielder at above.)

GEORGE MINNIKIN, at ye *KING'S HEAD* in St. Martin's-le-Grand, near Aldersgate.   1676

(See also under Paperstainers.)

ALEXANDER MONTGOMERY, at the *ANCHOR & CROWN*, in Cornhill, near the Royal Exchange.

1745

BENJAMIN MOORE, at the *PAPER MILL* in Newgate Street.   1758

AUSTIN OLDISWORTH, at the *GOLDEN BALL*, against Nicholas Lane in Cannon Street.   1710

CHARLES POWELL, at the *QUEEN'S HEAD & HALF MOON* against Bread Street, in Cheapside.

c. 1760

(Succeeded T. Atkins, *q.v.*, and followed by John Macklin in 1777.)

WILLIAM RIDGWAY, at ye *WHITE BEAR*, ye corner of Warwick Court, Holbourn.   1755

WILLIAM ROACH, at the *BIBLE & CROWN*, next ye Black Swan Inn, Holborn, near Fetter Lane end.   *c.* 1750

(Succeeded by S. Smith, *q.v.*)

JOHN SEAGOOD, at the *GOLDEN BIBLE*, the Northgate of the Royal Exchange.   *c.* 1760

WILLIAM SERJEANT, at ye *BIBLE*, in Great Newport Street, near Newport Market.   *c.* 1730

J. SHOVE, at the *MITRE*, opposite Furnival's Inn, Holborn.   *c.* 1760

JAMES SMITH, at ye *WHEATSHEAF*, in Newgate Street. 1744

SAMUEL SMITH, at the *SUN & WHEATSHEAF*, No. 6, Holborn, near Staple's Inn. *c.* 1770
(Successor to Mr. Roach, *q.v.*)

ALEXANDER STRAHAN, at the *GOLDEN BALL*, near St. Michael's Church in Cornhill. 1749
(He succeeded George Strahan who was at the Golden Ball in Cornhill from 1699—*c.* 1740. This house was burnt down in the Cornhill fire in 1748 and Alexander Strahan then moved to the above address.)

THE BELL

JOHN SUTTON, at the *QUEEN'S HEAD* in Barbican, near Aldersgate Street. 1752

ARTHUR TOOKER, at the *GLOBE*, in the Strand, over against Salisbury house. 1664

RICHARD WALKDEN, at ye *BELL*, on London Bridge, near St. Magnus Church. 1735
(Subsequent to the demolition of the houses on the Bridge in 1760 he was succeeded by his son John Walkden at the Bell, No. 7 in the Borough, Southwark, and later in Shoe Lane. In 1892 the firm was formed into a limited liability company and still exists in St. Bride Street under the name of Cooper, Dennison & Walkden.)

WILLIAM WARTER, at the signe of the *TALBOT*, over against Fetter Lane end in Fleet Streete. 1683

GEORGE WESTERMAN, at the *KING'S ARMS* in Black Swan Alley, London Wall, opposite the backside of Bedlam. *c.* 1750

THE TALBOT

THOMAS WHITTLESEY, at the Signe of the *GLOBE* in Gracious Streete, over against the Cross Keyes inn.* 1663

ROBERT WILSONN, at the *CROWN*, the corner of Nicholas Lane, Lombard Street. 1752

JOSEPH WOODGATE, at the *BIBLE & CROWN*, Within Bishopsgate. *c.* 1770

STAYMAKERS

CHEESMAN, (late Lee) at the *INDIAN QUEEN*, No. 38, Holywell Street, Strand. *c.* 1790

ELIZABETH CORBET, at the *NAKED BOY* (?), Tavistock Street, Covent Garden. 1761

THE GLOBE

---

* The Arms are those of the City of London and the Stationers' Company.)

SEVEN STARS

PAIR OF STAYS

THE BLEEDER

JOHN DEARMON, at the *SEVEN STARS*, in Bedford-bury, near Covent Garden.   *c.* 1750

THOMAS FIELD, at the *GOLDEN HEART*, in Shandois Street, Covent Garden.   *c.* 1770

H. S. H. [name and address wanting].   1692

WILLM. MENDHAM, at the *WHEATSHEAF & BODDICE*, against Gutter Lane, Cheapside. 1735

SYFRET, at the *GOLDEN LION*, in Dartmouth Street, Westminster.   1770

ROBERT TURNER, at the *WHEATSHEAF*, in High Holbourn.   *c.* 1760

MARY VARDEN, at the *CHILD'S COAT & ROSE*, in Houndsditch, near Bishopsgate.   *c.* 1760

WETHERHEAD, at the *LAMB & STAR*, Smock Alley, Bishopsgate Street.   *c.* 1770

SURGICAL INSTRUMENT MAKERS
See under CUTLERS, p. 58, marked ‡

SURGICAL & DENTAL OPERATORS

NATHANIEL BAKER, at the *GOLDEN SPURR*, in Round Court, St. Martin's-le-Grand, near Newgate Street.   *c.* 1700 (?)

SAMUEL DARKIN ye Elder, at the sign of the *BLEEDER*, next door to the Cow & Hare, in Church Lane, White-Chappel.   *c.* 1720

SAMUEL DARKIN the Younger, at the sign of the *BLEEDER & STAR*, the corner of Adam & Eve Alley, White Chapel facing the Church Yard Gate.   *c.* 1760

ALICE NEALE, at the *TURKS HEAD* Bagnio in James Street, Golden Square.   *c.* 1750
(Successor to J. Smith, cupper, 1731.)

WILCOX, at the *TURK'S HEAD*, in Newgate Street, over against Butcher Hall Lane.   1729

SWORD CUTLERS
See under CUTLERS

SAMUEL ALLEN, at the *DRAYMAN & JACKET* near Whitechapel Church.   *c.* 1790

EVANS, at the *GOLDEN FLEECE*, Smock Alley, Bishopsgate Street.   1780

KEAY, at the *GOLDEN FLEECE*, No. 77, Broad Street.   *c.* 1780

RICHARD KILBY, at the *OLD BLACK BULL'S HEAD & STAR*, next the George alehouse, in Monmouth Street and also at the *JOLLY SAILOR*, in White Lyon Street, near Monmouth Street, Seven Dyals.   *c.* 1760
(See K. Dawson under Slopsellers.)

I. G. PRATTEN, at the *GOLDEN ANCHOR*, No. 77 Shoreditch, near the Turnpike.   *c.* 1780

WILLIAM SCRAGGS, at the sign of the *THREE PIGEONS*, the upper end of Monmouth Street.   *c.* 1760

GOLDEN FLEECE

TALLOW CHANDLERS

SUSANNA COLLIN, (daughter to ye late Mr. Heny. Leeson, deceased) at the *BLACK BULL*, near the East end of the New Church, in the Strand.   1753

WILLIAM LEWIS, at the *SUN*, in Oxford Road, near Soho Square.   1759

BLACK BULL

TEA MEN

See also GROCERS

EDWD. ALDERSON, (successor to Mr. S. Roberts), at the *THREE SUGAR LOAVES*, No. 102 Oxford Street, Corner of John Street.   1802
(John Street was the south end of Portland Street.)

ANTROBUS, SEAMAN & ANTROBUS, at the *KING'S ARMS*, opposite Northumberland Street, in the Strand.   1787

ANTROBUS, GREEN & RUSSELL, at above   1809

THREE SUGAR LOAVES

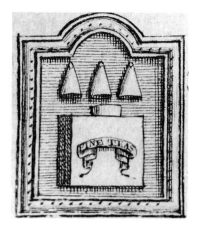

*GREEN CANISTER AND
THREE SUGAR LOAVES*

GRASSHOPPER

*THREE SUGAR LOAVES
AND CANISTER*

ANNE BARNARD, at the *CANISTER*, near Pope's Head Alley, Cornhill.   *c.* 1760

JOHN BARTON, at the *GREEN CANISTER & THREE SUGAR LOAVES* on Ludgate Hill. 1750

RICHARD BEACH, at the *FIGG TREE*, in Newgate Street.   1726

E. BEECH & CO., at the *CANISTER*, in Milk Street, near Cheapside.   *c.* 1770

BROWNE & CULLEY, at the *ANGEL & TEA CHEST* in Ludgate Street.   1766

THOS. CARRINGTON, at the *GOLDEN KEY*, opposite White Lyon Street, Norton Folgate.
                                             c. 1760

ROBERT CARTONY, at the *KING'S ARMS & GOLDEN BOTTLE*, opposite Somerset House, in the Strand.   1763
(Joseph and Robert Cartony were at the corner of Long Acre in Drury Lane in 1755.)

CARTONY & MICHELL, at the *KING'S ARMS & GOLDEN BOTTLE*, opposite Somerset House, in the Strand.   1773

DAVIDSON, at the *GOLDEN CANNISTER*, No. 66, the corner of Long Lane, West Smithfield. *c.* 1770

JOHN D'EPCKE, at the *GRASSHOPPER*, No. 112, Long Acre.   *c.* 1780

GEORGE DURSON, at ye *THREE SUGAR LOAVES & CANNISTER*, the corner of Water Lane, Fleet Street.   *c.* 1750

EDWD. EAGLETON, at the *GRASSHOPPER*, No. 9, Bishopsgate Street.   1781

FLETCHER, from Mr. Twining's, at the *GRASSHOPPER*, near Essex Street, Temple Barr. 1754

ANN FLIGHT, at the *GRASSHOPPER*, near Pope's Head Alley, Cornhill.   *c.* 1760

JOHN & BENJN. HANSON, at the *TEA CHEST*, No. 323 Holborn, opposite Gray's Inn Gate. 1768
(The firm continued at this address until 1825 and may be the precursors of the existing large firm of wholesale grocers and provision merchants, Samuel Hanson & Co. Ld. of 14, Eastcheap.)

Francis Kerton, at the *TEA TUB*, opposite St. Dunstan's Church, Fleet Street.   *c.* 1760

Maddock, at the *CROWN & PEARL* on Ludgate Hill.   *c.* 1770

Philip Margas, at ye *GOLDEN FAN*, in Bucklers Bury, near Stock Market.   1755
(A fashionable " India shop " mentioned by Prior.)

Mason & Sharman, at the *GREEN CANISTER*, No. 79 New Bond Street, three doors from Oxford Street.   1789

Thos. & Saml. Noton, at the *THREE SUGAR LOAVES*, two doors below Shoe Lane, in Fleet Street.   1748

Parkinson, at the *THREE GOLDEN SUGAR LOAVES*, in Rupert Street, near the Hay Market.   *c.* 1770

Wm. Prowett, at the *THREE SUGAR LOAVES & CANISTER*, on Holbourn Bridge, corner of Fleet Market.   1753

John Relph, at the *GOLDEN ANCHOR*, ye corner of New Turnstile, in High Holbourn.   *c.* 1760

William Sandys, (removed from Ludgate Hill) to the *TEA CHEST & CANISTER*, near the Horn Tavern in Fleet Street.   *c.* 1760

Isaac Thornton, at the *GRASSHOPPER & TEA CANNISTER*, the corner of Fleet Market, Fleet Street.   *c.* 1750

Wheler & Fox, at the *CROWN & CANNISTER*, in Cornhill.   *c.* 1760

White & Smith, at the *GOLDEN CANNISTER*, Pall Mall.   1788

William Xerxes, at ye *GREEN CANISTER*, in Jermyn Street, St. James's.   *c.* 1770

THREAD MAKERS

Egerton Amos & Spicer, at the *THREE PIGEONS & MITRE* in Fleet Street, near Serjeant's Inn.   1738

TEA TUB

THREE SUGAR LOAVES

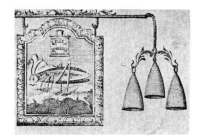

GRASSHOPPER & TEA CANISTER

3 PIGEONS & MITRE

*GOLDEN TEA KETTLE &
SPEAKING TRUMPET*

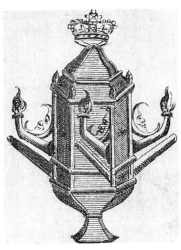

LAMP & CROWN

SPICER, FISHER & WELLS, at the *THREE PIGEONS & MITRE*, No. 52 Fleet Street. 1768

WELLS, FISHER, WELLS & HEADEACH, at above. 1784

THOS. SMITH, at the *THREE PIGEONS & SCEPTRE*, opposite Serjeant's Inn, No. 173 Fleet Street. 1791

TIN MEN & LAMP LIGHTERS

SAMUEL BEVINGTON, at the *GOLDEN TEA KETTLE & SPEAKING TRUMPET*, in Lombard Street. *c.* 1760

DURDEN, at ye *KING'S ARMS*, facing the Haymarket, near Pall Mall. *c.* 1760

ANTHONY DYCKHOFF, at the *LAMP & CROWN*, the corner of Middle Row, Holbourn. *c.* 1770
(Preceded by J. Haughton, *q.v.*)

SAMUEL ERRINGTON, at the *CROWN*, opposite the Church, in Church Street, Greenwich. *c.* 1760

JOSEPH GOAD, at the *SHIP*, near Alderman-Bury Postern, in Fore Street. *c.* 1770

JOHN HAUGHTON, at the *LAMP & CROWN*, the corner of Middle Row, by Holborn Barrs. *c.* 1750
(Succeeded by A. Dyckhoff, *q.v.*)

ABRAHAM HENSLEY, at the Sign of the *LAMP*, in Cheapside, near Fryday Street. 1784

JONATHAN HINCKES, at ye *LAMP & CROWN*, near Fetter Lane in Fleet Street. 1747

ROBERT HOWARD, at the *WHEATSHEAF & TRUMPET*, Smithfield Bars. *c.* 1760
(Succeeded by E. Post, *q.v.*)

JOSEPH HOWSE, at the *LAMP & CROWN*, near Dean Street, High Holborn. *c.* 1780

HENRY KEMP, at the *LAMP & CROWN*, opposite Durham Yard, in the Strand. *c.* 1760

JAMES LOVE, at the *ANCHOR*, next door to ye Black Swan Inn, Holbourn. 1759

Thomas Nash, at the *PLUME OF FEATHERS*, in Aldersgate Street.   *c.* 1770

Joshua Owen, at the *GLOUCESTER ARMS*, upper Mount Street, near Grosvenor Square.

1792

Thomas Patrick, at the *THREE HALF MOONS*, in Newgate Street.   1766

Edward Post, at the *WHEATSHEAF & SPEAKING TRUMPET*, Smithfield Bars. *c.* 1770
(Successor to R. Howard at above, *q.v.*)

Price & Marshall, at the *HOG & PORRIDGE POT*, No. 53, opposite Hatton Street, Holborn.

1777

Evan Richards, at the *CROWN & SEVEN LAMPS*, the corner of Cavendish Street, Oxford Road.   1769

Jonathan Tudway, at ye *THREE LAMPS*, Charing Cross.   1756

THREE HALF MOONS

TOBACCO PIPE MAKERS
See Pipe Makers

TOBACCONISTS & SNUFF MEN

Adlington, at ye *TOBACCO ROLL*, near ye White Hart, in St. Thomas's, Southwark. *c.* 1760

Allen & Pardoe, at ye *TOBACCO ROLE*, Russell Street, Covent Garden.   *c.* 1760

Bathurst, at ye *ANGEL & STILL*, ye corner of Love Lane, Billingsgate   *c.* 1770

James Beatty, at ye *HIGHLANDER*, behind St. Clement's Church, near the end of Butcher Row, without Temple Bar.   *c.* 1770

Briggs, at ye *GREEN MAN & STILL*, over against the Angel Inn, near St. Giles's Church.

c. 1770

Bullock, at ye *GREEN MAN & STILL*, at Ratcliff Cross.   *c.* 1750

TOBACCO ROLL

HIGHLANDER

DAGGER

RASP & CROWN

JOHN CATER, at the *BLACKMOOR'S HEAD*, facing Salisbury Court, in Fleet Street.   *c.* 1770

CROFTON, at the *DAGGER*, No. 61, Bartholomew Close, West Smithfield.   *c.* 1780
(Successor to Mr. Richard Ford, *q.v.*)

CROFTON, at the *DAGGER*, in Watling Street, No. 8, near St. Paul's.   *c.* 1760
(Successor to Mr. Richd. Ford, *q.v.*)
The Arms are those of the City of London and the Salters' Company.

DAVIS, at ye *COCK & TOBACCO ROLL*, in Golden Lane, Without Cripplegate.   *c.* 1770

DICKINS, at ye *SHIP & BLACK BOY*, at Parkers Lane End, in Drury Lane.   *c.* 1790

ECCLESTON, at the *VIRGINIA PLANTER*, near the Horn Tavern, Fleet Street.   *c.* 1760

EDWARDS, at the *GREEN MAN & STILL*, in Goswell Street.   *c.* 1770

FELTON, at ye *THREE TOBACCO ROLLS*, in Long Acre.   *c.* 1750

ALEXANDER FERGUSON, at ye *HIGHLANDER*, in Threadneedle Street.   *c.* 1760

RICHARD FORD, at ye *DAGGER*, upon Bred Street Hill, near Queen Hive.   *c.* 1740
(*cf.* C. Hampton, and Crofton.)

PETER FRIBOURG, at the *RASP & CROWN*, in the Hay Market.   1720

FRIBOURG, SAULLE & PONTET, at the *CROWN & RASP*, in Pall Mall, near the Haymarket.   1773

FRIBOURG & TREYER, at the *RASP & CROWN*, upper end of ye Hay Market, No. 34.   *c.* 1780

FRIBOURG & TREYER, No. 34, St. James's Haymarket.   1787
(Under this name, and with the old sign, the famous shop at the top of the Haymarket is carried on to-day.)

GOWAN, at ye *TOBACCO ROLL*, in Rose Street, near Covent Garden.   *c.* 1750

NATHANIEL GRANT, at the *HIGHLANDER*, in Angel Court, Westminster.   *c.* 1760

CARY HAMPTON, at the *DAGGER*, in Watling Street. 1725
(Successor Richd. Ford.)

JOHN HARDHAM, at the *RED LYON*, in Fleet Street, near Fleet Bridge. 1755
(A later bill, dated 1772, gives " the No. of the house 106." This bill is made out to Edward Gibbon the historian. Hardham's friendship with David Garrick is well known, likewise his "No. 37" snuff. He was succeeded by J. & G. Proctor about 1810 and in 1844 W. Kirk took the business across the street to No. 101, where the trade is still carried on under the style of John Hardham & Co.)

HIGHLANDER

WILLIAM HEBB, (1) at ye *HIGHLANDER*, ye corner of Pall Mall, facing St. James's Hay Market. *c.* 1765
(2) at the *OLD HIGHLANDER*, next door to Mr. Pinchbeck's, at the corner of Cockspur Street facing the Hay Market. 1772
(Successor to Mr. John Hatfield.)

JENNING, at the *BLACK LYON*, Piccadilly. *c.* 1760

JONES, at the *GOLDEN LYON*, in Tower Street. *c.* 1700

JOHN LAWRENCE, at ye *THREE PIDGEONS*, in Martin's-le-Grand. *c.* 1700

RICHARD LEE, at the *GOLDEN TOBACCO ROLL*, in Panton Street. 1745

MARGERUM, at the *BLACK BOY & STILL*, in Church Street, Hackney. *c.* 1760

BLACK BOY & STILL

THOMAS MARSHALL, at ye *BLACKAMOOR'S HEAD*, in Wapping, near ye Hermitage Bridge. *c.* 1700

MOOR, at the *WHITE HORSE*, Castle Alley, Royal Exchange. *c.* 1760

ROBERT NASH, at the *TOBACCO ROLL*, opposite Hatton Garden, Holborn. *c.* 1765

NOSS, at the *BLACK BOY & STILL*, in Fleet Street. *c.* 1750

PARKHURST, at the *ORANGE TREE*, in Fleet Street. *c.* 1740

HIGHLANDER,
THISTLE & CROWN

SHALLETT, at the *BLACK BOY & WHITE HORSE*, Without Temple Barr.   *c.* 1750

TURNER, at ye *TWO BLACK BOYS*, in Tower Street.   *c.* 1760

VINCENT, at ye *ROSE & CROWN*, in Tuttle Street, Westminster.   *c.* 1770

DAVID WISHART, at ye *HIGHLANDER, THISTLE & CROWN*, at ye upper end of St. James's Hay Market, in Coventry Street.   1720
(Wishart's sign is said to have originated the custom of placing a Highlander outside tobacconists' shops. In his case it indicated a Jacobite rendezvous. The Coventry Street shop was pulled down in 1880 and the business has since been carried on in Panton Street.)

JOHN YVE, at the *HIGHLANDER*, in Compton Street, So-ho.   *c.* 1760

TOOL MAKERS

JOHN JENNION, at the *THREE PLAINS* [*sic*], in Queen Street, near Cheapside.   *c.* 1730

THREE PLANES

JEREMIAH LOWEN & WM. MORGAN, at the *TWO AXES*, in Thunderbolt Alley, Windmill Hill, near Morefields.   *c.* 1720

JOHN UPCHURCH, at the sign of the *COOPER'S TOOLS*, in Little Eastcheap.   1765

TOY-MEN

JOHN BANISTER, at the sign of the *ORANGE TREE*, the corner of Cranborn Alley, in Little Newport Street, near Leicester Fields.   *c.* 1760

BELLAMY, at the *GREEN PARROT*, near Chancery Lane, Holborn.   1762

GREEN PARROT

PAUL DANIEL CHENEVIX, at the sign of the *GOLDEN DOOR*, over against Suffolk Street, Charing Cross.   1742
(" Mrs. Chenevix, the toy-woman of Suffolk Street," sold the Strawberry Hill property to Horace Walpole in 1748—(see *D.N.B.*) Mrs. Chenevix was daughter of Mr. Deard, *q.v.*)

COLES CHILD, at the *BLEW BOAR*, on London Bridge. 1756
(When the houses on the bridge were demolished in 1760, Child removed to Upper Thames Street.)

JOSEPH CRESWELL, at the *UNICORN*, in Suffolk Street (Charing Cross). 1770

WILLIAM & MARY DEARD, at the *STAR*, the end of Pall Mall, near St. James's Hay-market. *c.* 1740
(Deards' was a fashionable rendezvous during the early part of the 18th century and frequent references are found to it in the poems and letters of the period.)

ELEPHANT & RISING SUN

JAMES LEWER, at ye *ELEPHANT & RISING SUN*, five doors from Friday Street, in Cheapside. 1750

MRS. MARKHAM, at the *SEVEN STARS*, under St. Dunstan's Church, Fleet Street. 1720
(Succeeded by J. Pearson, *q.v.*)

*MARTIN, at the *THREE RABBITS*, near Durham Yard, in the Strand. 1737

JOHN PEARSON, at ye *SEVEN STARS & CROWN*, under St. Dunstan's Church, in the Strand. 1743
(Succeeded Mrs. Markham, *q.v.*)

ANN PENNALIGGAN, at the *THREE HERRINGS*, No. 75, in Gracechurch Street, next door to the Ship Tavern. 1793

THREE RABBITS

WALTER ROWBOTHAM, at the *RED M. AND DAGGER*, in Pope's Head Alley, against the Royal Exchange in Cornhill. 1731

ROBERT WAITE, at the *PARROT & STAR*, against Bow Lane, in Cheapside. *c.* 1720

TRUNK MAKERS

DANIEL BRADSHAW, at the *GOLDEN CUP*, in Fleet Street, near Temple Barr. *c.* 1760

JAMES BRYANT, at ye *TRUNK & BUCKET*, the corner of St. Paul's, facing Cheapside. 1756

RACHEL BRYANT, at same sign and address. *c.* 1765
(Wm. Bryant's Trunk and Bucket Warehouse was at No. 28, Ludgate Hill in 1790, and Nathl. Bryant, trunk maker, at 49, St. Paul's Churchyard in the same year.)

* The arms are those of the City of London and the Skinners' Company.

TRUNK & BUCKET

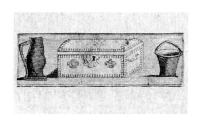

TRUNK & BUCKETS

THREE TRUNKS & BLUE BOAR

CHAPMAN & DRIVER, at the *KING'S ARMS*, in Cockspur Street, near Pall Mall.   1772

RICHARD DRIVER, at same sign and address. 1775

DRIVER & EYRE, at same sign and address and also at No. 70, Charing Cross.   1792

ISAAC EYRE, at same sign and addresses and also at No. 19 Cockspur Street.   1797

JOHN CLEMENTS, nephew and successor to H. Nickles (see below), at the *TRUNK & BUCKET*, at ye corner of St. Paul's next Cheapside [No. 5].   1755
(Succeeded by Robert Seabrook, c. 1790.)

SAMUEL FORSAITH, at *INDUSTRY & INDOLENCE*, in Long Acre.   *c.* 1770

NATHANIEL GLADMAN, at the *THREE TRUNKS & BLUE BOAR*, next door to Leaden-hall in Leaden-hall Street.   1723
(Succeeded by C. Townsend, *q.v.*)

THOMAS GRIFFITH, at the *ACORN* in Marylebon Street, near Golden Square.   1766

JNO. MERRIMAN, at the *TWO TRUNKS & CHEST*, in Leadenhall Street.   1767

HENRY NICKLES, at the *TRUNK & BUCKETS*, the corner of St. Paul's, next Cheapside Conduit.
          c. 1740
(The old-time toast of " Sweethearts and wives, not forgetting the trunk-maker and the elm tree at the corner of St. Paul's " is said to allude to H. Nickles who amassed a fortune of £20,000 before he died in 1750. He was succeeded by his nephew, J. Clements, *q.v.*, and later by R. Seabrook (1793).

WILLM. ROBERTSON, at the *THREE TRUNKS & TWO BUCKETS*, No. 44, New Bond Street, corner of Clifford Street.   1778
(This bill is made out to Edward Gibbon, the historian, when he was living in Bentinck Street.)

CHARLES TOWNSEND, at the *THREE TRUNKS & BLEW BOAR*, in Leadenhall Street. *c.* 1760
(He succeeded N. Gladman, *q.v.*)

PETER BARTLETT, at the *GOLDEN BALL*, in Prescot Street, Goodman's Fields.   1737

HOLMES & LAURIE, at the *GOLDEN KEY*, No. 2, in St. Bartholomew Close, near West Smithfield.   1773

JOHN RICHARDSON, at the *GOLDEN KEY*, Prescot Street, Goodman's Fields.   1748

TURNERS

JOHN ALEXANDER, at the *ELEPHANT & COFFEE MILL*, No. 29, in Crooked Lane, near the Monument.   1776

ELEPHANT & COFFEE MILL

ISAAC BARNES, at the *BLUE COAT BOY*, opposite Buckingham Street, in the Strand.   1777

EDWARD BEESLY, at the *KING'S ARMS*, opposite the Waxwork, in Fleet Street.   1787
(Mrs. Salmon's famous waxwork show was at the Golden Salmon, No. 189, Fleet Street.)

THOMAS BLAIR, at the *BLUE COAT BOY*, opposite Buckingham Street, No. 446, in the Strand.   1779
(Successor to Isaac Barnes, *q.v.*)

BENJAMIN BOOTH, at the Sign of the *ROCKING HORSE*, near Serjeant's Inn, Fleet Street.   1749
(The only other instance of this sign is also that of a turner—dated 1724.)

GERARD CRAWLEY, at the *COFFEE MILL & NIMBLE NINEPENCE*, adjoining to St. Michael's Church, in Cornhill.   1768

JAMES DANSER, at the *ELEPHANT & STAR*, the corner of Bow Church Yard, Cheapside.   *c.* 1760

*COFFEE MILL &
NIMBLE NINEPENCE*

SAMUEL JARVIS, at the *ROSE AND CROWN & FOWLER*, on Snow Hill.   1740
(Probably a maker of gun stocks.)

JOSEPH PATTERSON, at the *CROWN*, next Her Majesty's bookbinder, in New Bond Street.   *c.* 1710

*PAINTED FLOOR CLOTH
AND BRUSH*

PETER BOAT & DOUBLET

WHITE HART & COFFIN

TURNERS

ELIZABETH BARTON STENT, at the *TURNERS'
ARMS*, in Little Britain.   *c.* 1740
(Successor to Robert Stent.)

FRANCIS THOMPSON, at the *THREE CHAIRS*, in
St. John's Lane, near Hick's Hall.   *c.* 1730

ALEXR. WETHERSTONE, at ye *PAINTED FLOOR
CLOTH & BRUSH*, in Portugal Street, near
Lincoln's Inn Back Gate.   1763

CHRISTOPHER THORN (also maker of cricket bats),
at the *BEEHIVE & PATTEN*, in John Street,
Oxford Market.   1764

TWINE & ROPE MAKERS

JOHN BRADSHAW, at the *PETER BOAT*,* on
Fish Street Hill.   1768
(Later Bradshaw & Davidson.)

WILLIAM GOOD, at the *PETER BOAT &
DOUBLET*, on London Bridge.   1668
(This signboard is still in use by Messrs. Tull & Barker in
Creechurch Lane.)

UNDERTAKERS

WILLIAM BOYCE, at ye *WHIGHT HART &
COFFIN*, in ye Grate Ould Bayley, near Newgeat.
    c. 1680

EDWARD CHANDLER & SON, at the *NAKED BOY
& COFFIN*, in the corner of Turnagain Lane
by the Fleet Market, near Holborn Bridge. 1764

JOHN CLARKE, at the *FOUR COFFINS*, in Jermine
Street, near St. James's Church.   1725

JOHN FRYDAY, at ye sign of ye *FOUR COFFINS*,
in St. Martin's Lane, the corner of Burying
Passage.   *c.* 1750

ARTHUR GRANGER, at the *CROWN & COFFIN*,
in White Chapel.   *c.* 1720

WILLIAM GRINLEY, at ye sign of ye *NAKED BOY
& COFFIN*, at ye Lower Corner of Fleet Lane.
    c. 1730

* A Thames craft peculiar to fishermen.

ALEXR. HORROCKS, at the *WHITE BEAR*, against
Gray's Inn Gate, in Holborn.   1732

ROBERT LOW, at the *COFFIN & CROWN*, in
Pater Noster Row, Spitalfields.   *c.* 1770

ELEAZAR MALORY, at the *COFFIN*, in White
Chapel, near Red Lion Street end.   *c.* 1700

RICHD. MIDDLETON, at the sign of *THE FIRST
& LAST*, in Stonecutter Street on the West side
of Fleet Market.   1790

GEORGE PAGE, at the *FOUR COFFINS*, St.
Margarets Hill, Southwark.   1752
(Succeeded by Robert Green.)

ISAAC WHITCHURCH, removed from Fleet Lane to
the *THREE COFFINS*, by the Ditch side, near
Holbourn Bridge.   *c.* 1740

WILLM. WHITCHURCH, at ye *FOUR COFFINS*,
on Holborn Hill.   *c.* 1760

NAKED BOY & COFFIN

UPHOLSTERERS

JOHN BOOTHBY, at the *GOLDEN HEAD*, in
Norfolk Street, in the Strand.   *c.* 1750

JAMES BROWN, at the *KING'S ARMS*, the South
Side of St. Paul's Church Yard.   1768–1793

RICHD. CHILLINGWORTH & THOS. BURNETT, at
the *KING'S ARMS*, against the New Church in
the Strand.   1724

WILLIAM CLARKSON, at the *KING'S HEAD*, the
corner of Old Bedlam, Moorfields.   *c.* 1780

THOMAS CLOAKE, at the *GOLDEN LION*, No. 5,
in Lower Moorfields, near Old Bethleham.   1774

WILLIAM DARBY, at the *BEAR & CROWN*, in
Aldermanbury, near ye Church.   1770

JONATHAN FALL, at the *BLUE CURTAIN*, No. 5,
in St. Paul's Church Yard.   1763
(Successor to John Iliffe, *q.v.*)

CHARLES GRANGE & SON, at the *ROYAL BED*,
Snow Hill, near St. Sepulchre's Church.   *c.* 1760

WHITE BEAR

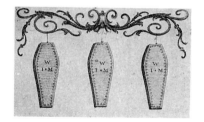

THREE COFFINS

CROWN & CUSHION

THE TALBOT

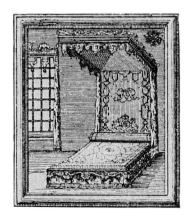

ROYAL BED & STAR

ELIZABETH HAWKINS, at the *ROYAL BED*, in New Bond Street, Hanover Square.   1767

NATHANIEL HEWITT, at the *CROWN & CUSHION*, near St. Thomas's Gate in the Borough of Southwark.   1768

JOHN HOWARD, at the *TALBOT*, in Long Acre, near West Smithfield.   1732
(The father of John Howard, the philanthropist and prison reformer (see *D.N.B.*).)

ELIZABETH HUTT & SON, at the *BLEW CURTAIN*, in St. Paul's Church Yard.   1741

JOHN ILIFFE, Successor to Mrs. Eliz. Hutt, at the *BLEW CURTAIN*, in St. Paul's Church Yard.
          c. 1760
(Succeeded by J. Fall, *q.v.*, who was followed by Thos. Silk, cabinet maker.)

WILLIAM JELLICOE, at the sign of the *CHAIR & ANCHOR*, in Fleet Street.   1770
(Successor to the Widow Smith.)

JENNINGS & WALKINGTON, at the *VINE*, in Long Acre.   *c.* 1770

ROBERT LEGG, at the Sign of the *LEG*, near Southampton Street, in Holbourn.   *c.* 1760

JOSHUA LEWIS, at the *THREE TENTS*,* in Fleet Street, by Fleet Ditch.   1725

PETER MARCHANT, at the *ROYAL BED & STAR*, near Fleet Bridge.   *c.* 1750

TIM⁰. MATTHEWS & ERASˢ. DELAFIELD, at ye *ROYAL BED & SUN*, near Salisbury Court, in Fleet Street.   1723

THOˢ. NASH, ELKINGᴺ. HALL & RICHᴰ. WHITE-HORNE, at the *ROYAL BED*, on Holborn Bridge.   1730

HENRY NEWTON, at the *THREE TENTS*,* the corner of Cullum Street, in Lime Street, near Leadenhall Market.   *c.* 1760

* Arms of the Upholsterers' Company.

SAML. PHENE & THOS. JONES, at the *GOLDEN PLOW*, the corner of Little Moorgate, London Wall. 1763
(Their successors, Phene & Williamson, removed from London Wall to New Bond Street in 1839.)

CECIL PITT, at the *RISING SUN & FOX*, five doors from the corner of New Broad Street, in Moorfields. 1754

CECIL PITT, at the *ROYAL TENT*, in Moorfields, almost fronting Bedlam Walk. 1763

PITT & CHESSEY, at the *ROYAL BED & STAR*, No. 12, in Moorfields. 1774
(Late Rodwell's, *q.v.*)

POPE & MACLELLAN, at the *POPE'S HEAD*, the corner of Harvey Court, near Half Moon Street, in the Strand. *c.* 1760

THOMAS PORTER, at the *KING'S ARMS*, in New Round Court, Strand. *c.* 1770

JOHN POTTS, at the *BLACK SPREAD EAGLE*, King Street, Covent Garden. *c.* 1760

JOHN PRICE, at the *THREE CHAIRS & CABBINET*, in Catherine Street, in the Strand. 1756

FRANCIS PYNER, at the *TENT*, near George Yard, Lombard Street. 1765
(Successor to Mrs. Powle from Three King Court, *c.* 1750.)

JOSEPH READ, at the *CHAIR & CROWN*, No. 78, Fleet Market, facing the Dial. 1771

JAMES RODWELL, at the *ROYAL BED & STAR*, the second door from the corner of New Broad Street, faceing Bedlam Walk, in Moorfields.
(Succeeded by Pitt & Chessey, *q.v.*) *c.* 1730

JOHN STURGIS, at the *ROSE & CROWN*, next door to the White Horse Inn, Fleet Market. *c.* 1760

HYMNERS TAYLOR, at the *CROWN & CUSHION*, over against Lord Monson's in Piccadilly. *c.* 1750
(Lord Monson acquired Sunderland House in 1746 and sold it to Henry Fox in 1763. It stood next to Burlington House; the site is now occupied by " Albany ".)

THREE TENTS

ROSE & CROWN

ROYAL BED & STAR

UPHOLSTERERS

ROBERT WEBB, at the sign of the *QUEEN'S HEAD & THREE TENTS*, in Bedford Street, Covent Garden. 1716

WILLIAM WITTON, at the *ROYAL BED*, on St. Margaret's Hill, in the Borough of Southwark. *c.* 1750

VARIOUS

TRADES UNSPECIFIED

RUPERT ATKINSON, at the *THREE NUNS*, in the Broad Way, Westminster. *c.* 1760

HENRY BREESE, at the *GOLDEN LION*, in Bow Lane, near Cheapside. 1749

THOMAS BRENTNALL, at ye *ROSE & CROWN*, facing the Market in Newgate Street. *c.* 1750

THOMAS BROWNE, at the *CRANE & ANCHOR*, in Friday Street. *c.* 1740

ELIZABETH CORBET, at the *NAKED BOY*, Tavistock Street, Covent Garden. 1763

WILLIAM HALBERT, at the *SEVEN STARRS*, Church Street, Greenwich. *c.* 1750

WM. & THOS. JESSER, at the *WOOLPACK*, Billingsgate. 1749

GEORGE POUGHFER, at the *GOLDEN BALL*, near the Church, in Broad Street. *c.* 1750

TOLFREY, FREWIN & WIMPEY, at the *STAR*, in Aldermanbury. *c.* 1760

E. WALKER, at the *HALF MOON & SEVEN STARS*, on Clerkenwell Green. *c.* 1760

WAREHOUSEMEN

ADAMS, at the *SEVEN STARS*, in Norris Street, near St. James's Hay Market. *c.* 1760

DICKINSON & GRAHAM, at the *HAND, GLOVE & CROWN*, in Bucklersbury. 1762

CRANE & ANCHOR

HALF MOON & SEVEN STARS

QUEEN'S HEAD & THREE TENTS

Jackson & Kluhl, at the *THREE CROWNS*, in Tavistock Street, Covent Garden. 1771

E. Smith, at the *PEACOCK*, No. 12, Tavistock Street, Covent Garden. *c.* 1770

Wolley & Blinkhorn, at the *GOLDEN LAMB*, in Bread Street, near Cheapside. 1763

WALLPAPER MAKERS
See Paperstainers

WATCHMAKERS
See Clockmakers

THREE KINGS

WAX CHANDLERS
See also Tallow Chandlers.

Isaac Barrett, at the *THREE KINGS*, opposite St. Clement's Church, in the Strand. 1758
(Succeeded by Barrett & Beaumont, No. 4, Haymarket, 1805.)

Eliz.ᵀᴴ Bedcott, at the *CROWN & BEEHIVE*, in Berkeley Square. 1761

William Bedcott, at above. 1757

Eliza Bick & Compy., at the *GOLDEN BEEHIVE*, opposite the Mansion House. 1758
(Later Bick & Cowan at above.)

B. Brecknell, at the *BEEHIVE*, in the Haymarket, near Piccadilly. 1787
(Later Brecknell & Turner, No. 31, Piccadilly.)

Chatfield, at the *KING'S ARMS*, in the Little Old Baily, near St. Sepulchre's Church. *c.* 1770

John Coggs, at the *RAVEN & SUN*, behind the King on Horseback at Charing Cross. 1747

Lewis Dupuis, at the *BEEHIVE & WAX CHANDLER*, in Beake Street, Golden Square. 1771

Lewis Dupuis, at the *BEEHIVE*, in Charlotte Street, Bloomsbury. 1783

CROWN & BEEHIVE

BEEHIVE & WAX CHANDLER

WAX CHANDLERS

THOMAS JONES, at ye *STAR & GARTER*, in ye Poultry.   1748

(Succeeded by Hannah Jones, at above, 1751.)

SOLOMON SAMMON, at the *BLACK BULL*, in Essex Street, in the Strand.   1751

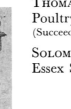

WEAVERS

SAMUEL COLE, at the *PEACOCK*, in Bedford Street, Covent Garden.   1768

JOHN COLLIER, at the *STAR*, in Wide-Gate Street, Without Bishopsgate.   1758

JAMES CRANCH, at the *SUN & STAR*, No. 10, Middle Moorfields.   1777

CHARLES GUILLUM, at ye *SUN*, in Horse Shoe Alley, Middle Moorfields.   1757

JNO. HALLETT & JNO. WILLS, at the *GOLDEN BALL*, Bow Lane, Cheapside.   1764

JOHN LAMY, at the *BLUE BALL*, in Gun Street, Spital Fields.   *c.* 1750

SPINNING WHEEL

JOHN RADBURNE, at the *SPINNING WHEEL*, in the Great Minories.   *c.* 1730

FRANCIS RYBOT, at the *CAT*, in Raven Row, ye further end of Smock Alley, Spittle Fields.   1777

(Preceded by Elizth. Rybot at above in 1726.)

WHALEBONE DEALERS

CROWN & WHALE

ELIZABETH BOWEN, at the *CROWN & WHALE*, over against the Bell Inn in Wood Street, Cheapside.   *c.* 1750

EDWARD TYSON & JNO. WHITELOCK, at the *BLACKMOOR'S HEAD & WHALE*, in Milk Street.   1749

WHIP MAKERS

ABRAHAM RIGHTON, at the *GOLDEN BALL*, Aldersgate Street, near the Bars.   *c.* 1740

NEHEMIAH WARD, at the *KING'S ARMS*, No. 198, High Street, Borough, Southwark.   *c.* 1760

GOLDEN BALL

ANN BADGER, at the *CHINA JAR*, in Cannon Street, near Gracechurch Street. *c.* 1760

GOULD & SQUIRE, at the *TWO SPIES*, No. 11, Catherine Street, Strand. 1784

EDWARD JEMMITT, at the *DISTILLERS ARMS*, against the Fountain Tavern in the Strand. *c.* 1750

JOHN MOORE, at ye *STILL & JUNIPER TREE*, the corner of Short's Garden, in Drury Lane. *c.* 1740

THOS. REEVES, at the *HOOP & GRAPES*, in Brick Lane, Spitalfields. 1764

THOS. WINSPEARE, at the *ANGEL & STILL*, near Holbourn Barrs. *c.* 1760

STEPHEN YATES, at the *WINE PRESS*, No. 23, in Watling Street, near Bow Lane. *c.* 1780

TWO SPIES

WIRE WORKERS

ELIZABETH AUBERY, at the *BIRD CAGE*, the corner of Savoy Gate, and Exeter Exchange, in the Strand. 1765–1773
(This bill is made out to Edward Gibbon, the historian, for " a strong parrot cage ".)

JOHN AUBREY, at the *BIRD CAGE*, the corner of Savoy Gate, and Exeter Exchange, in the Strand. 1745

PETT AUDLEY, at the *BIRD CAGE*, opposite Fetter Lane, in Holborn. *c.* 1765

WILLIAM BRIGHT, at ye *BLEW BOAR'S HEAD* in St. Michael's, Crooked Lane. *c.* 1740

GEORGE LEWIS CARR, at the *SUN*, in Little Britain. *c.* 1730

WILLIAM ELLYETT (successor to the late Wm. Bright), at the *BLUE BOAR'S HEAD*, opposite St. Michael's Church, in Crooked Lane. 1754

MILLIS & FFOSSICK, at the *BLACK HORSE*, over against the Church, in Crooked Lane. 1762

BIRD CAGE

BLACK HORSE

BLUE BOAR'S HEAD

WOOLPACK

RED LION & SEVEN STARS

ISAAC SMITH, at the *BLACK BOY & BIRD CAGE*, against Durham Yard, in ye Strand.   *c.* 1750

WILLM. SPARROW, at the *KING'S ARMS & BIRD CAGE*, opposite Durham Yard, in ye Strand.   1759
(Successor to Isaac Smith.)

WILLIAM WOOD, at the *GOLDEN LION*, in Noble Street, near Foster Lane.   1784

WOOLLEN DRAPERS

WILLIAM ADAMS, at the *GOLDEN COCK*, in Clare Court & White Horse Yard, Drury Lane.
c. 1760

JAMES ALEXANDER, at the *SUN & HALF MOON*, over against the corner of the Church Wall in Houndsditch.   1753

THOMAS BARLOW, at the *LAMB*, in New Bond Street, the corner of Bruton Street.   *c.* 1760

WILLM. BARRY & PHIL. BARNEVELT, at the *FLEECE*, in Fleet Street.   1727

PHILIP BARNEVELT, at the *WOOLPACK*, the corner of Water Lane, in Fleet Street.   1730

WILLIAM BARRY, at the *FLEECE*, in Fleet Street.
1732

JOHN BATEMAN & NATHL. NASH, at ye *RED LYON & SEVEN STARRS*, the West end of St. Paul's Church-Yard.   1735

GEORGE BINCKES & COY., at the *SEVEN STARS & KING'S ARMS*, in Bedford Street, Covent Garden.   1720
(Succeeded by Saml. Leech, 1752.)

DAVID CARNE & JOHN ELLISON, at the *NAKED BOY & WOOLPACK*, near ye New Exchange, in ye Strand.   1749
(See also Ellison & Carne, *q.v.*)

RICHARD CLEAVER, at the *FLEECE & WOOL-PACK*, opposite St. Peter's Church, in Cornhill.
1755

RICHARD & JOSEPH CLEAVER, at the *FLEECE &
WOOLPACK*, near the corner of Bishopsgate
Street, in Cornhill.   1765

JOHN COLLINGWOOD, at the *GOLDEN LION*, in
Fleet Street.   1746
(Successor to Noyes & Collingwood, *q.v.*)

STEPHEN COOPER & WM. ANDERSON, at the
BLUE BALL, in Grace-Church Street.   1768

JOHN ELLISON & DANIEL CARNE, at the *NAKED
BOY & WOOLPACK*, near ye New Exchange,
in the Strand.   1745
(See also D. Carne & J. Ellison.)

THOMAS FAWSON, at ye *GOLDEN FLEECE*, in
St. Paul's Church Yard, near Cheapside. 1740
(Succeeded by Richd. Fawson, 1760.)

NATHAN FEAR, at ye *GOLDEN BOY & WOOL-
PACK*, the corner of Black Moor Street, Drury
Lane.   *c.* 1740

THOMAS FENTON, at the *WOOLPACK*, No. 6, in
King Street Clothfair.   *c.* 1770

JOSHUA FLEATHAM & SON, at the *ROSE*, in
Cornhill.   1766
(Formerly Robt. Salter & J. Fleatham, 1725.)

THOMAS HARRIS, at ye *WHEATSHEAF & DOVE*,
in Monmouth Street, corner of White Lion Street.
                                        c. 1750

JOSEPH HEWATSON, at the *GOLDEN FLEECE*,
in Lombard Street.   *c.* 1760

PETER HODGSON, at the *WOOLPACK*, in Grace
Church Street.   *c.* 1750

WILLM. JACKSON, at the *NAKED BOY*, in ye
Poultry.   1754
(Preceded by Wm. Humphrys, 1722.)

JOHN JOHNSON, at the *HAND & SHEARS*, in
the Borough, Southwark.   *c.* 1760

JOSHUA JONES, the *NEW ADAM & EVE*, No. 76,
corner of Bagnio Court, Newgate Street. *c.* 1780

NAKED BOY & WOOLPACK

GOLDEN FLEECE

HAND & SHEARS

GOLDEN LION

NAKED BOY & ROSE

BLACK SWAN & PARROT

SAMUEL LEECH, at the *SEVEN STARRS & KING'S ARMS*, in Bedford Street, Covent Garden. (Preceded by G. Binckes, *q.v.*)   1748

NATHANIEL NASH, at the *RED LYON & SEVEN STARS*, the West end of St. Paul's Church Yard. (Preceded by J. Bateman & N. Nash, *q.v.*)   1741

NEWLAND & THIRLWELL, at the *ROYAL OAK*, in Monmouth Street.   *c.* 1770

WM. NOYES & JNO. COLLINGWOOD, at the *GOLDEN LION*, in Fleet Street.   1742

CHRISTOPHER PERKINS (successor to above). 1762

WILLIAM RICHARDS, at the *GOLDEN FLEECE*, in Great Castle Street, Cavendish Square. *c.* 1770

EDWARD SETCHALL, at the *NAKED BOY & ROSE*, in White-horse Yard, Drury Lane. *c.* 1750

JOHN SHORT, at the signe of the *BLACK SWAN & PARRAT*, in Cannon Streete.   1654

JOHN & WALTER TANCRED, at the *GOLDEN KEY*, in Henrietta Street, Covent Garden.   1768

TICHBOURNE & DOUGHTY, at the *LAMB*, in the Poultry.   *c.* 1760

JOHN WALLIS, at the *WOOLSACK*, opposite New Rents, in St. Martin's Le Grand, near Cheapside. *c.* 1760

ENOS WHITELY, at the *CROWN & SWAN*, No. 23, St. Martin's Le Grand.   *c.* 1780

WRITING MASTERS

JOHN AYRES, at the *HAND & PEN*, near St. Paul's School, in St. Paul's Church Yard.   1680

GEORGE BICKHAM, at the *CROWN*, in James Street, Bunhill Fields.   1741

JOSEPH CHAMPION, at the *GOLDEN PEN*, in Old Change, Cheapside.   1732

WILLIAM CHINNERY, at the *GLOBE & SUN*,
Chancery Lane. 1762

EDWARD COCKER, " dwelling in Paul's Church
Yard, betwixt the Signes of the *SUGAR LOAF*,
and the *NAKED BOY & SHEARS*, right over
against St. Paul's Chaine." 1657
(Author of Cocker's *Arithmetick*.)

T. COOKE, at the *TWO GOLDEN PENS*, next
door to St. Paul's School, in St. Paul's Church
Yard. 1710

PETER GERY, at the *RAINBOW*, in Fleet Street.
1665

RICHARD GETHING, at the *HAND & GOLDEN
PEN*, in Fetter Lane. 1616

SAMUEL LANE, at ye *HAND & PEN*, in Ball
Alley, in Gravel Lane, near Houndsditch, Without
Aldgate. 1699

THOMAS OLLYFFE, at the *HAND & PEN*, in
Fetter Lane. 1701

JOHN RAYNER, at the *HAND & PEN*, in St. Paul's
Churchyard. 1709

JAMES SEAMER, at the *FLOWER-DE-LUCE*,
corner of Mitre Court, in Fleet Street. 1676

GEORGE SHELLEY, at the *HAND & PEN*, in
Warwick Lane. 1699

CHRISTOPHER SMEATON, at the *HAND & PEN*,
over against Somerset House, in the Strand. 1685

CHARLES SNELL, at the *GOLDEN PEN*, in Foster
Lane. 1694

WILLIAM WEBSTER, at the *HAND & PEN*,
corner of Cecil Court on the Pavement, in St.
Martin's Lane. 1714

ELEAZAR WIGAN, at the *HAND & PEN*, on Great
Tower Hill. 1696

HAND & PEN

RAINBOW

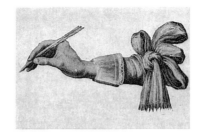

HAND & PEN

SAINT GEORGE AND THE DRAGON

INDEXES

A separate Index of Shopkeepers' Names is given on pp. 198–220.

For reference to the various Trades, the reader should consult the alphabetical lists contained in the Abridged Directory, pp. 28-185.

A separate Index of Shop Signs is given on pp. 188-197.

For reference to the various Trades, the reader should consult the alphabetical lists contained in the Abridged Directory, pp. 28-185.